Represented Communities

Represented
Communities

FIJI AND WORLD

DECOLONIZATION

*John D. Kelly and
Martha Kaplan*

THE UNIVERSITY OF CHICAGO PRESS
CHICAGO AND LONDON

John D. Kelly is associate professor of anthropology at the University of
Chicago. He is author of *A Politics of Virtue: Hinduism, Sexuality, and
Countercolonial Discourse in Fiji* (1991), also published by the University of
Chicago Press. Martha Kaplan is associate professor of anthropology at
Vassar College. She is author of *Neither Cargo nor Cult: Ritual Politics and the
Colonial Imagination in Fiji* (1995).

The University of Chicago Press, Chicago 60637
The University of Chicago Press, Ltd., London
© 2001 by The University of Chicago
All rights reserved. Published 2001
Printed in the United States of America
10 09 08 07 06 05 04 03 02 01   1 2 3 4 5

ISBN: 0-226-42988-1 (cloth)
ISBN: 0-226-42990-3 (paper)

Library of Congress Cataloging-in-Publication Data

Kelly, John Dunham, 1958–
    Represented communities : Fiji and world decolonization / John D. Kelly
and Martha Kaplan.
        p.   cm.
    Includes bibliographical references and index.
    ISBN 0-226-42988-1 (alk. paper)—ISBN 0-226-42990-3 (pbk. : alk.
paper)
    1. Decolonization 2. Nationalism 3. Decolonization—Fiji. 4. Fiji—
Politics and government. I. Kaplan, Martha, 1957– II. Title.

JV51 .K455 2001
325.9611—dc21

                                                                00-013098

⊚ The paper used in this publication meets the minimum requirements of the
American National Standard for Information Sciences—Permanence of Paper
for Printed Library Materials, ANSI Z39.48-1992.

Contents

Preface

Decolonization constitutes the nation-state as we know it, and decolonization is not well understood. There is a middle distance between the present and history, as Eric Hobsbawm has written, "a no-man's land of time" (1987:3), thirty to seventy years before the present. Neither generally remembered nor yet well reconsidered, these times pose a challenge to scholarship. Decolonization shows the marks of this twilight. When its ideologies of independence and modernization are juxtaposed with its starker realities, bitterness often dominates analysis. And we think that some basic issues for understanding decolonization—such as the rise of the UN model of the nation-state and the force and influence of American power in the decolonizing process—still require far more critical attention.

Frantz Fanon, writing in the midst of the Algerian War, before U.S. involvement in Vietnam, perceived a basic emerging dynamic: the United States advising its allies the European powers "to decolonize in a friendly fashion," while the latter acted with haste wherever an actual liberation movement manifested; "a veritable panic takes hold . . . for God's sake let's decolonize quick" (Fanon 1963:79, 70). But Fanon still held on to the dream of a free and independent nation, held on to a distinction between decolonization and true liberation, a distinction that actually renews the UN utopia despite its critical force. Decolonization sits in the twilight of history but is even harder to see because it also rests doubly in the shadows. In the shadows of periphery, it is further obscured by its looming historical successor, the Cold War. When the Fanons of the world gained their reputation and aura as potential revolutionary socialists, the issues surrounding decolonization were swept into the battles for hearts and minds between the alleged First and Second Worlds. The ex-colony nation-states became the Third World. Decolonization was not a phenomenon of the Cold War. The Cold War with its Third World was only an episode in the continuing history of the nation-state, a history fundamentally structured by decolonization. To understand the present, we suggest that scholarship attend more closely to the processes, some still continuing, wherein the utopian idea of a nation-state gets routinized in actual places. This book is about this process, especially in the realities of one place, the Fiji Islands.

This book brings together some of our writing on the nation-state, representation in colonial and postcolonial communities, and the tragedies and ironies of recent history in Fiji. It is based on ethnographic field research and archival research. Reflections on Fiji's realities as a postcolonial nation-state, especially after the 1987 coups, have led us to an increasingly systematic critique of dominant approaches in the anthropology of nationalism, especially Benedict Anderson's *Imagined Communities*. In fact these reflections have led us to polemic, reasoned we hope, and also to a real alternative framework for approaching nation-states, decolonization, and dilemmas in contemporary politics. In this book we will be using historical ethnography of Fiji to discuss decolonization in reality.

We do not apologize for the urgency and political positioning of our writing on Fiji. Since 1982 we have worked in and on Fiji, Martha Kaplan primarily with ethnic Fijians, John Kelly with Indo-Fijians. We have come to regret such ethnicized separations in scholarship (which are quite typical) as one small manifestation of the problems that Fiji faces, and we try now, whenever possible, to write against these divisions. The chapters of this book are essays written between 1991 and 2000. We first planned this volume in 1998 and wrote its introduction that year, when we recognized that the included essays made a coherent set and that the theory and ethnography would strengthen each other. Each essay has been slightly revised to remove repetition and occasionally to update historical references. Chapter 6 has been fully redrafted to address the situation in Fiji as of early July 2000, in the midst of Fiji's third coup d'état.

Writing about history anthropologically creates dilemmas in terminology. In general in this text, we use "Indo-Fijian" rather than "Fiji Indian" or "Indian" to refer to Fiji citizens of South Asian descent. Generally we use "ethnic Fijian" to refer to Fiji citizens descending from the Pacific Islanders resident in the island group when the British arrived. To project this usage back into the era before citizenship creates anachronism, and other incongruences also arise with quoted materials past and present. In the colonial-era English-language documents, the terms most frequently found are "Indian" and "Fijian," and "Fiji Indian" emerges far earlier than "Indo-Fijian." "Indo-Fijian" is largely, perhaps exclusively, a coinage of the nation-state era, and "ethnic Fijian" emerges only in the 1980s and 1990s. Therefore, in the chapters about events midcentury, we sometimes use "Fiji Indian" as well as the anachronistic "Indo-Fijian," and we use "indigenous Fijian" (a term with a politics we discuss inter alia). Conversely, colonial usage continues in many consequential ways after independence. Notably, Fiji's constitutions starting in 1970 have required these citizens of Fiji to register as "Fijian" or "Indian." When describing these constitutions, and in other cases when quoting or paraphrasing, we use these terms set in place in the colonial era but revert to "ethnic Fijian" and "Indo-Fijian" when writing in our own voice. And, after all, we are out to question presumptions that these are natural communities in any sense.

More generally, in this book we advocate a punctuation of time for scholarship on nations and nationalism that differs in basic ways from the one found in texts such as *Imagined Communities*. We argue that there is both less and more to the nation-state and its genealogy. On the one hand, the nation-state is less: we see the nation-state as emerging much later in history, especially in the UN era, and we see it as a contingent, particular political form, less inevitable and necessary than it appears to be in theories that equate it with "modernity." On the other hand, the nation-state has more in its genealogy. Its complex roots include a bourgeois-Christian form of redemption built into its "self-determination" utopia, something that is far more than an artifact of horizontal equivalences generated by print capitalism. And, more important for its complexity in reality, the nation-state's roots also include communities that exist not merely in any imaginary, but also in institutions of representation whose actual histories matter. Crucial to understanding postcoloniality is both what is less and what is more here: the recent, specific imposition of the nation-state form of "self-determination," and the complex historic depth and continuing, dynamic reality of colonially constituted institutions of community representation.

Acknowledgments

Acknowledgments are due to many different people and institutions. Over the past two decades, many people in Fiji have generously shared time and insights on Fiji past and present. To them, first and foremost, people who have spent hours and days of their time with us, who have invited us to rituals and meetings, who have shown us private archives or directed us to documents in public ones, who have introduced us to others, who have patiently and carefully explained ongoing events, who have disagreed with us when we were wrong and have suggested things to us that we had not considered, we express our most profound gratitude. Under the best of circumstances, it is difficult for ethnographers to balance the intrusiveness of acknowledgment to particular individuals, given the questions of privacy and confidentiality that can be entailed. Under the present circumstances, we choose not to even name particular places. We know this errs on the side of failing to recognize the contributions made to this work by real people, but Fiji's political future is sufficiently uncertain that we would rather err in this direction.

We acknowledge permission for research from the Fiji Government in 1984–85 and 1986 and from the Republic of Fiji in 1991. We thank the late S. T. Tuinaceva, archivist, for permission to use the records of the National Archives of Fiji and greatly appreciate the assistance of the staff at the archives, especially Margaret Patel. (In our references, we use the designation CSO to refer to minute papers in the Colonial Secretary's Office series, and the reference numbers used by the archive. At times, archival sources cannot be specified because the Fiji Government required as a condition for archival research using the Colonial Secretary's Office confidential minute paper series that these files not be identified as the source of information.) The Fiji

Museum has been unfailingly hospitable to us, and we thank past museum directors Fergus Clunie and Kate Hindle and staff. Over the years we have also appreciated the collegiality shown by faculty and library staff at the University of the South Pacific.

We acknowledge funding support for research and writing from the following institutions: SSRC, Fulbright-Hays, NSF, Institute for Intercultural Studies, Wenner Gren, Princeton University, Vassar College, and the University of Chicago. We would also like to thank our colleagues in the Departments of Anthropology at Princeton University, the University of Chicago, and Vassar College for years of scholarly collegiality.

At multiple levels, the text is a collaboration. We have been working with each other as scholars since 1980, pursuing research in and about Fiji for close to two decades. In this book, chapters 2, 3, and 4 were originally written by John Kelly and chapter 5 by Martha Kaplan. But each of these chapters incorporates research and writing insights by both of us. Chapters 1 and 6 are jointly authored.

Several of these chapters began as papers at conferences. We thank the following conveners and institutions and acknowledge the contributions of interlocutors at these conference events: "Nationalism and National Culture in Melanesia," session organized by Robert Foster, annual meeting of the Association for Social Anthropology in Oceania, March 1991 (chapter 5); "Global Transnationality," conference organized by Arjun Appadurai, Chicago Humanities Institute, February 1995 (chapter 3); "Globalization and the Construction of Communal Identities," conference organized by Birgit Meyer, Peter Pels, and Peter Geschiere, WOTRO, the Globalization Project, and the Research Centre "Religion and Society" at the University of Amsterdam, March 1996 (chapter 2); "Communalism and Migration: Ethnic Conflict in Indian Ocean States," conference organized by Crispin Bates, University of Edinburgh, June 1997 (chapter 4). Versions of chapter 5 were also presented in colloquia at the anthropology departments of Bryn Mawr College, University of Hawaii, and Vassar College, and a version of chapter 1 was presented at the workshop "The Sociology and Cultures of Globalization," University of Chicago. We would also like to thank Pinar Batur-VanderLippe for inviting us to write the article that was an early version of chapter 6.

Versions of each chapter have been published elsewhere, and we acknowledge permission for inclusion in this volume. Parts of chapter 1 will appear as "Nation and Decolonization: The Need for a New Anthropology of Nationalism," *Anthropological Theory* (forthcoming); reprinted by permission of Sage Publications Ltd. Chapter 2 appeared as "Time and the Global: Against the Homogeneous, Empty Communities in Contemporary Social Theory," *Development and Change* 29, no. 4 (1998): 839–71; reprinted by permission of Blackwell Publishers Ltd. Chapter 3 appeared as "Diaspora and World War, Blood and Nation in Fiji and Hawai'i," *Public Culture* 7, no. 3 (1995): 475–97. Chapter 4 appeared as "'They Cannot Represent Themselves': Threats to Difference and So-called Community Politics in Fiji from 1936 to 1947," in *Community, Empire and Migration: South Asians in Diaspora*, edited by Crispin Bates (New York: St. Martin's Press, 2000), 46–86; reprinted by permission of Macmillan Press Ltd. Chapter 5 appeared as "'Blood on the Grass and Dogs Will Speak': Ritual Politics and the Nation in Independent Fiji," in *Nation Making: Emergent Identities in Postcolonial Melanesia*, edited by Robert Foster (Ann Arbor: University of Michigan Press, 1995), 95–125; reprinted by permission of University of Michigan Press. Parts of chapter 6 appeared as "Race and Rights in Fiji," in *The Global Color Line: Race and Ethnic Relations from a Global Perspective*, Research in Politics and Society, vol. 6, edited by Pinar Batur-VanderLippe and Joe Feagin (Stamford, Conn.: JAI Press, 1999), 237–57; reprinted by permission of Elsevier Science.

We thank the Fiji Ministry of Information for permission to reprint photographs taken by Robertson Ramsay (Rob) Wright as Fiji's Government Photographer in the 1940s and 1950s. We also thank Peter Thomson for his permission to reproduce the Rob Wright photographs from *Fiji in the Forties and Fifties* (Auckland: Thomson Pacific, 1994). We thank the Fiji Ministry of Information and the National Archives of Fiji for permission to reprint the photographs of Kisan Sangh leaders in 1941 and of celebration in Fiji of Bharat Mata (Mother India) Day in 1947. We thank the estate of A. D. Patel for permission to reprint two photographs of A. D. Patel and Swami Rudrananda, and the National Centre for Development Studies, Australian National University, for permission to reproduce them from Brij Lal's book *A Vision for Change: A. D. Patel and the Politics of Fiji* (Canberra: National Centre for Development Studies, 1997). Finally, we would like to thank Brij Lal for his help in locating photographs of A. D. Patel and in identifying Kisan Sangh leaders in the Kisan Sangh photograph.

We are grateful for the collegiality of several scholars in and of Fiji, especially Pio Manoa, Paul Geraghty, Subramani, Vijay Naidu, Stewart Firth, Brij V. Lal, and Don Brenneis. For their insights into the history of colonial Fiji, we particularly thank Fergus Clunie and Margaret Patel, both of whom have been interlocutors from the beginning of our archival work. Henry Rutz has generously shared his own research materials and experiences with us, and we return often to his trenchant analysis of 1980s political discourse in Fiji (Rutz 1995). We have also learned much from Stewart Firth's survey of decolonization in the Pacific (Firth 2000). Robert Foster is a good friend and colleague, and for years we have benefited from his works on the anthropology of nationalism (Foster 1991, 1995b). However, we are entirely responsible for the interpretations we offer in this book.

Finally, we would like to underline the impact of the thinking of our teachers Marshall Sahlins and Bernard Cohn on this and most of our works. Sahlins first suggested Fiji to us and taught us to think about culture, history, and power nonreductively. He taught us to find culture in the dynamics of real history and to find power in the dynamics of real culture, local and global. Barney Cohn taught us to think seriously about colonialism and about the knowledge and power issues in scholarship itself. Just as much as our Fiji studies reflect multiple influences of Sahlins's ongoing historical ethnography of Fiji, so also our research is informed and oriented by Cohn's ongoing studies of the British in India, the British Empire, and colonial societies in general. And most importantly, in this book we begin to take up the challenge of Barney Cohn's long-standing insistence that American cultural anthropologists take seriously the realities of American power in the twentieth century. We dedicate this book to Marshall Sahlins and Barney Cohn.

ONE

Nation and Decolonization

ON THE ACTUAL ORIGINS OF NATION-STATES

When the twentieth century began, the world did not consist of "nation-states." In fact, this locution was not generally known. "Nation-state" does not appear in the *Century Dictionary and Cyclopedia* of 1911, though "nationhood" does. It does not appear in *Funk and Wagnall's New Standard Dictionary of the English Language* in 1938, 1949, or even 1959, though "nationhood" and "nationwide" do. It does not appear in Oxford's *New English Dictionary on Historical Principles* of 1888 or the 1931 *Oxford Universal Dictionary*. At the beginning of the twentieth century, the world did not consist of nation-states but, instead, was mostly made up of European empires. In that world, liberal and republican conceptions of popular sovereignty were well known, widely distributed, and controversial. Some republics had forced their way to independence from European empires. And liberal reforms had recast many governments in Europe itself into more democratic order, with or without violent revolutions, and always without abandonment of their remaining colonies. But other organizing ideas were less disputable. Especially among Europeans, their descendants, and those they ruled, debates over the constitution of government were conducted in terms of Enlightenment social and political theories, with the virtues of all political possibilities measured against the realities and necessities of "civilization." It was a world in which conceptions of civilization, race, and progress established both the cultural logic of empires and the context for deliberation over the possibilities and limits of democracy and "home rule." We no longer live in that world.

THE LEXICAL ENIGMA

Dictionaries are quite limited, generally, as a source for cultural and political information. But in this case they have an interesting story to tell. The 1989 *Oxford English Dictionary* tracks the lexeme "nation-state" back only to 1918, in J. A. R. Marriott's treatise *European Commonwealth*, published in the year of the Versailles treaty negotiations. But Marriott himself, at least by 1927, was projecting back the existence of nation-states in England, France, and elsewhere in Europe to the fifteenth and sixteenth centuries (1927:11) and, at the same time, connecting it with another key term: the "modern," as in "the modern state," part of Marriott's 1927 title. Similarly, the next instance cited by the 1989 *Oxford English Dictionary*, Julian Huxley and A. C. Haddon's *We Europeans*, also connected the nation-state to Europe, the "modern," and sixteenth-century origins (1935:11, 187). There are two things we think important here: the lateness of the coining of the term, and the quickness with which consensus emerges that it is connected to "modernity" and has early modern roots.[1]

We are aware that the late arrival of the hyphenated noun "nation-state" into the dictionaries is not proof of the nonexistence of nation-states in earlier periods. Discussion of the "national state" as a type of state clearly preceded the twentieth century, for almost obvious reasons, especially in German while Germany became one. But we would argue that these "national states," even when constituted, were far from the states of United Nations–era ideology. The young Max Weber articulated the passion of the nineteenth-century European nations for self-assertion, competition, violence, and domination of one another, their plain advocacy of the interests of a home race in an agonistic world: "We believe that those nations which today fail to mobilize their economic future for national greatness do not in fact have a future" (1989 [1897]:219). In Germany the "national state" was advocated as a desirable type of state at least since the days of Kant, Clausewitz, Fichte, and Hegel, but hardly without controversy (pace Balibar and other Fichte-centrists, one has to note, for example, Nietzsche's celebration of Richter and Goethe's disdain for "Fichte's mendacious but patriotic flatteries and exaggerations" [Nietzsche 1989 (1886):178]). Even by the late nineteenth century, despite Ernest Renan's now-famous dissent, the premise that nations were first of all races, and races in a more or less Darwinian competition, was close to universal (connecting theorists as diverse as Nietzsche, the bombastic Treitschke, and the young Weber). In any case, there was no lexical standardization of "national state" in English, while, as we shall see, the concept of "nation" was almost invariably associated before World War II with "race." According to Istvan Hont, there is no standardization of *Nationalstaat*, "national state," *even in German* until the unification in the second half of the nineteenth century; for example, Hegel's expression in the *Philosophy of Right* translated by Knox and then by Nisbet as "nation state" "was '*das Volk als Staat*,' the 'people *qua* state,' and not 'nation-state'" (Hont 1995:228 n).[2]

How late, exactly, did this "nation–state" become self-conscious and insistent on its "modernity," insistent so routinely on its "early modern" roots? In a comparable case, Keith Tribe (1981) has demonstrated that the idea of "industry" as complex machine-driven manufacture, rather than "industry" as individual bodily exertion, did not arise until well into the nineteenth century, and that the idea of an "industrial revolution" was constituted several decades after the alleged event (see also Williams 1976). But the nation-state's alleged emergence and its lexical routinization are separated by centuries. This is not just some owl of Minerva flying at dusk. Nor is it merely some *post festum*, "after the feast," analysis mistaking historical phenomena for universals (cf. Marx 1977:168, on the commodity). This big blank glossed vaguely as "modern," stretching from the sixteenth century to the mid-twentieth, is a motivated amnesia. It is a repression of imperial history.

NATION AND PERIODIZATION

In sum, the overwhelming tendency to suture "the nation" to "the modern" occludes imperial history and the significance of decolonization. In contrast, consider the connections between decolonization and the inception, both lexically and practically, of the nation-state as the paradigmatic political unit. It is not hard to date the point at which the nation-state was routinized in and for global politics. This dating is sufficiently easy, in fact, that it astonishes us that the periodization is not already commonplace in the anthropology of nations and of globalization. Before 1945, debates about future political alignments were varied and ideological. The Communist International and others calling for revolution were rivaled by many other visions of "the new order" and "the new world order." Both the Treaty of Versailles and the League of Nations were major steps toward the realization of the actual future order of nation-states, mutual reliance of nations on states and states on nations.[3] But even after this Europe-focused institutionalization, the principle of national self-determination was widely treated as flawed or limited, fatally abstract, and either temporary (as for Lenin[4]) or largely unworkable (as for Smuts[5]). In fact, the political debates from the 1900s through the 1940s were as utopian as were the debates about monarchy among philosophes and reformers in France, England, the Atlantic colonies, and elsewhere in the decades leading up to 1776 and 1789. But the final transition from utopian and ideological imaginaries to institutional realities and necessities was just as clear. In the twentieth century the watershed was the end of the Second World War—the inception of the world of United Nations.

Since 1945 the local is framed by a different global: a global of formal horizontalities and symmetries (one nation-state one vote), and a civility based upon allegations about nature (human rights, needs, freedoms), not culture (or civilization). At issue here is not just the Cold War, but also and more fundamentally the framework of commitments that kept the Cold War cold. War itself had been banished; at least, all legitimate war between nations or states.[6] And once this world was fully routinized, its premises could be rediscovered as new theory. A scholar, Benedict Anderson, could even propose that at core nations were not, as young Weber had it, survivors in a predatory world, groups whose signature was quest for power, but, rather, that nations were *communities,* communities of a particularly horizontal kind, intrinsically seeking to live in horizontal symmetries both internally and externally.

This collection of essays presents not only a sustained critique of Benedict Anderson's theory of nationalism, but also an alternative account of the dialogical dynamics of contemporary global political predicaments. Our argument in this book is threefold. First, we critically engage existing scholarship on the nation, especially the "imagined community" approach. We argue that Benedict Anderson and others mistakenly project the post–World War II nation-state, especially in its utopian formal symmetries, onto the actually existing nations and nationalisms of past centuries, leading to significant distortions and amnesia, especially in the analysis of postcolonial predicaments. Second, we seek to explain our approach to periodization, the punctuation of time. This entails both our sense of the watershed at World War II (which we first recognized following Dower 1986)[7] and our approach to the dialogical (*not* dialectical) processes relating local and global, and relating one global order to the next. In short, we recommend the abandonment of the concept of "modernity" and all its oversimplifications, distortions, and occlusions. Third, we want to propose a new theory of the post–World War II "new nations" and the global and comparative dynamics of decolonization. Along with many other scholars of postcoloniality, we feel that understanding postcolonial national dilemmas requires a serious grasp of colonial social, cultural, and political histories. Along with many other scholars of colonial societies, we feel that the history of political processes in colony and metropole need to be better integrated. But also, we feel that the institutionalization of the United Nations idea needs to be figured more critically into our understanding of the politics of community representation in the newly decolonized states in the twentieth century. In fact, the idea of "community" had an active life in the colonial era, which it is a major purpose of this book to reexamine.

In sum, we pose the following reconception of the dynamics of decolonization: against the *inceptive* approach to nationalist thought, the story of a new politics ex nihilo, and against the *exit story* narration of decolonization, that decolonization is primarily the end of something, we will track dilemmas, changing as global politics reconfigure, in local negotiations and struggles over *community representation*. Against the inceptive story, the idea that nations as imagined communities were a new, higher form of consciousness awakened by "modernity" and by a modular nationalist ideology, we will argue for the importance of colonial institutions of representation, and especially that *community was a fundamental political institution* precisely within the European, and especially British, colonial systems. That colonies were spaces filled by multiple communities, and communities of different characteristics and levels of civilization, of course made communal self-government merely a dangerous impossibility—as long as the imperial alternative made more sense. Colonially-routinized communities were precisely the materials, highly problematic in their fit, out of which nations could then be fashioned, with varying successes, to fit the slots in the new world order as it actually came into being: slots for new national communities. Decolonization, then, was not an exit from the aggressive world of dynamic imperials and civil hierarchies, since all that exited were the colonizers, not the apparatus of political institutions. But it was a superimposition, with varying degrees and types of local embrace, of the new political scheme from the top down. Decolonization was an entry, with considerable baggage, into a new world order with its own delimiting determinations for civil and political practices, its own rigid protocols for delimiting the scope and realm of collected political will. If we tell the story as the exiting of tradition and the inception of modernity (the story is reiterated omnipresently: modernity coming later, perhaps incompletely, in the lagging parts of the world), then we lose sight of some basic dynamics here, including both the particularities of the global cultural logic of this new global order of "communities" and its descent from political structures that were (not modern, not traditional, but) intrinsically colonial. Dilemmas and struggles over nation and political representation in postcolonial societies, then, can be windows into global political dynamics of the highest importance.

While this chapter and also chapter 2 will focus on theoretical issues and some high-profile political events and structures, the rest of the chapters focus on local political engagements with global forces and changes. The chapters address consequential political events in many places. However, they will also provide—across a dense, ethnographically precise lattice of analyses of events and relations in colonial and postcolonial Fiji—a sustained analysis of one particularly interesting case of continuing crisis in the constitution of a nation-state. Fiji's traumatic, continuing failure to self-constitute illuminates the limits and contradictions of the United Nations plan, and in fact led us to see its significance. The argument hinges neither on the generalizability nor the exceptionality of Fiji's history, but rather uses Fiji to illustrate the gains we make when our anthropology of nationalism centers the twentieth century on decolonization and its aftermath rather than on utopian nation-state ideology as modernity's inevitable modular culture.

DIALECTICS AND DIALOGICS

For many of his readers, Benedict Anderson's *Imagined Communities* provides a highly useful global history within which to locate critical study of particular nations and nationalist movements. We will describe and criticize Anderson's argument in more detail in chapter 2. Here, we want to focus on his dialectics. Frequently, scholars whose commitment in their own work is to the irreducible significance of local forces have found Anderson's vocabulary flexible and apparently unconstraining: imagination, community, print capitalism, and a modular form of nation free for pirating. They do not always examine the aspiration Anderson shares with many others, both Marxist and non-Marxist (Fukuyama also comes to mind) to locate the nation as part of some sort of general stage of history.[8] Dialectical accounts of nationalism can be connected to simple or complicated models of modes of production (such as Anderson's print capitalism) or to more intrinsically ideological stages, such as some sort of generalized modernity (an idea lately making a strong comeback, despite the withering critiques, such as Tipp 1973, of earlier "modernization" models). While it might strike some that any periodization of global history must involve some sort of dialectic, some general model of successive social necessities developing out of contradictions in prior stages or eras, we sense more shortcutting and wishful thinking than rigor in most allegations of inevitability, necessity, and grandiose causality.

The dialectical tradition is, as we understand it, a scholarly quest for explanatory synthesis by capture of a background causal dynamic with a finite number of interdependent elements (e.g., Marx's forces and relations of production, Hegel's subject and object, etc.; for trenchant critique of Hegelian history, see Duara 1995). We support an anthropology more dialogical in the Bakhtinian sense. For Bakhtin and others, history as a dialogical process is an open series, with neither absolute priorities of level nor finite numbers of subjects and objects involved. In a dialogical account, even global history is a series of planned and lived responses to specific circumstances that were also irreducibly constituted by human subjects, creating not a single vast chain of "the subject" changed by "the object" and vice versa, but a dense, complex network of individual and collective subjects continually responsive to one another. These constitutive, irreducibly subjective dialogics add enormous contingency and complexity to what dialectic there is between material realities and human societies. That there is a history of forces of production is obviously true. But even if there is a sense in which, as Marx argued, material conditions and transformations can be separated from ideological forms and described "with the precision of natural science" (1978 [1859]:5), we still find most felicitous Marshall Sahlins's depiction of their actual dialectical relationship, that is, as Sahlins puts it, that "the cultural design improvises dialectics on its relationship to nature" (1972:33).

Critics of dialogicality often argue that the emphasis of dialogical approaches upon subject-subject relations leads to neglect of asymmetries and objectifications of power. They expect a dialogical approach to emphasize concord or agreement, very local dualities of conversation, and symmetric situations, as against larger apparatuses of power. This is neither inevitable nor even likely, if one attends to dialogical processes in history. As we see it, a dialectical approach is always anxious to spot in any analytic situation the underlying causal variables it privileges, and to sort any set of facts into the subsuming logic of its dynamic totalization. We think a dialogical approach is more capable of understanding both symmetries and asymmetries in history, without prior commitment to ultimate causes. In place of the dialectical commitment to totalization, in place of the premise that some kind of totality is always already there, our approach to the dialogics of power takes an important cue from Weber, the importance of routinization,[9] and has as its premise that powerful systems come into existence sometimes, but never only on their own terms.

For an example, let us unearth a few aspects of the history of capitalism neglected in the Marxist dialectic merely by adding one irreducible additional dimension. (We step back for a moment from this book's topic, decolonization as the dialogical routinization of the nation-state, to make this brief illustration.) Consider how much is gained if military relations and initiatives are not subsumed in the dynamic of forces and relations of production. Capitalism, far from being a "stage" of European (and therefore world?) history after "feudalism," was an increasingly dominant mode of production, exchange, and consumption in Asia for many centuries before it transformed Europe (Abu Lughod 1989; Frank 1998). Europe's rise to preeminence in capitalism, and much change within capitalism itself, intertwined with European state and imperial histories always attendant to military considerations. In particular, military history must be understood to grasp Europe's invention of joint-stock companies, with all their unintended consequences. The genealogy of capitalist corporations—those crucial capitalist institutions so woefully understudied by critical scholarship endlessly refetishizing the commodity form—finds more strands that lead to colonial adventures than to anything in the history of agricultural relations in Europe. And, to jump ahead in time and move closer to this book's topics, the crucial emphasis on a United Nations of formally egalitarian peace at the World War II watershed was the consequence of the ruinous experience of two quickly successive world wars. If you want to spot some sort of ripening or rotting contradiction between capitalist forces and relations of production in those wars, we can't stop you. But we think there is a better way to focus on processes of routinization, of what was globally objectified in the aftermath of the world wars, than to search for the underlying necessities of any dialectic.

We think Weber identifies far more clearly than Marx the crucial institutional nexus in which societies have so consequently improvised on their relationships with productive forces and processes: coercive apparatuses, especially legal apparatuses that devise and enforce contract law (Weber 1978:317–19). This leads to a central irony in our project. Benedict Anderson, a political scientist, has encouraged a turn in scholarship on nationalism toward an "anthropological" vision attending to narrative, imagination, and quotidian experiences. Many scholars have grasped this "anthropological" imaginary as a vague dialectical supplement to materiality that they see centered in means of production. In our view, the vague dialectic of culture and political economy should be replaced by a more specific tracking of dialogically wrought institutional transformations, precisely by not encapsulating representation in an "anthropological" analysis (in Anderson's sense). In our view, current theorists can and should reconnect representation to what Weber calls "means of coercion" and reconsider especially the constitutive powers and limits of law, and the dialogical processes by which regulations are regulated.

We are quite prepared to accept, in line, generally speaking, with Weber's conclusion about the relations between law and economy, that a dynamic instability perdures when capital dominates processes of production. Markets in general, and markets in capital in particular, have great use for the calculability that comes with powerful legal regulation, not least to protect great and risk-laden investments. But nevertheless they have also an even greater use for schemes that lead to growth via exploitation, manipulation, and other overcoming of legal limitations. Efforts to sustain the former against the endless pressure of the latter, Weber argues, favor a further legal improvisation, "the monopolization and regulation of all 'legitimate' coercive power by *one* universalist coercive institution" (1978:337). Does this make the nation-state inevitable as capital markets advance? Weber argues that not even "the state" was indispensable, but that this tendency led toward some form of it, and in any case that "an economic system, especially of the modern type, could certainly not exist without a legal order with very special features which could not develop except in the frame of a public legal order" (1978:336). To put it simply, what form of state? Nation-states? One world government? Empires? A monopoly on law and order—enforced how? If the tendency is toward unitary coercive institutions, then there is nothing obvious about the breaking up of empires into nation-states. But then again there is much that is not obvious about the actual post–World War II routinization of the nation-state. And in sum, we think it is an emergence that can better be understood dialogically, as fundamentally connected to specific contingent conjunctures in the history of individual and collective subjects, than as some dialectical determination of inherent tendencies of capital. If it was determined, in any sense, by developing material forces, we would point toward forces of coercion, not forces of production. But we would still see it as in crucial ways improvised in its determination. In this light, let us consider some fragments of the dialogues that eventually routinized the idea of a globeful of egalitarian, community nation-states.

THE UNITED NATIONS SYNTHESIS

What made the idea of a United Nations vitally important? How might it have been otherwise? What precedents, and what anxieties, made deep, horizontal comradeship both within and between nations into a necessity, a global moral absolute? Historian Prasenjit Duara has written that "what is novel about modern nationalism is not political self-consciousness, but the world *system* of nation-states" (1996:157). We agree. And we think that this "world *system*" became real when "nation-states" became real, both the term and the referent, in the construction of the United Nations.

Harry Truman's first public appearance as president of the United States came on June 26, 1945. By this date, firebombs had already destroyed Berlin and Tokyo, and the plans to use atomic weapons were in place. Truman was at the Opera House in San Francisco, for the official signing of the United Nations Charter.

> They were there, he told the delegates, to keep the world at peace. "And free from the fear of war," he declared emphatically, both hands chopping the air, palms inward, in rhythm with the words "free," "fear," and "war." (McCullough 1992:401)

Long before the United Nations charter was signed amid general fanfare about world peace and brotherhood, the Communist International had announced a goal of general equality of self-determining nation-states. Self-determination for all nations was a goal articulated by Lenin before Wilson made his way to Versailles; in 1928 the International declared that its task was to ensure the recognition of the rights of all nations, irrespective of race, to complete self-determination. . . . Wide and armed struggle against the imposition of any kind of limitation and restriction upon any nationality, nation or race. Complete equality for all nations and races. (Quoted in Tinker 1977:40)

Comparing these two quotations of elite, even propagandistic fragments of discourse, what distinguishes Truman's new world from the International's is the commitment to peace as a means as well as an end. The 1928 Communist International was still squarely advancing the plan for a "war to end all wars," a phrase coined by H. G. Wells to describe the British plan for World War I as he originally imagined and hoped. Wells was in fact one of the first to propose that the world faced either annihilation from increasingly destructive European weapons and war aims or else a new regime of peace, an argument he began to offer even before the turn of the century. But Wells envisioned as the "new world order," a phrase he also put into political circulation, not the Roosevelt-planned, Truman-instituted United Nations, but a global federation, a world state with policies set by benevolent scientists.

As Tinker (1977) argues, Franklin Roosevelt and Winston Churchill were in no position to go as far as the colony-free Communist International did, toward promising equal nations for all people. Neither Roosevelt's "Four Freedoms" goal announced in January 1941 (freedom of speech, of worship, from want, from fear) nor their September 1941 Atlantic Charter setting joint war aims proffered nearly as clear a promise of independence or equality for colonies, especially after Churchill announced that point three, promising "the right of all peoples to choose the form of government under which they will live," did not imply British withdrawal from India (Tinker 1977:42). But of course, the general idea of a brotherhood of free, equal, self-determining nations began with neither Roosevelt nor Churchill, the Communist International nor Wells. Among major diplomatic programs, it can clearly be traced to World War I, Wilson's Fourteen Points, and the League of Nations (and see Hobsbawm 1990 on the Versailles conference as the first moment when standing as an independent, self-governing state was forced upon territories, specifically the various Eastern European and Baltic fragments of the destroyed Austro-Hungarian Empire). And what eventually evolved into the idea of a British Commonwealth of Nations began earlier than this; in the wake of the various breakaways in the new world, London granted measures of "home rule" as an expedience to avoid white-settler colony independence movements. Wars were of course involved here as well.

It was not difficult for leaders among the colonized to develop their own utopian visions of national and global self-rule (as in *swaraj*, "self-rule," to cite the Indian National Congress concept) long before the Communist International came courting favor. As early as 1874, Kristodas Pal wrote in his newspaper, the *Hindoo Patriot,* about the egalitarian democratic possibilities he perceived in events elsewhere:

> Our attention should . . . be directed . . . to the introduction of constitutional Government for India. . . . If the Canadas could have a Parliament, if such small and little advanced Colonies as Prince Edward Island, [and] Newfoundland . . . could have elected councils, surely British India has a fair claim to similar representation. . . . Home Rule for India ought to be our cry, and it ought to be based upon the same constitutional basis that is recognized in the Colonies. (Quoted in Moulton 1991:225)

In 1874 an intellectual among the colonized in India could articulate the idea of symmetric constitutionalism as a political telos. Allan Hume, first general secretary of the Indian National Congress, even argued in his pamphlet *The Star in the East* (1886) that popularly controlled "Responsible Government" was the "only goal for which it is worth the while of any civilized nation to struggle."

Hume argued for self-rule as the "only goal," and Pal argued for "the same constitutional basis" in all the colonies. But it would be rash to essentialize a single concept of the liberal state out of such articulations, and to project the core, hybrid political category of the United Nations world, the "nation-state," back into these voices. Hume, the Communist International, and Gandhi had consequentially different visions of ideal world order; consider a vision of Gandhi's also from 1928:

> My ambition is much higher than Independence. Through the deliverance of India, I seek to deliver the so called weaker races of the earth from the crushing heels of Western exploitation in which England is the greatest partner. If India converts, as it can convert, Englishmen, it can become the predominant partner in a world commonwealth of which England can have the privilege of becoming a partner if she chooses. India has the right, if only she knew, of becoming the predominant partner. . . . I want India to come to her own and that state cannot be better defined by any single word than "*swaraj.*" . . . India's coming to her own will mean every nation doing likewise. (Gandhi 1986:255)

Swaraj for Gandhi meant self-rule in a religiously resonating form of self-knowledge, self-control, and self-development, for individual, nation, and world. Against independence, Gandhi always called for interdependence. Like H. G. Wells's original "new world order" (a socialist world government dominated by scientific planning), Gandhi's world commonwealth led by Indian *swaraj* did not become real. Wells and Gandhi were each, in their own way, prescient to insist on a world order abandoning war as a legitimate political tactic, but both sought far stricter curbs on capitalist exploitation than United Nations planners would abide.

Anderson projects back in time the United Nations model of the nation-state, including its premises of symmetry, horizontality, and quiescence, precisely because of his dialectical method, trolling the nineteenth and twentieth centuries only for the discourse that fits his model. He not only homogenizes nationalists, but, more markedly, ignores even the most mainstream criticisms of liberal proposals. In effect, for England he remembers the Liberals but not the Whigs or Tories. Surveying dialogically, we can not only spot vaguely emergent trends for which we supply the teleology, but also seek specific engagements and rejoinders. We cannot here, of course, inquire into all the specific effects of the interactions of political movements within and across the British Empire, the Communist International, and the United States. But for example consider, within the British Empire, what Edward C. Moulton provides for Hume:

> While British Liberal Radicals such as Hume and Wedderburn, who were in the forefront of the Congress cause, strongly believed that liberal political principles were universally applicable and ideally suited to India's situation in the 1880s, the leaders of the Liberal Party in Britain, including Gladstone and Ripon, were less enthusiastic.... Conservatives and Unionists, who dominated political office in Britain around the turn of the century, tended to be thoroughly behind Salisbury in his opposition to any recognition of the electoral principle in the selection of legislative councils in India. The key to this dominant line of thinking was pithily expressed by Dufferin when he wrote: "you cannot apply constitutional principles . . . to a conquered country [such as India], inasmuch as self-government and submission to a foreign Sovereign are incompatible." (Moulton 1991:249)

The frame of "a public, legal order," Weber tells us, was necessary for a capitalist economy to function. When the likes of conservative leader Disraeli responded to liberal propositions, both at home and abroad, the issue of public legal order, its benefits for the British nation, and what it took to sustain it couldn't have been engaged more directly. For a single example, in 1878 Disraeli announced the need to mobilize army reserves, against Liberal opposition, and justified it with reference to conflicts in Eastern Europe:

> Public law is set aside . . . for Heaven's sake, that [this] lunacy might not imperil the British Empire! . . . Its flag floats on many waters; it has Provinces

in every zone; they are inhabited by persons of different races, with different religions, different laws, manners, customs. Some of these are bound to us by the tie of liberty, fully conscious that without their connection with the Metropolis they would have no security for public freedom and self-government. Others united to us by faith and blood are influenced by material as well as moral considerations. There are millions who are bound to us by military sway, and they bow to that sway because they know that they are indebted to it for order and justice. But, my Lords, all these communities agree in recognizing the commanding spirit of these Islands that has formed and fashioned in such a manner so great a portion of the globe. My Lords, that Empire is no mean heritage; but it is not a heritage that can only be enjoyed—it must be maintained—and it can only be maintained by the same qualities that created it—by courage, by discipline, by patience, by determination, and by a reverence for public law and respect for national rights. My Lords, in the East of Europe at this moment some securities of that Empire are periled. (*House of Lords Hansard,* April 8, 1878:773–78)

Disraeli's nation had a duty, he felt, to arm for war and to face the attendant expenses, in order to maintain its national rights and the public order of its dominion. Disraeli's empire was constituted of a wide variety of "communities," complex in its multitiered hierarchy and types of political consciousness, but simple in its dependence for order and justice on the great commanding spirit of a particular nation. The quiescent communities of empire were not seen as nations equal to that at its center, but were seen as perpetually in debt to the ordering power of that great Britain. In the empires, public order followed from the routinized asymmetry between colonizer and colonized, the perpetually war-ready great power of Europe and the indebted, quiescent communities they ruled.

A dialogical analysis does not lead, inevitably, to an epistemology of mere contingencies, "partial truths," and limitless differences by perspective. Dialogical processes can still lead to definite results with truly global consequences, such as the invention of joint-stock companies, or the ending of the Raj, or the nation-states of the United Nations. The empires with their great powers engendered wars between them, which, in time, became world wars. And the outcome of world wars was Harry Truman's vision of peace in San Francisco and the historical synthesis that, we think, made vital the "nation-state" itself. The aggressive, predatory, social Darwinist "nations" of the European nineteenth century had had their day. But the "communities" that empires had worked so hard to render so quiescent would be expected to remain quiescent in Truman's world, to accept the new formal symmetries, including their place on the map and at the UN table, as "nations" imagined in a new framework.

BACK TO THE DICTIONARIES

Another perspective on the relationship of nations and states before and after World War II can be found with a brief return to the dictionaries and a look at definitions of "nation," rather than "nation-state." From a superficial point of view, we could be accused of vast overstatement. Is it a mere accident that there is no entry or mention of "nation-state," when, for example, even as early as 1888 the first definition of "nation" in Oxford's *New English Dictionary on Historical Principles* included ". . . usually organized as a separate political state . . ."? Consider also, for example, the second definition of "nation" in the *Century Dictionary and Cyclopedia:*

> 2. In a narrower sense, a political society composed of a sovereign or government and subjects or citizens, and constituting a political unit; an organized community inhabiting a certain extent of territory, within which its sovereignty is exercised.

If we quoted only these segments, then imperial period thought would sound very "modern" indeed, nations characterized as sovereign communities. But the *Century Dictionary* spoke to very different foundational ideas in its first definition:

> 1. In a broad sense, a race of people; an aggregation of persons of the same ethnic family, and speaking the same language or cognate languages.

And the full, first Oxford's *New English Dictionary* definition of 1888, similarly:

> 1. An extensive aggregate of persons, so closely associated with each other by common descent, language, or history, as to form a distinct race or people, usually organized as a separate political state and occupying a definite territory.

The *Century Dictionary* definition suggests separate uses, broad and narrower, which the *New English Dictionary* combines with "usually"; in both cases, a "race of people" or "a race or people," common descent, and shared language come first and are the true foundations. Usually a state, or more narrowly, a people with a state, but always a race or people of shared descent. Again, challenges to this ranking were available at the time. Renan's 1882 lecture "What Is a Nation?" rejected race, language, and territory as bases for nationality, invoking instead shared memory and political will. This argument eventually became famous, as the article on the "nation" in the 1968 *Encyclopedia of the Social Sciences* declared. But it did not reach the dictionaries so fast. The news could only reach the dictionaries after that crescendo of failure of nations seeing themselves as races destined to dominate empires, the global catastrophes following the Nazi effort to found an Aryan Third Reich, and the Japanese effort to build a Co-Prosperity Sphere with the Yamato race as nucleus.

In many senses, it is Benedict Anderson himself who deserves credit for insisting upon annihilation of the shared-descent definitions of nation, for insistence that the nation is first of all imagined, ideal, and realized in codependence with a state. Yet in this, we think, he is the theorist observing at dusk, theorizing the world order of quiescent nation-states built decades before by the architects of a United Nations in the rubble of the Second World War—and theorizing them not as twentieth-century contingencies but as a modern necessity. To Anderson, the disconnection of nation from race or descent group and its connection to the state was, ironically, not a historical development but something intrinsic to the nation. The fact of the Nazis notwithstanding, he found scholarship seeing any connection between nationalism and racism simply "basically mistaken" (1983:148).

We turn now to how this United Nations utopia was made real.

DECOLONIZATION AND AMERICAN POWER

People and politics gradually and sometimes abruptly realigned to new global realities after World War II. Not only the United Nations, but a vast new constellation of intertwined global institutions, all both political and financial in their reach, emerged quickly after the war: the World Bank, planned originally in the U.S. Treasury Department in 1944 in order to orchestrate reconstruction loans; the first GATT, General Agreement on Tariffs and Trade, an idea launched out of the U.S. State Department's Division of Commercial Policy in early 1943 (Freeland 1972:36); proposals for an International Trade Organization and an International Monetary Fund, both launched out of Anglo-American planning sessions of 1945. All came to embody, in economic policy, the doctrine that the Americans were already calling "multilateralism," the principle of general rather than binarily negotiated rules for international trade. The new global institutions were products of literal dialogue among official representatives of the powerful nations of the globe. But the locations of the most significant negotiations and inaugurations—Bretton Woods, New Hampshire; Dumbarton Oaks in Washington, D.C.; San Francisco, California, signing the charter for a UN to be built in New York—suggest the degree to which the United States dominated the planning of the postwar world. And the Americans' multilateralist transformation of the globe was not merely abstractly embodied in these institutions. The Americans had serious leverage over England's economy after the war, via the vast British war debts and even vaster needs for reconstruction loans, and used it to open wider the doors into the world's most important protected economic network. Richard Freeland summarizes:

> Britain was not only one of the world's largest international traders, but also the dominant member of the single most important commercial system in the world, the Commonwealth trading bloc (or sterling bloc). This was a network of commercial arrangements or "Imperial Preferences" among the nations of the Commonwealth that enabled them to trade with each other on terms far more favorable than those available to other countries. Prior to the war the sterling bloc and North America had accounted for about one half of the world's trade. Agreement between the U.S. and Britain could largely determine the future of international commercial practices. The elimination of Imperial preference by the Commonwealth trading bloc was the single most important commercial objective of the American program for the implementation of multilateralism. (1972:18)

By 1945 the British had known for more than a century that free trade tended to benefit the most capable and most efficient national economies.[10] Nevertheless, given their other needs, they could put up only limited resistance. In short, they were hoisted on their own petard, and their empire faced more pressures, quickly, than merely the depletion of its resources by the world war and the well-organized anticolonial political movements. It is no wonder, and no mere matter of social evolution, that things fell apart for the British and other European imperials so quickly.

The United Nations idea quickened and oriented the anticolonial movements at least as dramatically as the discourses of liberal political economy had remade the case against slavery in Britain in the early nineteenth century. One can conclude that each marked the emergence of a new hegemony, institutional changes purveying a new common sense serving the new dominant class and nation. But "hegemony" stories can be as resistant to real specificity as any other dialecticism. We seek to underline a more specific moral: that it is time to configure decolonization as more than the end of something, postcoloniality as a space not merely outside something, but also the superimposition of something, the reconfiguration of local civil hierarchies into the terms of a new global plan for political order. And we want to underline that it was an American plan. It is no paradox to say that the United States, while a minor overseas colonizer, was the world's leader at decolonizing.

Not everything here was new, and the American plan was certainly not an Adamic monologue (in Bakhtinian terms), that is, not a self-contained and self-adequate discourse but rather something organized by its responses to others. The United States sought from very early on to fashion itself a republic in a world of empires, fearful of domination by outside powers, cognizant of the unstable precedent of the Roman republics, and aggressive, even predatory, in its own new ways.[11] Even from the days of the Monroe Doctrine, U.S. leadership voiced skepticism of imperial entanglement, both for others and themselves, and favored innumerable military interventions in the Americas over the building of an empire. Over time the United States elaborated a clear alternative general plan, combining the sheer real estate acquisitions of "manifest destiny" with demand for "open doors" everywhere else. The American preference for territories over colonies was well established long before the "annexation" of Hawai'i in 1898. Even the apparent large-scale exception—the deliberate Republican Party venture into overseas imperialism, claiming the Philippines, Cuba, and Puerto Rico after picking a fight with Spain—in fact showed clear marks of particularly American strategy. The predatory military logic of these conquests is incompletely appreciated when they are treated as a generic exercise in Western imperialism. It is no accident that the United States, when it chose to take possession, went long on geostrategic island groups but never bothered with large, expensive, densely populated insular territories, for example, China or even Mexico. In the decade before the acquisitions, Alfred Thayer Mahan vigorously argued for the necessity of expansion of American sea power, especially for a chain of coaling stations across the Pacific (i.e., as it came to be, especially Hawai'i, Midway, Guam, and Manila) and in the Caribbean leading to the forthcoming canal. To protect its national right to global trade, Mahan advised the nation to develop its global reach, its power to keep the crucial sea lanes open, and to project military force against enemies. Direct rule over others, or economic exploitation of conquered and governed peoples, was never the crucial element. For example, the Americans, concerned about expense, began their withdrawal from governance of the Philippines in the 1930s, long before even the fall of the Raj. But questions of military bases and rights of access were, and still are, always central.

The new nation-states, then, after 1945 are efficiencies of long-standing American strategies: self-determination, open doors, limited liabilities. The role of the United States in promoting and provoking decolonization has long been recognized by scholars of international relations (e.g., Louis 1977), but the full implications of it, no theory of nations and nationalism has yet addressed. Even the most critical anti-American analyses, even the rhetoric of the Vietnam era (see also Anderson 1991:148), has tended toward accusing the United States of imperialism and neocolonialism, accusations less wrong than imprecise: roughly as accurate, and illuminating, as it would be to explain the British Empire as kingdomism and neofeudality.

THE TRUMAN DOCTRINE AND THE NEW NATIONS PROJECT

To raise Vietnam, finally, is to remember also the Cold War. In fact, the ramifying pressures and dramatic conflicts of the Cold War have distracted scholarship from the more basic features of the new arrangements worked out in the postwar world, arrangements now reemerging (global GATTs, World Bank or IMF "bailouts," etc.) as if from nowhere in particular, fresh sprung from the Gods. Some fragments of diplomatic history again can suggest how tightly the Cold War was wound into, and interruptive of, the American plan for the postwar world. On October 9, 1944, while Franklin Roosevelt expressed "extreme satisfaction" with the results of the conference at Dumbarton Oaks, drafting the United Nations charter, Winston Churchill was arriving in Moscow, to secretly negotiate the division of the Balkans into Soviet and Anglo-American "spheres of influence."[12] Roosevelt reported to the American public that the plans established at the Yalta Conference in early 1945 "spell the end of the system of unilateral action and exclusive alliances and spheres of influence and balances of power and all the other expedients which have been tried for centuries—and failed" (quoted in Freeland 1972:43). It was not quite true, yet.

Karl Polanyi, as he wrote *The Great Transformation* during World War II, anticipated the collapse of "self-regulating" capitalism with as much certainty as did the 1919 Communist International, which had declared imperialism to be "capitalism moribund and decaying." Polanyi perceived the rise of protectionist imperial economic policies as the inevitable outcome of efforts of strong metropolitan powers to protect themselves from the vicissitudes of wholly free markets. The pattern Polanyi perceived could be described as one specific version of the more general dynamic that Weber identified toward a unifying regulative authority, and in that light in the twentieth century could be described as the collapse of four such orders: the one engineered by the British, imagining themselves a new Rome (see Kaplan and Kelly, forthcoming), the even more starkly racial projects of the Germans and of the Japanese, and, finally, the Soviet system that imagined itself postcapitalist. Or better, the twentieth century could be described as the collapse of these four efforts to provide a unitary regulative authority for large segments of our planet, and the success of a fifth, audacious enough to force a plan upon the whole of it. It was not only Polanyi who failed to perceive the powers that would be marshaled by the American plan. Where the war itself destroyed the Japanese and German plans, and the British were forced by their need for reconstruction loans to break up some of the most important of their "imperial preferences,"[13] the Soviets were less impressed and more resistant. Both during and after the war, the Soviets diagnosed the world economic situation far differently from the British or Americans, deploying the kind of political economic analysis, vent theory, that had held empires to be necessary to matured, collapsing capitalism. Defending their right to set independent and protective trade policies for their sphere, they argued both during and after the war that the real objective of the Americans was to rely on free markets to hinder the industrialization of the rest of the world. Unlike the Western European allies, who viewed the United States as the lender requiring placation, the Soviets expected the United States to wallow in a postwar crisis of overproduction. They "expected that America's need to export would force the extension of credits to the USSR without Soviet concessions, a view that deprived the US of one of its key negotiating points" (Freeland 1972:52).

In short, for the Soviets things did not go well, but it was not until the 1980s that the Soviets and their allies were led to see the virtues of the American planned multilateralism. For final snapshots of the difference between this American plan and all that had gone before it, let us remember not only the Truman Doctrine and American anti-Soviet hysteria, but also Churchill's vision of the Cold War, in contrast to Truman's. By March 12, 1947, Harry Truman officially replaced Roosevelt's optimism about an end to spheres of influence and balances of power with a new, Manichean vision that quickly became known as the Truman Doctrine:

> At the present moment in world history nearly every nation must choose between alternative ways of life. The choice is too often not a free one.
>
> One way of life is based upon the will of the majority, and is distinguished by free institutions, representative government, free elections, guarantees of individual liberty, freedom of speech and religion, and freedom from political oppression.
>
> The second way of life is based upon the will of a minority forcibly imposed upon the majority. It relies on terror and oppression. . . .
>
> I believe that we must assist free peoples to work out their own destinies in their own way. (Quoted in McCullough 1992:548)

A year later he specifically identified "the Soviet Union and its agents" as the force that had "destroyed independence and democratic character of a whole series of nations in Eastern and Central Europe" (McCullough 1992:608).

This Manichean vision treated the emerging Cold War specifically not as a great power rivalry or the waxing and waning of spheres of influence, but as a struggle between two types of nation, one free and the other under thrall. Even though the term "totalitarian" became ubiquitous in descriptions of the Soviet political system, an umbrella to smear it by connection to discredited Japanese and German aggressions, the Truman Doctrine still asserted, in fact, the permanent existence in every nation of a majority favoring the "free institutions" of the American plan. The "second way" was always the work of foreign influences and, at most, an internal minority.

The Truman Doctrine startlingly naturalized the free nation, with its roster of institutions, both as what any nation would choose if choosing freely, and as what Eastern and Central Europe had had before destructive forcible impositions by the Soviets. This is the script against which Hobsbawm has emphasized the shallowness of the actual history of nation-states in Eastern and Central Europe. But in a strange, important concomitance, to Truman the sense was crucial that a new era was making real some new general rules. If we compare Truman's political will with Disraeli's, we find very interesting similarities and differences. Each is certain that they speak with real knowledge of the true requisites and wishes of a vast number of nations, and each plans geopolitically. But where Disraeli raised the stick, Truman broke open the bank, flooding his specific crisis spots not, first of all, with troops but with aid; as Truman himself famously put it, "We must be prepared to pay the price for peace, or assuredly we shall pay the price of war." And when it did come to war, a contrast between Truman's and Churchill's sense of the issue is most illuminating. On July 19, 1950, Truman told the American public, on television, of its duty to respond to an "act of raw aggression." The North Koreans had violated the UN Charter, and though the United States would make the principal effort to save the invaded nation, the Republic of South Korea, they would fight under a UN command and flag. And this, he said, was a "landmark in mankind's search for a rule of law among nations" (quoted in McCullough 1992:792). Perhaps not quite for everyone. Churchill, the man who had brokered spheres of influence with Stalin while the Americans planned their multilateralist future, parsed the sides and issues somewhat differently, within his own, imperial vocabulary. Reunited with Truman in January 1952, and again prime minister of England, Churchill apologized for loathing Truman's leadership in 1945. "I misjudged you badly. Since that time, you more than any other man, have saved Western civilization" (McCullough 1992:875). In fact, something important was happening, more generally, to the very concept of civilization, the great colonial alibi, in the new world order. It was pluralizing, into civilizations—thus Churchill could speak of a specifically Western civilization. But it was also becoming a thing of the past, assimilating with the concept of tradition, against a conception of a modern, universal present in which everyone, equally, was or wanted to be free.

The Truman Doctrine provided cogent reasons for projecting the nation-state as both natural and desirable, the natural choice of every people modern and free, past present, and future. Even before actual decolonization was earnestly under way, the new Manichean story rivaled the critique of colonial domination itself. The Cold War drama rivaled decolonization and, with the aid of scholars especially in the United States, buried it in stories of tradition versus modernity, in studies of the needs, dangers, and dramas of modernization and development (see also Pletsch 1981). In anthropology in particular, even Columbia University materialists, scholars most sensitive to the long, complex history of European capitalist imperialism, could launch conceptions such as "deculturation," projecting a vast binary break between a more particularistic, culturally insular past and a more conscious, disillusioned present. Meanwhile, among self-proclaimed "idealists" led by Robert Redfield, the capitalist empires faded from view altogether, sunk with barely a ripple into the folk-urban continuum, and areas came to be known by their great and little traditions and degree and potential for modernizing, a vision dominated explicitly by the tradition–modernity binary. Civilizations, recast as traditions, however great, became the heritage of the past, and capitalist colonial institutions were doubly disguised: if there were chains to be cast off, these traditions were the ultimates, especially after formal decolonization in fact, and the very richness of great traditional heritage in the face of iron cages of modern practical reason enabled new forms of doubt, irony, and regret about all liberations.

The new nations project led by Fallers, Geertz, and others, clearly the high point of the anthropology of nations and nationalism before Anderson, was not without its insights. In particular, McKim Marriott's acute observations about the processes by which elites of new nations fashioned national narratives deserve more attention than they have received.[14] But the most influential scholarship of the project embedded the nation in the modernization narrative, especially Geertz's essay "The Integrative Revolution," wherein race, the preeminent principle of colonial capitalist divisions of labor, reemerged as a primordialist value of tradition-minded others, in a list with blood, language, locality, religion, and tradition. Geertz called them "the gross actualities" that, to a great extent in the new states, "their peoples' sense of self remains bound up in" (1973b:258). Geertz's analysis was as unclear on the way a specifically imperial past had bound those peoples' "sense of self" to a legally and economically rendered gross actuality of race, as it was on the specifics of an American plan for global legal structure that Geertz simply considered "modernity." The point is not merely that the new nations project was intertwined in Cold War assumptions about freedom and unfreedom, good and evil, and that this aspect of it embarrasses post-1960s anthropologists and explains our reluctance to examine connections to it. The more important point is that when the Cold War–period American anthropologists elaborated a distinction between tradition and modernity, the actual dynamics of decolonization were occluded by alleged necessities of modernization. In this way, these anthropologists were active participants in the routinization of the nation-state itself.

THE NATION-STATE AND ITS SCHOLARS

The palpable failure of the "new nations" paradigm articulated by Fallers, Geertz, Shils, and others has led anthropologists to Anderson's *Imagined Communities*, as if this vaguely Marxist study of dynamics of nationalist ideologies could provide an alternative baseline, in positive critique of Marxism, for a new anthropology of nationalism unfettered by a catastrophically naive past. But in fact, Anderson's argument reproduces precisely what was worst about the "new nations" paradigm before it: an unexamined evolutionism, a vague sense of necessity and inevitability to nation-states and national community, and an unfortunate peripheralization of colonial political dynamics, inadequately rectified by a new chapter in the second edition and in more recent writings.[15] *Imagined Communities* has provided a Marxist platform for a rerun of modernization theory. The anthropology of nationalism could use, now, an alternative to *Imagined Communities*.

These essays critique *Imagined Communities* and present an alternative approach to the study of nationalism. Against Anderson's depiction of a modular cultural idea of the nation as a kind of "imagined community" connected to "print capitalism," now globally, these essays stress the history of colonial reliance on conceptions of "communities" among the colonized as both an alibi for differences of rights and powers in law and as a vehicle for limiting and channeling political aspirations. At issue then is not imagined communities but represented communities, "communities" renewed in their existence not only by representations in the semiotic sense, but also by representation in the political, institutional sense. The shift from focus on diffusely totalized imaginaries to a dialogical semiotic terrain is itself important, enabling clearer recognition of representations by others as well as by selves in the constitution of possible and impossible nations. As Stuart Hall has argued, no identities without representation; so also, no communities without representation. But more crucial (and certainly connected) is representation in the other, more directly political sense of delegated powers of spokesmanship in actual political apparatuses and engagements: congresses and parliaments official and unofficial, elected and appointed, labor union leadership, committee constitution, the quotidian and intercessive works of lawyers and other advocates. As against Anderson's focus on synchronized and synchronizing news reading and pilgrimages of bureaucrats, deliberately quietistic portrayals of group-making dynamics, this book insists on examining conditions of possibility for effective political representation, crises in claims to

the proper organization of spokesperson standing in confrontations and negotiations—strikes, boycotts, legal cases, elections, commissions—and their
relationship to the ontics of community existence. What exactly are those
newspapers reporting on? Even rituals, especially national rituals, are sites
of complex negotiations of representations in both senses, as we shall see.

At least since Hymes 1969 and Asad 1973, anthropologists and other
scholars have tried in good faith to reconsider critically the connection of
their work to colonialism and imperialism. The overwhelming tendency of
critical scholarship has been to combine critique of American power and that
of the European empires in categories of "the West" and "the modern." In
this Benedict Anderson is hardly alone. In *Orientalism*, for example, Edward
Said portrays Americans as mere neophytes following in European footsteps,
declares the "parallels" between European and American imperial projects
"obvious," and repeatedly depicts the United States as accidentally achieving
power after World War II, "when the United States found itself in the position recently vacated by Britain and France" (Said 1979:16, 295, 290). Some
real insights have followed for study of "nations" from punctuating time at
1776, 1789, and 2000, by highlighting their Enlightenment emergence and
then a crisis of the late twentieth century, whether assessed in terms of "post-
modernity," "late capitalism," or "globalization." However, as theorists as
diverse as Dipesh Chakrabarty (2000) and Max Weber (1949) have emphasized, the reality of scholarly practice is that scholars commit to simplifying
punctuations that both limit and make possible their insights. If we put more
weight on 1945 than on either the Enlightenment or alleged crises of the
millennium, we get a very different and, we think, more enabling view of
global political forces. This point, and some of our intellectual debts, can be
clarified by discussing some of the best literature on nations and nationalism
written after *Imagined Communities*.

The most sustained critical commentary on Anderson's model, attentive
to issues of colonialism and postcoloniality, is that found in the works of
Partha Chatterjee. Anderson is surely wrong when he tries to dismiss the
issue of "derivative discourses" as a "bogey" (1998:117). In the same piece,
Anderson renews precisely the kind of argument that led Chatterjee to pose
his trenchant question. As Anderson sees it, Europe is the fount of national
institutional logic: "By the beginning of the century the 'electoral' mode of
population enumeration has assumed such normalcy in the metropoles that
it penetrated silently even into the colonial autocracies, where it could only
have long-term subversive effects" (126). "Silently"? "Could only"? The
sense of the irreversibility of metropolitan normalcy, the ineluctability of its
"penetrations," the lack of scope for agency, especially the passivity of the
penetrated except when they can only follow another given script—all this
is the stuff of Chatterjee's disquiet about nationalism as a derivative dis-

course. But for Chatterjee, the point is not that Anderson is wrong about all this. Chatterjee, like all the members of the Subaltern Studies school of historians, was challenged not just by Anderson, but also by Ranajit Guha's call, the year earlier, for an explanation of "the failure of the nation to come to its own" in postcolonial South Asia (Guha 1982; cf. Gandhi quotation earlier this chapter). Chatterjee has provided the most provocative series of answers to Guha's question of any member of the Subaltern Studies school, in a continuing effort to determine the implications of the fact that nationalism in South Asia is a derivative discourse, a sequence of efforts to adopt from the colonizing West. The course of his philosophical and historical inquiries has led Chatterjee to doubt social totalities, nation, state, or society, but also individuals, philosophical or naive, as the adequate starting point for imagining or discovering a nonderivative, nonhegemonized politics. He has come to celebrate the potential of the fragment, even to revive the *jati*, the caste, as a historical and potential unit of liberating struggle and to regard the Enlightenment, even modernity itself, as his nemesis. This is where Anderson has led him into a cul-de-sac.

Nationalism, and more particularly the nation-state, is a derivative discourse and an adopted nexus of institutions in South Asia. We agree with Chatterjee that theorists as astute as Gandhi are responsive to received ideas, in large part ideas received from the West. But from a dialogical point of view, nothing in that is particularly surprising. The desire for an Adamic, pristine point for departure, or any purity of alternative, is highly unpromising at best. The point can be made in reverse, to borrow a formulation of Korean sociologist Cho Hae-Joang, that to be colonized is to be required to use foreign things to live. The point is that in that sense (though clearly not in most other senses) we are all colonized in multiple ways. No one wholly invents their language, and only a group as deliberately forgetful as the colonizing Europeans could boast about their own unique civilization and neglect that everything from their semiotics and their number system to many basics of their print, military, and other technologies, much of their clothing patterns and materials and virtually all of their favorite foods were developed outside their own region.[16] The issue of derivative discourse gains its bite precisely when it is reframed within the simplistic fatalisms of a tradition-modernity-type, two-stage model. If one's nemesis is the entirety of European intellectual, social, and political history ever since Rousseau put pen to paper, then one has great reason for despair. But the nation-state, as sublime a reality as it is, should not be allowed to claim such a vast array of irreversible alliance. It is merely the currently successful product of twentieth-century U.S. economic leadership and military triumph, amplified by adroit and ruthless diplomacy. That is nemesis enough for a reorganizing global left, but on a planet with people who can still remember the defeat of the

Nazis, let alone Gandhi's nonviolent humbling of the Raj, it is a nemesis that can and should be taken head-on.

The mood, in current literature, is far from this optimistic. In the writings of many, one senses an iron-cage despair about current political prospects, or even, in such works as Stanley Tambiah's powerful *Leveling Crowds* (1996), a sober alarm over the privatization and proliferation of violence in the world's less functional nation-states. Tambiah, in his critique of the works of Subaltern Studies historian Gyanendra Pandey, also sounds another salutary warning, this one applying also to our project in this book. Pandey (1978, 1990) has researched and argued eloquently about the emergence of communalism, especially Hindu/Muslim communalism, in North India as a result of colonial policies and nationalist efforts to contest them. But too persuasively, Tambiah thinks. Not all of the political issues of the present can be laid to rest on the provocations and counteractions of the colonial period, especially fifty years after decolonization, Tambiah argues, and neither is it wise to imagine all ethnic histories and rivalries to be inventions no older than the colonial period. A skeptic of any monocausal schematic, Tambiah would have us distribute attention multiply, to the social-cultural long run, to the colonial period, and as well to the more proximate dynamics local and global when discussing more contemporary events. We take his point, but in these studies, we do connect contemporary crises to the colonial era, and more especially to the dynamics of decolonization: decolonization is crucial precisely because the contemporary crises are not the continuation of colonial-era communal conflicts, but rather the renegotiation of systems of representation under the pressures and within the limits of the new globally imposed model of nation-state.

David Scott has acutely described a post–Cold War impasse in postcolonial studies. In the wake of the collapse of the Soviet bloc and the failure to thrive of a long sequence of alternative third-path socialisms, from Nehru and Mao to Manley and Castro, "it is no longer so clear what 'overcoming' Western power actually means" (1999:14). We think that this is true especially when one punctuates time along the lines of Anderson's analysis of nationalism. Taking on nemeses like "the Enlightenment," "Western culture," "modernity," or "the (neo)liberal state" can lead one to the mood of the conclusion of *Imagined Communities,* sadly contemplating the wreckage of contemporary history. But what if "American power" no longer hides within "Western power"? What if critical scholarship seeks not the grandest nemesis but the dialogical history of much more particular, present political power, power still very much intact and alive? An American plan instituted in 1945 a network of global institutions that now thrive in a multicentered global linkage largely beyond the ken of its inventors. Its inventions have become lived and contested realities. We argue that critical scholarship on the nation-state could focus very productively on the era of decolonization and the United Nations, as the horizon for many real, present departures and initiatives.

THE CHAPTERS

Each an independent essay, the next five chapters nevertheless build an argument comprehensively as they proceed. Chapter 2 is the most squarely and polemically addressed to criticism of Anderson's work, and the last, chapter 6, is most comprehensive in articulating and exemplifying in real local detail the alternative approach we offer. Chapters 3 through 6 also build the lattice of ethnographic analyses of events in Fiji especially from the Second World War to the present.

Chapter 2: Time and the Global

Anderson relies much on Walter Benjamin in his portrayal of nations as parallel communities in "homogeneous, empty time." Beginning with Anderson's serious misunderstandings of Benjamin's arguments and imagery, this chapter argues that Anderson's model is one root of contemporary globalization theorists' oversymmetric portrayals of world political and ideological dynamics. Also reconsidering *Time and the Other*, Johannes Fabian's 1983 critique of evolutionary premises in anthropology, this chapter skeptically examines the replacement of Fabian's and existentialism's "the Other" with the new binary: local people versus (the largely implicit new class of) global people. Against Fabian's hope for a retotalizing dialectic of European self and the Other, this chapter argues for a dialogical, not dialectical, approach to global-local dynamics. And against Anderson's premise that homogenous, empty time is real, this chapter argues that calibrated asymmetries in global time were made real by colonial practices, that global "flows" still largely follow channels cut and opened in the European colonial era; that we have forgotten that glory and hierarchical self-assertion, not horizontal comradeship, were central to Europe's Rome-fantasizing imperial nations; that elite diasporas have replaced imperial conquests precisely in the wake of decolonization and the rise of UN ideology; and that Anderson's theory is an inadvertent expression of U.S. and UN ideology. Inter alia this chapter discusses the analyses of nation and empire of Ranajit Guha and Ruth Benedict and reconsiders Macaulay's minute on Indian education and Anderson's misunderstanding of it.

Chapter 3: Diaspora and World War, Blood and Nation in Fiji and Hawai'i

Blood can have extraordinary power in politics. This chapter concerns not the blood of descent but blood sacrificed, and its power to overcome political boundaries and to establish new ones. At the outset of World War II, close to half, roughly 45 percent, of the population of Fiji was South Asian by descent, and 37 percent of the population of Hawai'i was Japanese by descent. Both of these Asia-descended populations were introduced into their islands as labor for sugar plantations. At the outset of the war, Fiji was still a British colony and Hawai'i was a territory "annexed" by the United States. Despite fierce discrimination against them, in the context of the Pacific war between the United States and Japan, Japanese Hawaiians forced the United States to let them fight on the American side and parlayed wartime heroism and sacrifice in Italy into the foundation for claims to American citizenship. After the war, while most colonies demanded independence, Hawai'i voted overwhelmingly to become a state of the United States, and a Japanese-Hawaiian-dominated Democratic Party began a half-century of hegemony, bringing the New Deal to Hawai'i despite McCarthyist antagonism. In Fiji, Indo-Fijians followed the lead of the Indian National Congress to be skeptical of imperial war aims. In the face of efforts by local "Europeans" to use the emergency against them, they refused to support the war effort without government commitment to equality. And ever since, the question of their "loyalty" has been raised against them in local politics. Engaging recent science studies critiques of antirelativism—especially for the observation that the deepest objections to relativism concern not what it allows one to accept, but what it allows one to forget—and attacking the fetishization of identity in contemporary cultural scholarship, this chapter argues that memories of blood sacrificed are extraordinarily important in narrations of national past and future, and claims of right and place in contemporary politics.

Chapter 1: "They Cannot Represent Themselves"

This chapter explains the reaffirmation of race as the organizing principle of social life in Fiji during and after World War II, against the global trend against official racism that followed the war and the Holocaust. It does so by focusing on the logic of specific decisions in the midst of complex events: the refusal of Fiji's sugar company to negotiate the price of cane, and in fact its efforts to keep the price low, in order to maintain what it considered "normal"; the refusal of the Central Indian War Committee to carry out the Governor's wishes, and its decision to disband; and the decision of Ratu Sir Lala Sukuna, the highest-ranking Fijian in government service, first to accept and then to reject an offer by striking Indo-Fijian cane growers to give their cane to the government, in exchange for government taking responsibility for future price-setting. Explaining these events, this chapter sets out what we mean by "represented communities." "They cannot represent themselves" is part of a sentence of Marx's that Edward Said chose to make the frontispiece to *Orientalism*. As this chapter details, Said misunderstands

Marx's discussion, which concerns not only the semiotics of discursive representations, but the institutions by which collective will gains its spokespeople, representation as in voting systems and so on. This chapter draws on both senses of representation, and also on Gaston Bachelard's call for models that seek not to simplify but to render complexity intelligible, to argue that all communities require representation, that they never preexist their representation, and that there is no simple or natural form for such representation to take. We propose an approach to "community" cognizant of different but connected legal machineries constituting different kinds of community, sensitive especially to the importance of systems of "communal" representation in the European empires. We think that attending to colonial communities and the fate of their institutions of representation will better illuminate postcolonial situations than relying on a model of a simplex, modern form of nation to explain the options and choices of agents involved as colonial regimes were succeeded by new states. This chapter describes choices that doomed Fiji to continuing open and official racism.

Chapter 5: "Blood on the Grass and Dogs Will Speak"

This chapter chronicles the ritual politics of Fiji's decolonization, examining the ritual requirements of nationhood and the succession of efforts to fix a national political order in Fiji. Focusing on an eccentric Indo-Fijian prophet's unsuccessful efforts to create national rituals in the 1980s, it addresses the wider failure of a ritual order to sustain the (ostensible) social balances of Fiji's first constitution at independence in 1970. While the prophet's rituals changed little or nothing, the unsuccessful national celebrations and rituals of the 1970s were gradually supplanted in the 1980s by a Christian-chiefly ritual politics with deep roots in Fiji's colonial order, but no roles for Indo-Fijians. Following the 1987 military coups, the chiefly rituals of ethnic Fijians became unabashedly the foundation for ritual representations of state and nation. Nations require narratives, and narratives with key elements established beyond dispute; rituals are the vehicles for representing what is indisputably central as such. The radical changes of decolonization have been tangibly problematic, and the contradictions and shortcomings of post-colonies have been clearly visible, precisely on occasions of state ritual, when the nation must represent itself, freely, to itself and others.

Chapter 6: Constituting Fiji

This chapter ties together not only the critical but also the positive argument of the book, arguing for a new approach to locating the nexus of issues connecting identity, community, nations, and civil rights. We argue here against three approaches and in favor of a fourth, against (1) universalistic civil rights models, (2) indigenist models of communities of the *longue durée,* and

(3) the Andersonian image of the pirated, modal imagined community, in favor of (4) tracing histories of actually existing social contracts. Tracking deals struck between alleged representatives of social entities (nations, communities, empires, corporations, labor unions, etc.), both in terms of the institutionalized narrations of representation that define the deal makers' authority and the instituted narratives of the deals and their future use in constituting social order and boundaries, we hope to understand communities in terms of conditions of possibility that are definably historical. Past the scandal that these things are socially made, which is the end point of so much allegedly radical and deconstructive current scholarship, we seek to show how to understand why and how specific social constitutions are arranged and sustained, the dialogics of these deals and their institutionalization. The illustration is, of course, Fiji's history, from the Deed of Cession negotiations between British imperial officers and Fijian chiefs, and the negotiations between Fiji, India, and the Colonial Sugar Refining Company setting up indenture, to the Deed of Cession debate in 1946 affirming the deed as charter for the paramountcy of indigenous interests, to the 1987 coups, the 1990 and 1997 new constitutions for the Republic of Fiji, and, finally, the 2000 coups and their aftermath. We analyze literal constitutions and other constituting moments, to argue for an anthropology of nations and nationalism that takes seriously the manufacture of social charters, as well as colonial realities and legacies.

Time and the Global

AGAINST THE HOMOGENEOUS, EMPTY COMMUNITIES IN CONTEMPORARY SOCIAL THEORY

In short, *geopolitics* has its ideological foundations in *chronopolitics.*

—Johannes Fabian, *Time and the Other*

Comparison of others' attempts to setting off on a sea voyage in which the ships are drawn off course by the magnetic north pole. Discover *that* North Pole. What for others are deviations, for me are data by which to set my course. I base my reckoning on the differentia of time that disturb the "main lines" of the investigation for others.

—Walter Benjamin, "N (Re the Theory of Knowledge, Theory of Progress)"

Discourse on "globalization" is itself globalizing, from roots that are deeper in business and policy journalism than in the academy, and toward multiple futures trackable from no one vantage. As far as I can tell, its authors (now including me) tend to address it with an almost antinomic mixture of respect and aggression—respect for its sublime enormity and ubiquity, but also a sense of moral and political urgency to its specification, as two recent U.S. journalistic examples will illustrate:

Because this phenomenon we call "globalization"—the integration of markets, trade, finance, information and corporate ownership around the globe—is actually a very American phenomenon: it wears Mickey Mouse ears, eats Big Macs, drinks Coke. . . . [C]ountries that plug into globalization are really plugging into a high degree of Americanization. (Friedman 1996:A27)

* * *

How do you define the uniformity of thought prevailing in our societies? . . . My arrogance does not go so far as to offer a program to a movement that, anyhow, needs a vision, not a blueprint. But I am brave enough to suggest four points, four taboos that the movement will have to smash if it is not to be blocked by the diversions of official propaganda. The first is the assumption that the form the internationalization of the economy has taken—so-called globalization—is a natural and inevitable result of technological progress. Actually, it is the outcome of a deliberate policy: the extraordinary expansion of international transactions has more to do with the decision to free capital movements than with the invention of computers and modems. (Singer 1996:22)

Here I am more interested in what is similar about these texts than their differences. For Thomas L. Friedman, the foreign affairs columnist for the *New York Times*, "The only answer is multi-localism," not Daniel Singer's movement, both "multi-localism" and "Americanization" are precisely the sorts of thing that Singer, Europe correspondent for *The Nation*, seeks to dismiss as diversions. Yet both Friedman and Singer invoke not globalization but something someone was "calling" globalization, both rely on synecdochical icons (mouse ears, modems) to concretize vast process, and both give the underlying process two definitions—what it is and what it really is: first the globalization definition (Friedman's "the integration of . . . ," Singer's "the form the internationalization of the economy has taken"), and then the discernment of true underlying form: "Americanization" or "the decision to free capital movements."

I am not interested in dismissing globalization as a false front, false consciousness, mere surface, or even partial truth (though at times, as you will see, I feel all these ways about "identity"). I am more interested in what globalization is, than in what it really is, more interested in its implications for theory and method in social and cultural scholarship, than in playing the hero finding the secret core (though one cannot avoid both roles when things get serious). I will reconsider arguments akin to those of Friedman and Singer: Friedman's is anticipated in theories of "Westernization" and perspicaciously criticized by Ulf Hannerz; Singer's outrage against premises about natural and inevitable progress is anticipated by Walter Benjamin. We are well advised by both Friedman and Singer to remember, even when we focus on matters of culture and cultural globalization, that it all obviously has something to do with corporations and capital. But let us return to what globalization is, now not any alleged underlying thing called "globalization," but the theory, in the context of social theory.

Globalization theory, as I see it, distinguishes itself in social theory with an important premise, a new solution to the long-standing "units problem" for comparative social science.[1] Against presumption that societies, cultures, nation-states, or other units exist, that they are bounded, separate, discrete, and/or autonomous, the premise of globalization theory is that, at least at present, there are no absolute political, social, or cultural boundaries un-breached by global flows. Comparison, generalization, or any other modes of social theorizing, whether about economics, religion, kinship, or politics, must then address not separate examples or discrete cases, but rather phenomena that are densely and dynamically interconnected. So, now what? As Hannerz has put it, the problem now is "grasp of the flux" (1992:267).

Against the absurd prospect of writing the world, the search is on for conceptions of social realities that are supple enough to handle this flowing and flowed-at mode of being. If we neglect, here, deliberately reductionistic approaches claiming foreknowledge of the real social foundations, common current tools for grasping the flows include concepts of identity, ethnicity, and nation as imagined community. Richard Fardon, for example, has recently argued that the conceptions of culture and society have come to seem "innocent dupes of the political triad" of nation, ethnicity, and identity, that representations of the very existence of cultures or societies are "a derivative fact," complicit in "the historical plots" of nationality, ethnicity, or identity, and the agents possessing and possessed by them (1995:7–8). Fardon's description certainly captures the trend of contemporary scholarship, but the problem has not been solved. No matter how earnestly the new names avoid innocence by emphasizing explicit and implicit political interests, nothing, it seems to me, is less likely to solve the problem of "grasping the flux" than allowing new names to revitalize the old units and keep us operating as if the world is first of all a collection of nameable groups.

This chapter will address the limits I perceive to reliance on conceptions of identity, ethnicity, nation, and other forms of "imagined community" as a solution to the problem of describing either "local" or "flowing" social dynamics in an already globalized social field. It will proceed mainly by a critical rereading of *Imagined Communities*, Benedict Anderson's remarkable, now-classic reflection on nations and nationalism, with particular attention to the story of global history as Anderson tells it and to Anderson's use of Walter Benjamin's concept of "homogeneous, empty time."[2] Not to put too fine a point on it, it will be a polemic against Anderson's understanding of Benjamin's concept and its implications, and thereby an argument against an aspiration for global symmetries that I perceive as an unpromising feature of much current scholarship. Before turning to Anderson's arguments and images, however, I will offer a few more comments about space-time premises and the scholarly place of globalization theory itself: both the place globalization theory finds in genealogies of social theory, and the place globalization theory offers scholars in its world.

THE PLACE, SPACE, AND TIME OF GLOBALIZATION

More than fifteen years ago, Carl Pletsch published a powerful description and critique of the division of labor in the (Western) social sciences circa 1950 to 1975. His main point was that modernization theory organized social science research in the West and did so even though scholars were skeptical from the outset of the very idea of modernizing. Modernization theory informed the idea of First, Second, and Third Worlds, "the most primitive system of classification in our social scientific discourse" (Pletsch 1981:565) and justified the allocation of different kinds of scholarship to each—economists to the First World, for instance, area specialists to the Second, and anthropologists to the Third. General laws of human behavior were thought to be visible especially in the First World, where things and people were most developed and unconstrained by either ideology (as in the Second World) or tradition or culture (as in the Third). The Third World was destined to modernize and become either more like the First World or entrapped in ideology by the Second. Or so went the theory.

Pletsch argued persuasively that one could not simply "cast aside this conceptual ordering of social scientific labor," entrenched as it was in the research programs of disciplines. He called instead for criticism "in the Kantian, Hegelian, and Marxist sense": not only acknowledgment that the modernization theory and its three-worlds scheme was imbricated with the politics of the Cold War—that much was obvious, he showed, to everyone from the outset—but criticism that would "finally transcend it by devising another conceptual umbrella for social science that will serve all the useful purposes that the three worlds notion served, without its obvious defects" (588). Whether or not social history actually follows a Hegelian dialectic, something I doubt, Pletsch is surely right that social theory does.

In 1981 Pletsch predicted that a revolution against the paradigm was in preparation. I would argue that since then, not one but two alternative conceptual umbrellas have been proposed with both the potential breadth of reference and the conceptual simplicity (or "primitivity") necessary to be new transdisciplinary paradigms. Both are imbricated with changes in the social world, including the end of the Cold War, but neither, as yet, has been established institutionally: I refer, of course, to postmodernism, on the one hand, and globalization theory, on the other.

The topic here being globalization, I won't inquire very far into the unique history of postmodern social theory. Its history has already been written, always already, by postmodernists themselves. In fact, postmodernism has narrated its own story continually, self-consciously, and even obsessively. Drawn forth especially when both Third World hopes and Second World threats grew increasingly dubious, postmodernism has offered the drama of its own arrival as the concept capable of overcoming the drama of modernization. For this reason, despite real commitment to anti-essentialism and nonfoundational theorizing, it has trouble abiding without seeming at least as final, at least as much a claim to being the end of history itself.

The three worlds of modernization, as a classification scheme, presented first of all a geography. It was a geography connected to a history, but first of all a simple image or "primitive classification" of space. Postmodernism subsumed the spaces of modernization in a three-stage scheme of time, encompassing the dramas of modernization as a mere prelude to the creative destruction of the modern by the postmodern. Now, globalization returns us to space—finds in space a way out of the end of time.

To be clear here, all three of these "conceptual umbrellas" for social science are chronotopic (Bakhtin's term), conceptions that establish space-time possibilities. All project premises about both space and time, the configuration of human places and their possibilities past, present, and future. Nonetheless, what they distinguish, count, and name in the foreground varies extremely, an alternation with a clear dialogic. In a globe of blurring Cold War boundaries, a time scheme projecting a radically new future enabled subsumption of modernization's three worlds into the past; precisely as that future failed to objectify itself as a real and present new society arise calls for new kinds of observation of social relations in space. It has been fair for scholars to ask of postmodernism what were its premises about allegedly "other" societies in space, about cultural difference and colonial history (see, for example, Chow 1993; Kaplan 1995b; Spivak 1994; Stoler 1995). It strikes me as equally fair, and more interesting, to ask now what theories of time and history are possible within the premises of globalization. This, and not either deconstruction or defense of anyone's nation or identity, seems to me the intrinsic task for cultural scholarship in a globalizing world.

TO THE ANGEL OF HISTORY, THE NATION IS NOT AN IMAGINED COMMUNITY

So now we turn to Anderson's *Imagined Communities* in pursuit of the theory of global time and history that, I think, makes this text so influential among scholars. In Anderson's formulations, the nation is a community constituted by imagined rather than face-to-face relationships, especially by a sensibility of "deep, horizontal comradeship" (Anderson 1991:7), feelings fostered by print capitalism, especially novels and newspapers. "Print-language is what invents nationalism" (134) and, in turn, "nations inspire love, and often profoundly self-sacrificing love" (141). Thus Anderson argues, nations and nationalism are "cultural artefacts of a particular kind" (4), born in the break-away self-consciousness of the "creole pioneers," that is, the European colonies in the New World, then "awakened" in Europe and pirated into being elsewhere, a "modular" kind of cultural artifact, "capable of being transplanted" (4), "available for pirating" in the early nineteenth century (81), and "everywhere modularly imagined" after World War II (113). What we have here is not only a cultural theory of the nation, but also a story of an emergently modularized global culture, a story of capital-driven print languages rendering the world into synchronized, symmetrical units of imagined communal self-love.

In order to put Anderson's theory of the nation into bold relief, let us carry with us three other depictions of what distinguishes nations among human groups.

> So what, we may ask, is the just basis for a nation's claim to independence? Must a people first wander the wilderness for 2,000 years, suffer repeated per-secution, humiliation and genocide in order to qualify? Until now, history's answer to the question has been pragmatic and brutal: a nation is a people tough enough to grab the land it wants and hang onto it. Period. (Le Carré 1994)

This version of "history's" definition of the nation, from an op-ed newspaper essay by novelist John Le Carré (1994), is refreshingly uninterested in cog-nition, sensibilities, and experiences, and refreshingly interested in the will, of the typical active nation. Recalling, next, Ernest Renan's now-classic dis-cussion (1990 [1882]) of the nation as definable not by shared race, language, antiquity, or territory, but by shared memory and will, Le Carré's definition poses an interesting challenge to the scholarly tradition now following Bene-dict Anderson. Anderson's discussion of the nation has sent recent schol-arship in search of nationalism as a style of memory, imagination, and community, in search of expressions and elicitations of "deep, horizontal comradeship," and so on. As if nationalism was adequately understood as some kind of search for, realization, and enactment of some kind of identity. Is there more to matters of will, especially the importance of organized, in-stituted will, than is imagined in our current philosophies of identity?

Max Weber puts a similar insight more practically:

> Time and again we find that the concept "nation" directs us to political power. Hence, the concept seems to refer—if it refers at all to a uniform phenome-non—to a specific kind of pathos which is linked to the idea of a powerful political community of people who share a common language, or religion, or common customs, or political memories; such a state may already exist or it may be desired. (Weber 1978:393–94)

In this brief and far less-celebrated comment on the nation as a type of social group, Weber singles it out for a specific emotion, "this pathetic pride in the power of one's own community, or this longing for it" (394), group obsession with seeking, having, and revealing power and privilege.[3]

The estrangement of the nation as a social form is accomplished differently by this trio, Renan, Weber, and Le Carré, than it is by Anderson. If we understand the nation to be a collective, let alone collected, will to power, then we can expect far more from its praxis than the quiescent being of community, and similarly we have different questions about its poetics, the chronopolitical imaginaries that might collect and direct the wills. Quite concretely, we might inquire more into imaginations of the present and future as well as shared forgettings and memories. As scholars try to describe a globalizing world, to grasp the flows, we should not be naive about what historical imagery is for. Especially if we seek to understand the poetics and praxis of people in these flows, colonizers, migrants, and other diasporic peoples, and if we seek to accomplish practical things with these understandings—as I think we should—we might admit that by trying to grasp this flow, and to lead others to a general consciousness of it, we are also trying to interrupt other narratives of history, in Prasenjit Duara's phrase, "rescuing history from the nation."

In this sense, grasping the flow, finding and communicating present realities that transgress nation-state imaginaries, resembles what Walter Benjamin depicted as seizing a flash in a moment of danger, a praxis for historians (1968:255). The real task of the historian, Benjamin insists, was not to relive the past by empathy, not to set the present aside in order to recover (in a naive sense) the way it really was, and certainly not to locate and portray with a judicious evenhandedness the same number of details about each unit of time across equal units of space, as if human history were a story of progress across "homogeneous, empty time" (261). Instead, Benjamin calls upon historians to be cognizant of debts and danger, debts owed to the dead who struggled and sacrificed and danger in the present. This historian realizes that "*even the dead* will not be safe" (255) without historians' active intervention, that memory of losses and sacrifices will be lost or distorted in the interests of the presently powerful, and, most importantly, that memories of past struggles, the flashes seized, can become inspiration for political movements in the present and future.

Benedict Anderson relies on Walter Benjamin, and specifically on imagery from Benjamin's "Theses on the Philosophy of History," to provide much of the mood and some of the substance of his study of *Imagined Communities*.[4] Tracking the different moods and meanings that Anderson attaches to Benjamin's images will enable us to trace how far Benjamin's ideas actually orient the theorizing of Benedict Anderson and to spot, quite vividly, the chronopolitical vectors that are specifically Anderson's. In particular, to state my own thesis, Anderson's theory of the peculiarity of the nation as an "imagined community" depends upon his use of Benjamin's image of "homogeneous, empty time" (1968:261, 264): but Anderson insists upon acceptance of the reality of this chronotope, which to Benjamin was precisely the image of history that had to be refused.

We shall twice return to "homogeneous, empty time," but to open questions about mood and purpose, let us begin with the "angel of history," another image from Benjamin (1968), with which Anderson concluded the first edition (1983) of *Imagined Communities:*

> In all of this, China, Vietnam, and Cambodia are not in the least unique. This is why there are small grounds for hope that the precedents they have set for inter-socialist wars will not be followed. . . . [N]othing can usefully be done to limit or prevent such wars unless we abandon fictions like "Marxists as such are not nationalists," or "nationalism is the pathology of modern developmental history," and instead, do our slow best to learn the real, and imagined, experience of the past.

Of the Angel of History, Walter Benjamin wrote that:

> His face is turned towards the past. Where we perceive a chain of events, he sees one single catastrophe which keeps piling wreckage upon wreckage and hurls it in front of his feet. The angel would like to stay, awaken the dead, and make whole what has been smashed. But a storm is blowing from Paradise; it has got caught in his wings with such a violence that the angel can no longer close them. The storm irresistibly propels him into the future to which his back is turned, while the pile of debris before him grows skyward. The storm is what we call progress. [Benjamin 1968:257–58]

> But this angel is immortal, and our faces are turned towards the obscurity ahead.

To sense some tension between Anderson's own tropes and Benjamin's, consider the progressivism of Anderson's forward-facing scholar doing his or her "slow best," who hopes to do something eventually useful "to limit or prevent wars," and the scholar-heroes envisioned in Benjamin's thesis, seizing flashes in moments of danger, "man enough to blast open the continuum of history" (Benjamin 1968:262). Anderson asks in the first line to the preface of the second edition, "Who would have thought that the storm blows harder the farther it leaves Paradise behind?" (xi). I think Benjamin would have, the Benjamin who announced that "it is our task to bring about a real state of emergency" (1968:257). Where Anderson declares himself "haunted by the prospect of further full-scale wars between the socialist states" (1991: xi), Benjamin seems haunted, instead, not by active nationalists or indeed by the fascists, but by the specter of quiescence among the exploited. What, then, is Benjamin's hopelessly aware angel of history doing for Anderson's text?

Clearly, a pathos of nationalism is located especially, for Anderson, in socialist nations. Anderson's text begins and ends with the wars in Indochina, wars "of world historical importance" because the belligerents were "revolutionary" states engaging without plausible denial in "conventional" war (1991:1). Anderson sees and measures out nationalism—strange and important to notice—first of all, neither, for example, as an anticolonial civil force nor as a pressure of a United Nations world-spirit, not as a bourgeois ideograph nor as a modern necessity, but instead as the demon responsible for derailing "regimes whose independence and revolutionary credentials are undeniable" (1), derailers of world history. The nation first commands Anderson's attention as the killer of a utopian political aesthetic.

Thus while pathos abounds, we find quite different foundational resentments directed at nationalism by Anderson than, for example, by Le Carré. The assignment of pathos in Le Carré's plain tale is the more easily accounted for (and I hope not caricatured, for it cuts close to my own commitments) in the Nietzschean template for ("slave") philosophies based on resentment: the politically weak intellectual, morally sympathetic with the weak of the world, will tend to find ordinary political quests for power not good but evil, especially when they succeed. Anderson, more complexly, blames nationalism for the collapse of a political dream revealed as a fantasy, the virtuous revolutionary state, and yet locates nations first of all in the social imaginary and the explosion of the fantasy in "world history" (cf. "world historical" quoted above). He then refuses Tom Nairn's depiction (quoted in Anderson 1991:5) of nationalism as the modern pathology, favoring instead this "slow best" research into the nation as experienced. The result is a fascinated delineating of the real effects of the nationalist imaginary, a delineation now undertaken by an army of scholars and still overarched with a vast sense of disappointment and disillusionment.

Benjamin's own pathos finds a third vector, not directed at the nation or nationalism. Benjamin, the most flamboyant in his resentments, attacks especially (not fascists but) Social Democrats, for their narcotic doctrines of gradualist progress:

> The concept of the historical progress of mankind cannot be sundered from the concept of its progression through a homogeneous, empty time. . . .
> History is the subject of a structure whose site is not homogeneous, empty time, but time filled by the presence of the now. Thus, to Robespierre ancient

Rome was a past charged with the time of the now which he blasted out of the continuum of history. The French Revolution viewed itself as Rome reincarnate. . . .

The awareness that they are about to make the continuum of history explode is characteristic of the revolutionary classes at the moment of their action. . . .

We know that the Jews were prohibited from investigating the future. The Torah and the prayers instruct them in remembrance, however. This stripped the future of its magic, to which all those succumb who turn to the soothsayers for enlightenment. This does not imply, however, that for the Jews the future turned into homogeneous, empty time. For every second of time was the strait gate through which the Messiah might enter. (Benjamin 1968:261, 264)

For Benjamin, the idea of living in homogeneous, empty time is pathetic, and the agents promoting it were evil. The pathos of the angel—unable to intervene, awaken the dead, make whole what is smashed—is not his final word. Tellingly, the angel appears far closer to the final word of Anderson's essay than he does in Benjamin's theses. Benjamin ends here with the Messiah and allies the historian not with the angel (not doing "our slow best to learn the real, and imagined, experience of the past" [Anderson 1991:161]), but with the Messiah, shaping "a conception of the present as the 'time of the now' which is shot through with chips of Messianic time" (Benjamin 1968:263). What exactly it means to figure the agent of revolution as the Messiah is something that Benjamin scholars might never settle,[5] but Benjamin's scorn is palpable for this conception of homogeneous, empty time, the Benjaminian image that, above all, Benedict Anderson found useful.[6]

GATES THROUGH TIME AND SPACE

So Benjamin offers us, as the antidote to the Social Democrats' "homogenous, empty time" of slow progress and deep, horizontal symmetries, an image of intellectually fostered, but class-based, anti-evolutionary messianic moments. When the French Revolution exploded the continuum of history by viewing itself as Rome reincarnate, this "tiger's leap into the past . . . this same leap into the open air of history is the dialectical one, which is how Marx understood the revolution" (Benjamin 1968:261). Recalling that, for Anderson, the scandal of ordinary war among purportedly "revolutionary" states marked the end of utopian illusions, perhaps we should reluctantly agree with Anderson as a rewriting of Benjamin, into the deeper pathos in which the homogeneous and empty is the real, and historian intellectuals can only partner with the angel. Or can we find things between the theological and the null? Even if we don't want to rely on Messiahs, revolutions, or dialectical tiger's leaps, can we still find gates through time and space, and space-times neither homogenized nor emptied? Probably almost everywhere.[7] But let us content ourselves, for this chapter, with two descriptions of diasporic people, by intellectuals themselves enmeshed in the histories of movement. Both concern the configuration of space and time in the British Empire, the first chosen, perhaps perversely, as an example of a failed effort to homogenize and empty a history of human labor flow, the second, a return to one of Anderson's paradigmatic figures.

Benedict Anderson's reflections on nationalism focus on shared memory, and he added a chapter to the second edition (1991) on the strangeness of the obliged amnesias that stabilize national narratives. In the Fiji Islands, I find a striking instance of an amnesiac recollection of diasporic passage that was a literal effort to orient a national memory. Could anyone narrate the colonial exploitation of labor diaspora within the frame of inevitable gradual progress? Yes, of course; and doing so—to transpose Benjamin's objection to the tactics of the Social Democrats—can lead the diasporic population (like "the working class") to "forget both its hatred and its spirit of sacrifice, for both are nourished by the image of enslaved ancestors rather than that of liberated grandchildren" (Benjamin 1968:260). This message was published by the Honorable Vivekanand Sharma, member of Fiji's Parliament, in a supplement to the *Fiji Times* (May 12, 1979), Fiji's leading English-language (and simply, leading) newspaper. The supplement commemorated the centenary of the first arrival of indentured South Asians to Fiji, where their descendants have become half the population. One would never know, from Sharma's tone, that politicians among the ethnic Fijians, the other half of Fiji's population, were already increasingly encouraging of ethnic Fijian nativism and resentments against "Indians" or Indo-Fijians. The first of Fiji's pro-ethnic Fijian, anti-Indo-Fijian military coups was five years and two days away.

> Pioneering has always been a major element in the development of resources for the good of mankind and there are numerous examples of this in history. The Christian Bible tells of how the prophet Moses led his people out of Egypt into the promised land across the Nile where today after decades of toil flourishes the land of Israel.
>
> In the History of India itself there were mass migrations of people from Asia Minor to North India and from North India to the Deccan Plateau. In recent history there have been pioneering movements from India to Mauritius, Trinidad, South Africa, British Guyana, Surinam and Fiji.
>
> All of these movements have been in search for a better opportunity to enjoy life in its fullest sense. In many cases it has involved hardships that have

been conquered and those of us who are living in Fiji now are reaping the fruits of the efforts of our forefathers. Our chosen land is a land of peace, of freedom, of religion, and of opportunities. It is our duty today to continue with the good work done by those whose memory we treasure so much to ensure that our children and all those who follow them will have the same opportunities that were created for us.

People who move inherit the earth. All they have to do is keep up the good work, "in search for a better opportunity." If Benjamin would find pathos in the pleasure taken in the present and expected in the future as an arrival across a continuous progress, and if Anderson might find pathos in the simultaneous, purposeful remembrance and forgetting of past hardship and (here displaced) conquest, I fight a virtual anger at the mildness of this political will. We should fight such anger, in the interests of a clearer understanding. In Fiji, after the Indo-Fijians forced independence onto both the British and the ethnic Fijians and before the coups interrupted all stories of evolving constitutional democracy in Fiji, Indo-Fijian politicians had persistently tried to shape the nation in this romance of development (see also Kelly 1988a). Abandoning all grievances and pleading for community and future prosperity, abjuring their hatred for their intimate enemies the British, the Indo-Fijians had hoped to evade the hatred of the ethnic Fijians. It didn't work; few among the ethnic Fijians have yet come to see themselves as partners with immigrants in a world of flows in search of better opportunity and continuous progress, and one hears fewer serious efforts, in recent years, to tell the story this way.

Benjamin underestimated the fascists in his attack on the Social Democrats, as much as Sharma underestimated the Fijian nationalists in his nervous triumphalism about Fiji's freedoms. Of course, there is a sense in which the Indo-Fijians have maintained "the same opportunities" for their children, since Indo-Fijians had almost as little actual political power in 1979 as they do at present. Nonetheless, something very odd is going on, not only in Fiji but in many other places in the world, in the willed forgetting of the exploitation and violence of colonial labor history in some narrations of diaspora, in diaspora narratives of "opportunity" and "progress" that abandon the power of memories of sacrifice. There are many varieties of transnational, diasporic pathos, not only willed forgetting but also remembering, for example remembering a "promised land" across intervening millennia. Dilemmas in the representation of diasporic flows cannot be understood, I suspect, except in relation to dilemmas in the collecting of political will. For now, though, what has been demonstrated is that homogenizing and emptying the diasporic passage, the assertion of a shared, evolving prosperity-world, can be a desperate and even doomed tactic in some localities, even if it draws upon the tropics of the European Social Democrats that Benjamin hated and Anderson thought already universal.

What we shall seek next are the means to imagine transformations taking place as things "flow" that do not fit any Hegelian script: changes that are not merely progressive, arrested, or regressive, not merely gradual or revolutionary, not merely big or small movements in one field, but, rather, other kinds of interruptions, eruptions, and especially connections of social time and space. In this search we shall be well served by other tools to measure and describe. Thus I defer our second diasporic self-narrative, a British one, until after we develop a new descriptive concept.

SEA CHANGES

Both Ruth Benedict and Ranajit Guha resort to a Shakespearean allegory, the "sea-change," to characterize transformations that they find particularly significant. First, Benedict, in her World War II ethnography of Japan, *The Chrysanthemum and the Sword:*

> I found that once I had seen where my Occidental assumptions did not fit into their view of life and had got some idea of the categories and symbols they used, many contradictions Westerners are accustomed to see in Japanese behavior were no longer contradictions. . . . Virtue and vice as the Occident understands them had undergone a sea-change. The system was singular. It was not Buddhism and it was not Confucianism. It was Japanese—the strength and the weakness of Japan. (1946:19)

Benedict also uses other metaphors for the same process of change.[8] More interesting for us, she connects these breaks in the flow of translation, these "sea-changes" experienced by anthropologists and others, to the larger and longer history of cultural flows and change that Benedict, Boas, and most of the Boasians were interested in:

> A tribe may share ninety per cent of its formal observances with its neighbors and yet it may have revamped them to fit a way of life and a set of values which it does not share with any surrounding peoples. In the process it may have had to reject some fundamental arrangements which, however small in proportion to the whole, turn its future course of development in a unique direction. (Benedict 1946:9)

Anything that flows across cultural boundaries can undergo a sea change as it is fit into a different way of life and set of values. The process itself can turn future courses of development in unique directions.

To me this sounds much like the global process Ulf Hannerz has labeled creolization. Of course Benedict, more than most of the Boasians, had a commitment to the unity of a cultural pattern that puts her work out of step with commitments in globalization studies to privilege heterogeneity, to imagine all boundaries porous, and to render locality more complexly and contingently. Few would now follow her lead in privileging the whole culture as a unitary agent, and I don't doubt that the premises of globalization oversimplify the world less than hers did. Equally, however, it would be wrong to accuse her of seeing cultures as either ahistoric or hermetically sealed; in fact, the evidence is ample that she, like her teacher Boas, was fundamentally interested in this process of sea change, in which transcoursing values both get changed and make changes, without one grid for their history or vector to their "development."

The Shakespearean source of the "sea-change" metaphor is *The Tempest* 1.2:

> Full fathom five thy father lies,
> Of his bones are coral made,
> Those are pearls that were his eyes.
> Nothing of him that doth fade
> But doth suffer a sea-change
> Into something rich and strange.

Things rich and strange, made by their refashioning after transcursion into a new context. Bruno Latour, among more recent social theorists, is fascinated by the way objects brought into being for a purpose, with their function inscribed into their form, can then gain a life of their own, new functions that further affect their form; subjects too. Full cognizance of this fundamental similarity, in fact, undermines the absolute separation of subjects and objects, Latour argues. If indeed one abandons anchors—if one resents nautical play, "grounding" is also an adequate, slightly more abstract image—like Benedict's presumption of the always ongoing whole culture, then, following Latour, one finds a world in which all similarity and difference is made, negotiated, renegotiable, a world both multiply ordered and orderable, and inexhaustibly chaotic as well. A world without stability in functions or telos even for well-made subjects and objects, without one direction for progress. Rich and strange indeed (though some might argue that Weber already described it).

Let us counterpose this supercreolizing sea-change world, which could in its own kaleidoscopic way be homogenized and in some sense empty, with a different scholar's "sea-change." Hannerz's classic contrast of global process pitted "creolization" as a world pattern against "Westernization," the sort of world vision ambiguously promoted by Benedict Anderson in his conceptualizations of modal, pirated nationality and nationalism, "cultural artefacts" with "formal universality" (Anderson 1991:4–5). Anderson does open the door to a more creolizing reading. He carefully insists that "once created, they became 'modular,' capable of being transplanted, with varying degrees of self-consciousness, to a great variety of social terrains, to merge and be merged with a correspondingly wide variety of political and ideological constellations" (4). Depending upon how we imagine these mergers, then, we would seem to place the world proliferation of nationalism and nationality somewhere on a Westernization-creolization spectrum, and somewhere between stable modules of form, and merger mush.

"Merging and being merged with" does not quite get us to the kinds of rejections and contentions observable in Fiji and elsewhere. Ranajit Guha observes a different sea change when the British devised the so-called "Permanent Settlement," a land-tenure rule for a conquered territory, Bengal:

> By tracing the intellectual ancestry of the Permanent Settlement to the very beginnings of Political Economy, it also helps to throw some light on the latter as it moves along an important, if obscure, part of its trajectory. Physiocratic thought, the precursor of Political Economy, was an implacable critique of feudalism in its native habitat and proved to be a real force in undermining the *ancien regime.* Ironically, however, while being grafted to India by the most advanced capitalist power of that age, it became instrumental in building a neofeudal organization of landed property and in the absorption and reproduction of precapitalist elements in a colonial regime. In other words, a typically bourgeois form of knowledge was bent backwards to adjust itself to the relations of power in a semi-feudal society. . . .
>
> Political Economy was not the only body of knowledge to have suffered a sea change under conditions of colonialism. There were other systems of thought too which the western bourgeoisie had relentlessly used in their struggle against feudalism during the period of their ascendancy in their own societies but which they modified and compromised all too readily in order to find a social base for their power in the conquered lands of the Asian continent. Capitalism which had built up its hegemony in Europe by using the sharp end of Reason found it convenient to subjugate the peoples of the East by wielding the blunt head. (Guha 1981:6–7)

A "sea change under conditions of colonialism" involves something more than merging or even creolizing. It involves a reconsideration of its tools according to new needs by a transcoursing agency.[9] Under the Permanent Settlement, Bengal gets endowed with a tradition suited to the needs of new rulers and foisted as continuous with an alleged despotic oriental past, a land-tenure system of "permanent" rights and duties. The terms and descriptions of political economists are deployed to distill a legal feudalism for Bengal, even while in Europe this new discourse on political economy is a vital tool in the deliberate dismantling of "unfree" feudal regimes.

Bengal was fixed in a tradition by a modern-minded colonizer, and not its own tradition, but a useful tradition, an almost caricatured feudalism as remembered by those who were its implacable foes in Europe, and a feudalism improved to stabilize both colonial relations and company incomes.[10] Regardless how much actual bad faith there was in the colonizers' construction of a legal memory of the past of the colonized, clearly a variable in actual colonial history, there was omnipresent a will to make the colonial law work efficiently, and to that end, to match up found law in some workable way with the needs of the colonizers' present. Further, Guha's main point, the retooling also most radically affected the most radical of the new political discourses of the colonizers' home social order. The growing range of enlightenment freedoms, let alone the deepening formal horizontality of democratic comradeship, were precisely what the conquered societies could not be "ready for," without negating the manifest reality of conquest, sedimented in the new old institutions. In British Bengal the idea of a "permanent" settlement was perhaps most extremely articulated, but, in a larger sense, it was clearly not unique to Bengal. In Fiji another colonial permanent settlement still lives: proponents of the paramountcy of Fijian chiefs, an aristocracy deliberately made by British-administered customary law, still continually refit horizontality, plurality, and even democracy into service to their hierarchy, but not without struggle.

So, we have here a specific kind of sea change, a sea change worked by colonial agency, that does not fit onto the Westernization-creolization continuum. It is a change that neither fits the local into the procrustean bed of a universal nor is a creole localization, is not merely a reproduction of the modal form nor merely a reformulation of it by admixture with local forms, materials, and agencies. It is a change worked on imported tools to meet the new needs of a transcoursing political will, Europe finding modernity in and for itself while also finding feudalism elsewhere. Almost needless to say, this is precisely the sort of process that makes the connected global space-time of European world rule in the eighteenth and nineteenth centuries something quite other than a homogenizing, emptying force. Here, reconsidering another argument of Anderson's will help clarify.

In his chapter "Official Nationalism and Imperialism," Anderson describes Thomas Macaulay's minute on education, its aspiration to use education to create "a class of persons, Indian in blood and colour, but English in taste, in opinion, in morals and in intellect" (Anderson 1991:91). Anderson concludes, "It can be safely said that from this point on, all over the expanding empire, if at different speeds, Macaulayism was pursued" (91). Flatly not true. In the wake of the 1857 Sepoy Rebellion, that is, the "Mutiny" and its threats, the British Raj massively backed away from the goal of Anglicizing India (see especially Cohn 1983). In many later colonies, such as Fiji, paternalist planning never contemplated an effort to eradicate difference between indigenous Fijians or Indian so-called "coolies" and British culture and sentiments. English-language education for the Indo-Fijians, in particular, overwhelmingly followed from their initiatives against much resistance. To Anderson, the official nationalisms of the world failed inevitably because they were contradictory amalgams of two different types of structures, nation-states with their deep, horizontal communities and dynastic realms with their hierarchy, foundering in practice on the career limits placed upon civil servants among the colonized. Macaulay, then, must have been confused? Disingenuous? This brings us to Macaulay, our second narrator of global chronopolitics, himself enmeshed in a diaspora.

GATES THROUGH TIME AND SPACE, AND THE WILL TO USE THEM

It is telling, to begin with a coda, that in Anderson's account, the fact that Macaulay was a Whig need never come up. The England toward which Macaulay sought to Anglicize India, insofar as Anglicizing India was really his goal, was far from the "deep, horizontal comradeship" of Anderson's imagination. Deep comradeship, perhaps, but in the minds of the Whigs, let alone the Tories, hardly horizontal.

Anderson trolls the history of the late eighteenth and early nineteenth century fishing for the emergent liberal democrats. Referring to the American Declaration of Independence and to the new calendars of the French Revolution, Anderson toys with the idea that time itself was absolutely punctuated, directly invoking Benjamin: "A profound feeling that a radical break with the past was occurring—a 'blasting open of the continuum of history'?—spread rapidly" (Anderson 1991:193). It is certainly true, to focus on England, that "the Liberal creed" (to use Karl Polanyi's phrase) rode with the new science of political economy to an extraordinary popularity and influence in early-nineteenth-century England (see, for example, Polanyi 1944; Semmel 1970). Many liberal texts became famous, such as James Mill's "Essay on Government," a highly abstract, modularizable argument for deeply horizontal democracy. But so too did the responses of worthy opponents, in an England that never gave up either Lords or Crown. Writing in 1829, a year after Mill, Macaulay was derisive about much in Mill's now-classic liberal argument. He began by attacking the utilitarian audience celebrating it as in general, ordinary men, with narrow understandings, and little information. The contempt which they express for elegant literature is evidently the contempt of ignorance. We apprehend that many of them are persons who, having read little or nothing, are delighted to be rescued from the sense of their own inferiority, by some teacher who assures them that the studies which they have neglected are of no value . . . smatterers, whose attainments just suffice to elevate them from the insignificance of dunces to the dignity of bores. (Macaulay 1860b:670)

This derision of the liberal audience fit the context of rivalrous Whig versus Liberal journals of opinion, but it also pointed directly toward the core of the critique Macaulay then developed. Macaulay, the soon-to-be great historian, was as aware as Benedict Anderson that the Liberal argued for a radical break with the past, its literature and wisdom, in the light of a new dawn.[11] Where Mill tried something impossible, to "deduce the science of government from the principles of human nature" (681), Macaulay argued instead for actual research into the past and present in line with the methods of science.

Proceeding thus—patiently, diligently, candidly—we may hope to form a system as far inferior in pretensions to that which we have been examining, and as far superior in real utility, as the prescriptions of a great physician, varying with every stage of every malady, and with the constitution of every patient, to the pill of the advertising quack, which is to cure all human beings, in all climates, of all diseases. (683)

Macaulay was not, as he pointed out vigorously, arguing in favor of monarchy or aristocracy because he was attacking Mill's argument for democracy. If two conceptions could summarize what he did seek to favor, I think they would be civilization and liberty, the classic Whig commitment being that each produced the other. Macaulay insisted: "Civilized men, pursuing their own happiness in a social state, are not Yahoos fighting for carrion" (678), and to know their interests and thus their motives, we have to know their civilization, not merely their human nature.

It now gets particularly interesting for those of us well read in our Anderson. Let us recall that Macaulay's civilization of literature and liberty was doomed, in Anderson's model, to either naively or disingenuously dangle the prospect of horizontal community across imperial spaces actually determined by hierarchy. We discover, reading Macaulay, that he was actually quite impatient with Mill's conception of *community*, for its naïveté about value and time. Mill had announced a solution, democracy with frequent elections, for the problem of rendering the interests of government identical with those of the community. On these terms, Macaulay observed:

We are rather inclined to think that it would, on the whole, be for the interest of the majority to plunder the rich. . . . [W]e have to notice one most important distinction which Mr. Mill has altogether overlooked. Throughout his Essay, he confounds the community with the species. He talks of the greatest happiness of the greatest number; but when we examine his reasonings, we find that he thinks only of the greatest number of a single generation. (679)

To Macaulay, the government either served or threatened not merely the community of the present but also the past and future, either improving or undoing "the work of so many ages of wisdom and glory," "taste, literature, science, commerce, manufactures" (680). In that light, horizontality would invite disaster. Macaulay concluded:

The higher and middling orders are the natural representatives of the human race. Their interest may be opposed, in some things, to that of their poorer contemporaries, but it is identical with that of the innumerable generations which are to follow. (680)

We could inquire into the affinities between Macaulay's vision and the principles of Maastricht and of America's New Democrats—skepticism of redistributive government, commitment to protect private wealth in the alleged interest of future generations—the politics of such interest to Singer, as quoted at the outset. But let us keep Macaulay, and his imagined civilization, in his own time, and follow him into India. What exactly was the education plan?

The line quoted by Anderson is the one widely remembered, but let us put it in its context. As Gauri Viswanathan (1989) has recently detailed, the debate in India not only concerned whether to teach vernacular texts or English ones, but also whether to teach the classics and the Bible as sources for Indian improvement, to use them in Indian schools as they were used in European schools. The solution advocated by Macaulay and others was to teach English texts, in order that England could play the civilizing role for India that Greece, Rome, and ancient Israel played for post-Renaissance Europe. Teach them to whom? The crucial, neglected context couldn't be clearer:

It is impossible for us, with our limited means, to attempt to educate the body of the people. We must at present do our best to form a class who may be interpreters between us and the millions whom we govern; a class of persons, Indian in blood and colour, but English in taste, in opinions, in morals, and in intellect. To that class we may leave it to refine the vernacular dialects of the country, to enrich those dialects with terms of science borrowed from the Western nomenclature, and to render them by degrees fit vehicles for conveying knowledge to the great mass of the population. (Macaulay 1972 [1835]:249)

To Macaulay, Anglicization was not the end, but the means, the most convenient way to produce fit vehicles for conveying knowledge. The target was not to make all or any of India into something like or part of Britain, but rather to lead the Indian upper class to become guardians and fomenters of a civilizing process. Was Macaulay disingenuous, or naive, about what outcome would follow from success in such a process? He professed not to be, in his speech on the East India Company charter in 1833:

> It may be that the public mind of India may expand under our system until it has outgrown that system; . . . that, having become instructed in European knowledge, they may, in some future age, demand European institutions. . . . [I]t will be the proudest day in English history. To have found a great people sunk in the lowest depths of slavery and superstition, to have so ruled them as to have made them desirous and capable of all the privileges of citizens, would indeed be a title to a glory all our own. (Macaulay 1833:192)

"Glory." Exactly what was Macaulay's vision of the nation, and why wasn't it a good idea to teach those students in India everything the English knew and loved about Rome?

For all his commitment to teaching English "taste, opinion, morals, and intellect," Macaulay could not have wanted the Indians to become English in essential ambition, English in political will. In a less-celebrated Macaulay speech, concerning war with China in 1847, Macaulay vividly described what the English seized at a moment of colonial danger:

> I was much touched . . . by a passage in one of Captain Elliot's despatches. I mean that passage in which he describes his arrival at the factory in the moment of extreme danger. As soon as he landed he was surrounded by his countrymen, all in an agony of distress and despair. The first thing he did was to order the British flag to be brought from his boat and planted in the balcony. The sight immediately revived the hearts of those who had a minute before given themselves up for lost. It was natural that they should look up with hope and confidence to that victorious flag. For it reminded them that they belonged to a country unaccustomed to defeat, to submission, or to shame; to a country which had exacted such reparation for the wrongs of her children as had made the ears of all who heard of it tingle; to a country which had made the Dey of Algiers humble himself to the dust before her insulted Consul; to a country which had avenged the victims of the Black Hole on the field of Plassey; to a country which had not degenerated since the great Protector vowed that he

would make the name of Englishmen as much respected as ever had been the name of Roman citizen. (Macaulay 1910:267–68)

Obviously, aspiring to be Rome could only be modular in a world doomed to extraordinary frustration. It is hardly clear, pace Anderson, that Macaulay was simply the modular Englishman. More has been written than can be rehearsed here, about conflict in British imagination between Athens and Sparta, and between remaking Jerusalem and reincarnating Rome. Let us simply note that whether it was an effect or a cause, regardless of how it fit into the sea changes of empire, this England, living up to the vow of the Protector, seeking the legacy of Rome, this imagined England was no mere community. There is a geopolitical will here, an image of the past that is more than the story of community origins and an image of the future that is more than making home secure. There is, to borrow again the term from Johannes Fabian, an arrogant chronopolitics directly informing the imperial agents, reproduced and ramified in their work upon their intellectual and institutional tools. No doubt, in the many European empires across time, there were actually several varieties intertwined, with differences and tensions, for example, between those remaking Jerusalem and Rome, having multiple possible outcomes, even before the creolizing impact of various "local" interests and powers. In short, the point for globalization theory so far is that European colonial empires not only increased and channeled global flows, but also worked temporal sea changes widely across the globe. Now, what about those "Others," those "locals"?

CHRONOPOLITICS, SCHOLARLY

Here Johannes Fabian's 1983 critique of temporal premises in anthropology, *Time and the Other,* can help us name some cardinal dilemmas in the tracing both of global chronopolitics and of the place of new scholarship in it. These days, one more often hears about the "local" than "the Other." One hears even about "local people," people awkwardly, implicitly contrasted with some other kind of people, usually unnamed, but obviously including the writer and reader. If not "global people," perhaps "transnational." All this may be the transformation, into spatial coordinates, of the practices in scholarly time reckoning critiqued by Fabian, making his argument well worth attention even if it might, itself, have to suffer a certain sea change when we consider scholars in relation not to "the Other" but to the global.

The thesis of *Time and the Other* is that anthropology, to Fabian's day, was guilty of what he calls allochronism, complicit with and legitimizing of colonial and neocolonial global relations. "Allochronism" means denial of coevalness, and by "coevalness," in turn, Fabian means "a common, active 'occupation,' or sharing of time" (1983:31). He seeks, in short, "ways to meet the Other on the same ground, in the same Time" (165), a meeting that should be confrontational and ultimately dialectical; thus his final gloss on "coevalness": "a dialectical concept of Time" (182). At least as much a new Hegelian as Pletsch, Fabian seeks a praxis for scholars to make the ground of coevalness, on which in turn the confrontation of Europeans and others could produce a new synthesis. "Anthropology as the study of cultural difference can be productive only if difference is drawn into the arena of dialectical contradiction" (164).

In Benedict, Fabian correctly perceives a champion for a style of analysis he condemns: a cultivator of "Gardens of Culture."[12] This, interestingly, leads him to a misrepresentation of her politics, cloaked in his own explicit allochronism: in Benedict's 1946 *Chrysanthemum and the Sword,* we are told, "the spirit of the times is aptly expressed." Benedict, writes Fabian, did not question "the legitimacy of 'being American to the hilt'" and aided unreflectively in a national effort "to bring the enemy down and, soon after, establish effective control and assure transformation of these values toward the model of the anthropologist's society" (Fabian 1983:47–48). Fabian is right that Benedict (and Mead, Bateson, and many others; see Yans-McGlaughlin 1986) sought during World War II to help bring the enemy down, but his characterization of her goals in 1946 (though fairer as estimations of some of the other Boasians he depicts) underestimates her intentions and self-consciousness in ways of interest to us here. In fact, Benedict sharply criticized plans to Americanize Japan.

> What the United States cannot do—what no outside nation could do—is to create by fiat a free, democratic Japan. It has never worked in any dominated country. No foreigner can decree, for a people who have not his habits and assumptions, a manner of life after his own image. The Japanese cannot be legislated into accepting the authority of elected persons and ignoring "proper station" as it is set up in their hierarchical system. They cannot be legislated into adopting the free and easy human contacts to which we are accustomed in the United States, the imperative demand to be independent, the passion each individual has to choose his own mate, his own job, the house he will live in and the obligations he will assume. (Benedict 1946:314)

This argument is central to her book. Where most anthropological writings, including Fabian's, presume a transnational audience of students and scholars, Benedict wrote for (and reached—her book was a best-seller) a different specific audience: the U.S. government and public. Acutely self-conscious that her audience in the United States was wielding enormous global power, Benedict sought to bring that audience to self-consciousness about the very existence of a specifically American culture. In order to demonstrate the contingent, cultural foundations of things that Americans took for nature or good sense, she used contrasts with Japan didactically—"The idea that the pursuit of happiness is a serious goal of life is to them an amazing and immoral doctrine" (192). She wrote against "protagonists of One World"—in fact, saying, "As Americans they urge our favorite tenets on all nations" (14, 16; note the way "our" binds both author and readers to a nonuniversalist, nonprivileged, but shared cultural commitment). She put her politics into a phrase, "making the world safe for difference." Here we come to her specific commitment, criticized by Fabian, that Americans can be Americans "to the hilt":

> The tough-minded are content that differences should exist. They respect differences. Their goal is a world made safe for differences, where the United States may be American to the hilt without threatening the peace of the world, and France may be France, and Japan may be Japan on the same conditions. (14)

Pace Fabian, Benedict's commitment is neither unreflective nor unreflexive. Her Americans can be American to the hilt only if they put away both their swords and their self-satisfaction.

Let us set aside the allochronic dismissal of Benedict's arguments as "the spirit of the times" and compare Fabian and Benedict as if contemporary, thereby constituting the kind of arena for dialectical confrontation that scholars are actually capable of producing. Fabian correctly observes that the holism in Benedict's theory of culture has little in common with "the emphasis on totality that originates in dialectical thought," that in dialectical thought, Fabian's approach, the "constituting acts are *negations* of cultural distance," and that this difference is connected to Benedict's "toughminded acceptance of radical cultural difference," against what she saw as "soft sentiments about One World and Universal Brotherhood" (Fabian 1983:47). However, Fabian is less observant about the more practical difference between the politics of his own and Benedict's essays. Like Fabian, Benedict was conscious of a global politics to her book, and, like Fabian, she sought to use scholarship to reshape the ground of group dialogues. Where the new Hegelian sought to shock scholars, via critique, into realization of their allochronism, thereby to lead them to prepare a new ground for coeval self and other dialectics, the student of Boas sought to shock the American public, via sea changes wrought upon their own key conceptions, into consciousness of American culture as one among many, thereby to lead them away from forcing their time and space onto others. "The world must be made safe for democracy," President Woodrow Wilson had announced to the U.S. Congress on April 2, 1917, when seeking the declaration of war that put the

United States into the First World War. Benedict's "world made safe for differences" is unmistakably a challenge to this classic official foreign policy pronouncement; but to what end?

Built into genre in Fabian's text, and also in this one but not in Benedict's, is at worst a premise that reforms of scholarly consciousness and praxis somehow intrinsically reshape world history, or at best a lack of explicit plans for intervention beyond academic arenas. At the core of Benedict's text, and research program, is engagement with actual power and thus "complicity" with it (as is so often said with a Pontius Pilate shudder). What, from Fabian's and Benedict's dynamic scholarly projects, might now flash up to address the dangers intrinsic to our contemporary globalization discourse? Should we be seeking a world safe for differences, or negation of distance in vigorous dialogues "on the same ground, in the same Time," or what?

Benedict's intervention into actual politics was both a strength and a limitation to her anthropology, precisely because all actual politics are in some sense local. While fully respecting her effort to thwart American triumphalism, we should note that this was, no matter how globally relevant, a locally directed political move that she made, a book designed to reshape American sensibilities. The idea of a "world made safe for differences" has other implications, much in the service of contemporary power elites, if it is to be globally applied as a general ethical standard. The same respect for differences that would limit the goals of American intervention could justify repression of many other forms of change, as for example when the military coup in Fiji that overturned an elected government was justified as protection for an endangered indigenous culture.

What then of Fabian's dialectical imaginary? A highly promising site to reenter his argument, in search of a means to address a world of global-local links and flows, is another of his citations of Ernst Bloch, an aphorism with which he begins his chapter including the critique of Benedict: "At any rate, the primacy of space over time is an infallible sign of reactionary language." If indeed the temporal promise of postmodernism, the overcoming of the telos of the modern, increasingly appears a dead end, is there a danger that the scholarly turn to globalization-style spatial reckoning will cover over important temporal processes, real and potential? Is "coevalness" or something like it the key to conceiving the temporal politics of globalization?

There is actually an important ambivalence in Fabian's imagery, between space and time and also thereby between symmetry and asymmetry, an outcome I believe of his effort to have his Hegelian dialectic and reflexivity, too. His main arguments reveal asymmetries beneath the apparent symmetries of others, especially allochronism within structuralism, functionalism, and relativism. His dialectical dream is both *symmetric* and *spatial:* a shared ground, same plane, coeval confrontation of self and other in an "arena of dialectical contradiction." He spots scholars making, remaking, and hiding asymmetries in time and power, and he wishes to stop them. But just so, when addressing realities of ethnography in context, Fabian shows that "the Other" cannot abide as a partner in symmetric, dialogic fantasy, but is, rather, an object manufactured by use and neglect of *asymmetric* realities, a real history of power. The critique insists on revealing realities of asymmetry, but the utopia is still a symmetry.

It seems to me that most scholars seek and privilege symmetries, on deep aesthetic and ethical grounds, leading notably to the great current satisfaction with the concept of identity. The virtues of symmetry are currently debated explicitly in science studies. Bruno Latour is a forceful advocate for a research method radically privileging symmetry, and there is much to be said for his vision of symmetry. According to Latour, a scholar should work hard to avoid privileging the truth or power either of his or her own conceptions, or those of one side, agency, or context in an actuality studied, in order, instead, to simply follow actual interdefinition of actors and chains of translations:

> The analyst does not need to know more than they; he has only to begin at any point, by recording what each actor says of the others. He should not try to be reasonable and to impose some predetermined sociology on the sometimes bizarre interdefinition offered by the writers studied. (Latour 1988:11)

Latour carries to a new extreme an attractive aspiration not to succumb to the insistent claims of Western knowledge and power, one that refuses either ethnocentrism or allochronism. Yet there is a problem.

The Latourian scholar, suspending his own arrogance and commitments of culture and knowledge, is also neglecting specific dimensions of what Talal Asad has called "translation as a process of power" (1993:179), specifically the existing pattern of flows to translation. Asad's critique of Ernest Gellner's essay on anthropological relativism could also apply to the otherwise quite different arguments of Latour:

> He fails to consider what cultural translation might involve when it is considered as institutionalized practice, given the wider relationship of unequal societies. For it is not the abstract logic of what individual Western anthropologists say in their ethnographies, but the concrete logic of what their countries (and perhaps they themselves) do in their relations with the third world that should form the starting point for this particular discussion. The dilemmas of relativism appear differently depending on whether we think of abstracted understanding or of historically situated practices. (179)

We could literally construct, if we focus as Asad would have us, maps of the flows of translation and translation skills in the globalizing world. The dynamic asymmetries in the weather patterns of discourse, the pressure systems of language and genre, would provide different images of globalization than would symmetric discovery of everyone's identity. If one path for scholarship on time and the global would lead from respect for differences through quest for symmetry to the reconfiguration of all history as confrontations over assertions and narrations of identity, quite a different direction opens here. What happens if we recast Fabian's argument without its symmetric, dialectical dream, within, instead, these strictures of Asad? Fabian's dialectic, in the Marxist branch, is already clear in its preference for critique over utopia, and with his emphasis on attending to actually existing power asymmetries, he would surely align here with Asad rather than Latour. What then for "coevalness," if we give up dialectical dreams and no longer grasp it for our telos? Rather than building a new common ground or finding a null point, Asad would have us begin with "political confrontations already in place . . . in an asymmetrically structured political terrain" (273). Let us reconsider time, and coevalness, in this terrain.

Recalling Fabian's first definition of coevalness, "a common, active 'occupation' or sharing of time," let us banish all utopian, symmetric, or dialectical "common ground" and seek the temporality within the "political confrontations already in place." What are the actual terms of trade in temporal consociality? Who controls what they share with whom, at what price? Is common occupation of a space-time always a matter of sharing? Consider not only buying and selling, but also imposition and Anderson's "pirating." Actual forms of active occupation? How about that by Britain of Bengal in 1757, and that by the United States of Japan in 1946? In sum, if not transplanted into abstract dialectical arenas, actual histories of negation of temporal distance and construction of common memory are likely to be rife with asymmetries of translation and institution.

This leads to the most important question about time and the global for contemporary globalization scholarship: Exactly when, and why, did who decide to share homogeneous, empty space-time, and the nation-state as a political form, with a globe full of Others? Who turned Others into "communities" of "locals," and why?

HOMOGENEOUS, EMPTY TIME

To paraphrase my frontispiece quotation from Walter Benjamin, I am convinced that other scholars setting off to explore and chart globalization have been far too attracted by the magnetic forces of nationalism, identity, and community. Whence the force in this attraction? "Discover *that* North Pole," Benjamin advises. Find "the differentia of time that disturb the 'main lines' of the investigation for others." Let us summarize a bit, both the disturbances I have spotted and the "main lines" I hope to lead you to doubt.

Disturbances: In Fiji, a living aristocracy of Fijian chiefs retains the power not to be impressed by arguments concerning progress, equity, or horizontality. As the most influential Fijian chief of the twentieth century, Ratu Sir Lala Sukuna, put it in his Annual Report as Secretary for Fijian Affairs in 1950, Fijian affairs were "based not on contract and freedom but on consanguinity and status" (quoted in B. Lal 1992:135). Assertions of rightful hierarchy are omnipresent in the discourse of ethnic Fijian nationalism, and any good account of their roots would have to emphasize not only creolizing reassertion of indigenous hierarchy, but also this happy redeployment of *Gemeinschaft* theory. If anything is an imagined *community*, this surely is. Guha has laid out the precise logic of such redeployment, the sea-change redeployment of European narratives of modernity, the careful construction of an imagined European past as colonial present and future, and the reasons for it. Finally, with Macaulay, in empire midstream, we find not a self-contradicting modernizer but a creolizing Whig with a civilizing mission, a self-conscious promoter of the glory of an empire folding both liberal political economy and Tory conservatism into new places in a Whig conception of an elitist, scientific, Rome-like civilization. In short, common active occupation of colonies by colonizers led to a civilization shared at a price: cognizance of its temporal hierarchy and your place in it. What happened to that time, in theory and reality?

Main lines, in theory: What happened to "homogeneous, empty time" in Anderson's custody? What general history is Anderson conveying? To recall, for Benjamin the idea of a general tide or flow of progress is the pathology, the crucial, narcotic delusion. "Nothing has corrupted the German working class so much as the notion that it was moving with the current" (Benjamin 1968:258). In turn, "the concept of the historical progress of mankind cannot be sundered from the concept of its progression through a homogeneous, empty time" (261). In contrast, *Imagined Communities* begins with profound disillusionment about Marxist revolutionary time, yet, as noted above, suggests that another revolutionary moment, that of the French and American Revolutions, was an actual "radical break," a "blasting open of the continuum of history." Let us look more closely at Anderson's depiction of this radical break.

Anderson quotes Erich Auerbach on a medieval Christian consciousness of a transtemporal kind of simultaneity in the connections between distant events existing eternally in Divine Providence, "something close to what Benjamin calls Messianic time" (Anderson 1991:24). Christian, Jewish, we could quibble, but let us follow Anderson to the main point: that "the very possibility of imagining the nation only arose historically when, and where, three fundamental cultural conceptions [this was the third], all of great antiquity, lost their axiomatic grip on men's minds" (36). Benjamin's hopes are Anderson's antiquity. "What has come to take the place of the medieval conception of simultaneity-along-time is, to borrow again from Benjamin, an idea of 'homogeneous, empty time' in which simultaneity is, as it were, transverse, cross time, marked not by prefiguring and fulfillment, but by temporal coincidence, and measured by clock and calendar" (24). Borrowing an image from Benjamin like a book from a library, Anderson has put to new use what Latour would call an entelechy, an item made real inscribed with its original purpose but capable of various translation and transformations by future actions. Benjamin, aware that "*even the dead* will not be safe" (1968:255), can do nothing to save his imagery from transformation into the marker of the triumph of the Social Democratic utopia. Benjamin suffers a sea change.

Anderson reglosses the crucial time conception as "horizontal-secular, transverse-time," a locution that has not come to rival Benjamin's original, but one that points better to important Andersonian claims: that nations imagine themselves among each other horizontally, across one clock moment existing simultaneously and evenly, symmetrically. There is an abstraction, in Asad's terms, to Anderson's treatment, an interest in "the very possibility of imagining the nation":

> The slow, uneven decline of these interlinked certainties, first in Western Europe, later elsewhere, under the impact of economic change, "discoveries" (social and scientific), and the development of increasingly rapid communications, drove a harsh wedge between cosmology and history. No surprise then that the search was on, so to speak, for a new way of linking fraternity, power and time meaningfully together. (Anderson 1991:36)

Now, let us remember Macaulay again. Macaulay's England was no mere nation among many figured transversely, symmetrically across time. It was, indeed, a prefigured fulfillment, living up to the Protector's vow to rival Rome and recognizing and reconfiguring an extraordinary amount of the rest of the world while doing so.

Where and when, exactly, was global space-time imagined to be homogeneous and empty?

Anderson's time duplex, ancient and modern, skips the crucial moment of colonial empires, empires whose sea changes made real, inscribed into social institutions, the temporal hierarchies of enlightenment evolutionism. As much recent research makes clear (see, for example, Abu-Lughod 1989; Chaudhuri 1990; Curtin 1984; Pollock 1996), in the "Old World" at least, these moments of occupation were redistributions of social relations in already existing cultural ecumene, whose now-lost space-time conceptions and institutions scholars have only begun to reconstruct. This problem is not fixed in Anderson's added chapter on colonial states. When it comes to its own amnesia concerning specifically colonial imaginations and institutions, Anderson's text should seem suddenly very familiar: in this sense, what Anderson's text is really reproducing is the story of modernization. The "three worlds" primitive complex as analyzed by Pletsch has been revised by Anderson in two major ways. First, virtually or perhaps actually anticipating the globalization viewpoint, Anderson dumps the segregating out of a "Second" World and downplays the Cold War. Second, very curiously, he has relocated a community, a kind of community, a *Gemeinschaft* of the imagination, not in the prior stage but in the later one. What are communities doing there at the end of evolutionary time?

Of course there are other ways to punctuate a general history of globalization, issues for inquiry that I have not raised. Most important, nothing I have considered addresses the patterns given to space-time by changing forms of money, trade, and capital. One could punctuate globalization, and even reengineer the concept of homogeneous, empty time, in relation not to late-eighteenth-century political revolutions, but rather in relation to later nineteenth-century antiteleology. One could imagine an increasingly purely quantified, highly anxious global time manifold, a world of quantified essences, materialism (especially Darwin's), a globe of uneven, compared rates of sheerly quantitative increase (for instance, increasingly precisely theorized, measured, and regulated rates of interest and return on investment). In this world, still, space and time were not, in all senses, homogenized or empty—nothing as neat, either, as a world system, but a gapped machinery only fixable by flows of capital, goods, and people, and more often moved through in lurches creating new instabilities. Still no transverse symmetry there, but definitely, in the primacy of sheer quantity, a homogenizing and emptying force stalking all other meanings.

This iron-cage emptying of utopian possibility is also important; many scholars portray nationalist imagined *Gemeinschaft*, in effect, fake community, as a kind of doomed protest against it. But I don't think this gets us wholly to our North Pole. We still don't know what happened to Macaulay's arrogance, his derision of community in favor of a relation to past and future generations, his quest for glory. Prasenjit Duara suggests something important when he emphasizes one of the themes that he thinks Anderson underplays: Duara is less convinced of the revolutionary break to nationalist mentality in the early nineteenth century, than of something significant taking shape in the twentieth: "What is novel about modern nationalism is not political self-consciousness, but the world *system* of nation-states" (Duara

1996:157). When, then, is a "system" of nation-states instituted? As Bernard Cohn has been saying for years, it is time we all looked more seriously at World War II and its aftermath.

A full account might start earlier, at least with the League of Nations, with attention also to more specifically European treaties, "concerts," papal bisections, and so on. Specifically in relation to the tempering of glory, however, and thus the ethical revaluation of colonization, one doesn't, in fact, get even a fantasy globe of Anderson's transverse symmetries until the United Nations—and then it gets systematized very quickly. A full account would recall Woodrow Wilson's valorization of "self-determination," his world that "must be made safe for democracy," but it is really the United Nations world in which such sentiments clearly rule out colonization, a world in which the formal symmetry of nation-states makes decolonizing the ticket of entry and promises substantive development at the price only of amnesia about colonial exploitation and in its place, shame at "backwardness."

Before the "world wars," ambitions could be open, from Protector's vows to elbow room, from manifest destiny to race wars (as Dower 1986 persuasively describes World War II in particular). Nations could have glorious destinies, and their states could have War Departments rather than Defense Departments. Then came the new system. In short, everything happened as if the United States, bomb in hand, commanded every nation in 1946 to henceforth imagine itself only as a community, to abjure all other histories and destinies, with demonization of all resistance from communism to Islam.

Here, precisely, is when, where, and why historic time was homogenized into transverse-symmetric progress stories and emptied of fuel for political will: so that nations won't aspire to conquer, colonize, or occupy one another anymore, now that glory is too dangerous. Only corporations, not nations, are free to pursue dreams of domination. Localities can be quiescent or in crisis. Against this grain, the paths out of locality, the new vents for human ambition, are those of the new elite diaspora. In relation to these trends, scholarship is arrayed variously. In 1946, aware of the stakes, Benedict self-consciously intervened on the side of Pax Americana, but deliberately to undermine its arrogance. (Just an ethnography? The cover of the first edition of *The Chrysanthemum and the Sword* bore a single sentence to depict the book's intent: "An investigation of the pattern of Japanese culture which suggests a program for new understanding among nations.") In contrast, Anderson's conscious heterodoxy challenges the revolutionary fantasies and dialectical dreams of Marxist intellectuals, with a sense of pathos that it took Benjamin's angel of history to convey. Addressing deep-felt disappointment in actually existing revolutions, rejecting the comforting idea that nationalism is the century's pathology, Anderson argues instead that the strange new communities were the century's culture (cf. his definition "in an anthropological spirit" [1991:5]). It was not his intention to become the arbiter of American orthodoxy, its leading global historian, to be Harry Truman in Marxist drag, any more than Benedict set out to bolster Japanese chauvinists. Nonetheless, trolling for deeper roots, Anderson has created the fictitious global genealogy of American geopolitics.

Especially now that scholars increasingly frame their research to explore the idea of global-local relations, rather than conceptions and categorizations of self and other, it does not help to aspire to symmetric or reflexive relationships, a simple common ground, between all localities, between all identities, or especially between people who can choose to flow globally and people who cannot. Amelioration, let alone anything approaching redemption, will not come from any general theory of identity or community. It will not come by way of either compassion or rebuke for the "identity politics" allegedly motivating all local crises. I think we should seek, instead, a clearer understanding of the asymmetries in global flows, including the actual dissemination of homogeneous, empty time, and all else that now sets the apparent limits to political possibility.

AFTERWORD: IMAGINED MODERNITY AND "THIS WORLD"

Our criticism of Anderson's work has focused almost exclusively on *Imagined Communities*. But a brief discussion here of a more recent article on seriality, Anderson's 1998 "Nationalism, Identity, and the World-in-Motion: On the Logics of Seriality," will enable us to pursue further some important themes concerning consciousness and "modernity" and will enable us to clarify, more philosophically, some key questions at stake here.

The concept of the modern began its lexical life as a shifter. Its referent was the present, the contemporaneity of the utterance, and in pre-Enlightenment English-language usage it frequently had a negative connotation. Only in the last two centuries, and especially in the twentieth, did it come to carry a presumption of superiority, in which modern and modernized phenomena were marked not by skepticism but the cachet of presumed superiority (Williams 1976:174).

Insofar as the modern is a shifter—and considering the notion of modernizing one's computer equipment, it is obviously still a shifter—the very possibility of a "modern era" is paradoxical, let alone a "modernity." Various versions of this paradox have long been staple fare for modern and "postmodern" art and literature (see, e.g., Berman 1988). But the simplifying and flattering possibility of arranging the history of culture more generally on a tradition-to-modernity axis has been one of the most fatally deluding practices in the history of social theory. And despite all the respect that he deserves for contributions on other questions, no doubt Max Weber merits singular blame for one of the most disastrous formulations of such an axis. Weber attempts to overcome the impossibility that is in fact intrinsic to attempting to stabilize the sense and reference of "modernity" by connecting it to another ill-considered conception, "this world," constituting the conception of, after all, a modern period inaugurated by the emergence of a unique form of human consciousness, finally attuned to this world and no longer, as in traditional societies, "otherworldly."

The pejorative deployment of the distinction between this-worldly and otherworldly consciousnesses, especially against religious enemies, goes back at least to Gibbon's *Decline and Fall of the Roman Empire*, in which the otherworldly Christians are blamed for the demise of the this-worldly virtues of the Roman citizens and soldiers that are said to hold the great empire together. Of course the resort to deixis begs the question of how one knows which categories better fit reality. (This world. You know, this one. This one here. No, not that other one, this one.) But the strange, insupportable premise that some cultures care to address the real world more than others has been so useful that it is invoked almost as frequently as, and all too frequently in fatal Weberian combination with, the alleged gap between traditional and modern consciousnesses.

Seriality, Anderson tells us, is always "basic" to "the modern imagining of collectivity." Seriality, we are told, can be bound or unbound, the former with origins in governmentality, especially censuses and elections, the latter with origins in the print market (1998:117). Together, seriality is two modes of understanding oneself or other things "serially," imagining them as units or instances comparable and contrastable to others in a series. In "the late colonial environment," Anderson argues, "a new grammar of representation came into being" (121). The shamelessness with which this model reinvokes the inceptive motif of modernization theory, people waking up to new powers of self-consciousness, is best simply portrayed with an extract from Anderson's analysis of a quotation from a 1952 novel in which Is, the teenage heroine, joins a revolutionary movement:

> The circle of Is's brothers, sisters, and parents is without series. But at the revolutionary moment, to which she makes her small contribution, she imagines herself, for the first time in her tender life, serially: as "a" woman, "a" typist, "a" free individual, "a" human being. This serialization so transforms her consciousness that everything now glows new to her. (128)

The idea of politics itself, Anderson argues, can only actually be grasped after this kind of breakthrough into seriality consciousness; it would have a "birth date" typically close to that of nationalism (120). Much here is simply implausible. That before the revolution, our young heroine was cognitively

incapable of realizing herself to have, and to be, a sister? That before censuses, elections, and print capitalism, all political phenomena would "heedlessly be glossed in the old vocabularies of cosmologically and religiously
sustained kingship"? (128) Let's call a single new witness, the *Arthaśāstra*, a
text on statecraft composed in non-Paninian Sanskrit in North India, perhaps in the third or fourth century before the common era. A vocabulary
presuming kingship, yes. Heedlessly? Without "seriality"? "Even an enemy
who helps is fit to be allied with, not an ally who does not act like one"
(7.13.27). Not very heedless, whether about the existence of categories in
general series or about the question of how to reevaluate memberships in
them.[13] Cosmologically sustained? "A king who is fully conversant with the
principles of statecraft shall understand the conditions of progress, decline
and no-change and apply the strategic method appropriate to each one in
order to weaken or overwhelm the enemy" (7.18.43).

The point is not merely that there can be more to noncapitalist, nonelec-
toral consciousnesses than is dreamed of in Anderson's philosophy. It is also
the implausibility of the claim that print capitalism is uniquely this-worldly,
"that newspapers everywhere take 'this world of mankind' as their domain,
no matter how partially they read it" (120). Comparing texts before and after
the great transformation, we are told, "one notes a deep, surely unconscious
shift in the semantic load" of words meaning "world." "Its prior meaning
was something close to 'cosmos,' a natural, vertical universe arranged hierar-
chically from the Deity, or deities, down through kings, aristocrats, and peasants, to fauna and flora and the landscapes. . . . [I]n the quite new sense of
'world,' a horizontal universe of visible and invisible human beings from
which volcanoes, demons, water buffalo, and divinities had vanished" comes
into being (119). It is baffling why we should consider more "this-worldly"
a deeply horizontal imagination of a totality only of humans, as against a
world including landscapes with water buffalo and other flora and fauna. So,
too, is the notion that the word "world" in newspapers generally refers to
human beings only.

What is clear, in all this, is that for Anderson, "this world," "horizontality" "the nation," "modernity," and "the glow of transformed consciousness"
all belong in one series, starkly opposed by "cosmos," "hierarchy," "kingdoms," "tradition," and "heedless use of old cosmologically sustained vocabularies," and that, at least according to this article, history's great transformation follows from "a new grammar of representation." It is not surprising
that, armed with this duplex for coding all human experience, he is doubtful
that diasporic experience is more than an extension of the modern (131), one
of the two kinds of grammars of representation in his series. But how modern, after all, by his own terms, can his own thought be? Is Anderson, with
regard to his crucial categories, really capable of the glow of seriality? Cer-

tain practices "have displaced the cosmos to make way for 'the world'" (117). The world, as against the cosmos. Not even merely the new world, as for example in "the new world order," let alone, "a world." In sum: Is Anderson really capable of serially cognizing "this world," or "the world" as merely "a world"? Is he capable of expecting his own perception to be cultural? Let alone dialogically constituted? Or, as all the weight of his argumentation would suggest, is "the world" that replaced the cosmos, the world that is horizontal and series defined et cetera, somehow unique in its reality? Is his commitment to a particular secularist egalitarian cosmology of his own conscious or unconscious? Either way, to have his great divide, he cannot locate himself on the privileged side of it. A consciousness of participation in a unique "modernity," heedlessly committed to the referential superiority of its own conception of "this world," is clearly committed to its own parochial hierarchies. Anderson himself thus "lacks any universal grounding" at least as much as the diasporic wanna-be cosmopolitans whose credentials he determines to doubt (131). Or to put it less polemically, from here we will leave theorizing "modernity" to others, since we doubt the utility of the paradoxical concept, and propose to pursue, with less ambition to specify a deep, universal tectonics, not so much some grammars of representation in general as some actual, active institutions of representation and the dialogics of their changing particulars.

THREE

Diaspora and World War, Blood and Nation in Fiji and Hawai'i

In this chapter I reopen some old questions about the politics of blood and its power to create political limits.

At the outset of World War II, close to half, roughly 45 percent, of the population of Fiji was of South Asian descent. The Fiji Indians, or Indo-Fijians, were largely the descendants of the so-called coolies brought in by British colonizers to work on sugar plantations. At the outset of World War II, 37 percent of the population of Hawai'i was Japanese by descent, largely descendants of laborers brought in by American settlers to work on sugar plantations. At the outset of the war, Fiji was still a British colony and Hawai'i was a territory "annexed" by the United States. Nothing in this chapter will be particularly new as ethnography or history. In particular, I do not claim extensive expertise about Hawai'i and draw from the work of other scholars, most notably Gary Okihiro.[1] For Fiji as well, fuller accounts of World War II exist, written by Brij Lal and others. The objective here is to think about what we already know, about the making and unmaking of political possibilities.

One kind of political power that is sometimes alleged to reside in blood concerns descent. Claims of priority for primordiality are frequent, by which I mean claims of privilege for the genuine locals, who are usually depicted as more innocent and deserving than those who have moved in later, especially if, as much discourse on race puts it, the former have kept their blood "pure." In the Pacific this kind of blood is well known, basic to tourism everywhere; designations like "Hawaiian" and "Fijian" can be ambiguous and might mean anyone born there, but "pure" Hawaiian and "pure" Fijian are not. They refer to natives in the classic sense.

Across the globe a romance is building for the defense of indigenes, first

64

peoples, natives trammeled by civilization, producing a sentimental politics as closely mixed with motifs of nature and ecology as with historical narratives. The residents of nation-states that once were colonial powers and/ or of nation-states that were made mainly by remembered immigration are increasingly enchanted by images of autochthone humanity. In Pacific tourism, where the authentic luau and other native "feasts" and cultural performances are carefully packaged commodities, this romance of the genuine locals is omnipresent. But its salience in local politics varies. In Fiji's politics the romance of the indigenes has a long history and was deployed to defend the coups of 1987, which overturned an elected government and threw out a constitution (and is again the theme in the coup of 2000). An open commitment to privilege indigenous Fijians was built into the constitution "promulgated" after the 1987 coups (and in 2000, a yet more pro-indigene constitution is promised).[2] In Hawai'i multiple indigenous nationalist movements emerged in the 1990s, but none has come close to taking hold of the center of state power.[3]

This chapter is not about these kinds of blood politics. My primary focus here is not the sentimental island breezes of a Pacific romance, however much or little they shake up the local political architecture. I shall focus on a different politics of blood, also crucial to rights for diaspora people, and to conditions of political possibility for global transnationalism. "We need to think ourselves beyond the nation," argues Arjun Appadurai (1993:411). But blood, which is to say, discourse about blood, ties us down and holds us in or out—and not only the kind of blood you are said to be born with, but also the kind of blood you shed. In his article on nationalism, Ernest Renan argued more than a century ago that the memory of blood that was shed had more to do with nationalism than any blood of "race." I shall address here the effects of global war in the mid-twentieth century on the political prospects and national affiliations of people moved vast distances in the colonial labor diasporas of earlier decades and centuries: thus, the Pacific theater and some of its theatrics of bloodshed.

To name something of what is at stake, then, I ask, have we fully plumbed the way wars set limits to transnationality? "Which side are you on?"—the great labor strike question—is a question that war can even more starkly pose. Let us now trace some of its effects.

THE SIGNS OF LOYALTY

A picture is at least a thousand words. Few have done more than Ulf Hannerz to generate the images of cultural complexity, a global ecumene, and transnational culture flow: a Swedish calypso song winning a European folk music contest, while on Nigerian television the evening news in English and Hausa is punctuated by funeral commercials. Consider in contrast some events in the Hawaiian Islands, an American-ruled territory, in 1941, in the weeks after the Japanese navy destroyed the ships at Pearl Harbor. I quote Okihiro:

> "Almost every Japanese family had a thorough housecleaning, and all objects which were kept for sentimental reasons were pulled out of trunks and destroyed." Family shrines connected with Buddhism, photographs and letters that linked individuals with Japan, Japanese books, magazines and records, and flags and emblems were all burned and buried. Japanese discarded kimono and geta (raised wooden tongs) for Western dress, shoes, and stockings; women trimmed and curled their long black hair. So pervasive was the need to conform that Japanese who persisted in wearing kimonos were seen by fellow Japanese as defiant of Hawaii's military rulers and a threat to the community's well-being. . . .
>
> Japanese-language schools and newspapers were closed by military order; Shintoism was banned; and although Buddhism was officially permitted, nearly all its priests were interned in concentration camps and its adherents threatened. . . . [M]ost temples closed their doors. (1991:229–30; Okihiro initially quotes Kawahara and Hatanaka 1943:38)

On the mainland, Japanese Americans were themselves summarily removed to camps; in Hawai'i, only about fourteen hundred were interned, mostly prominent men. Half of these were rounded up immediately following the attack, people whose names were on a list already prepared by military intelligence with help from the FBI. Though labeled "subversives," they included leaders of pro-American movements, and Christians as well as Buddhists. The households they left behind overturned their inner hierarchies in fear. As Dennis Ogawa describes, the Nisei, the American-born generation, took control over the Issei, those who emigrated from Japan:

> Disciplinary rules from the children such as "don't talk in Japanese," "don't use the telephone because you don't speak English," "don't wear a kimono," and "don't bow like a Japanese" reversed authority roles in the home. . . .
>
> As one Issei said, "We are afraid. We don't know what to do. Even our own children won't let us go out. If we go out, we will be the focus of hate and revenge. So we stay in the home." (1978:319, 317)

Here the new generation, capable in a cultural sense of switching, melding, and remaking codes, did something very different. Under some circumstances, people in kimonos can eat poi, kimchi, and hamburgers at the beach. Under others, "the Japanese flag in photographs of Japanese-language school graduations or weddings were carefully blackened" (Ogawa 1978:315). An intrinsically transnational generation, in a ruled territory at stake in a war, disciplined itself, its seniors, and its children to a U.S. nationalist hypercorrectness. The American military had been attempting to discipline the Japanese in Hawai'i for decades. For example, Commander W. H. Hartt Jr. of the American Fourteenth Naval District told a conference for young Japanese leaders (called "Conference of New Americans") in 1930 that there was a "necessity for unambiguous alignment on one side or the other of the citizenship issue. You have been asked to get off the fence when most of you probably did not realize you were on one. If this advice was sound five years ago, it is clear that it is still sounder today" (Okihiro 1991:150). Until the outbreak of war, response to this pressure was not monolithic. Many worked to promote Buddhist "churches" and Japanese-language schools, while others campaigned for Americanization, until war transformed a productive cultural swirl into a frightened mimicry.

MEANWHILE IN FIJI

And yet irony looms. In the peaceful, prosperous, postwar U.S. state of Hawai'i, time came again for Buddhist temples (though not with the same demographics), and with booming Japanese tourism, time also came for a Japanese Hawaiian immersion in Japanese language and culture. But only the ethnic Hawaiian nationalists, in the present political scene, cast any aspersions on the civil roots of immigrant-descended citizens.[4] In Fiji, on the other hand, the Indo-Fijians were as free in the years of World War II to resist the British imperial cause as the Japanese in Hawai'i had been free in the 1920s and 1930s to resist American bombast. They were, of course, not entirely free, but free enough to weigh the political costs. But something very different happened in Fiji, and for at least a decade now, it is the Indo-Fijians who live in fear.

There is no doubt that the British in Fiji felt a threat to empire and, briefly, to Fiji, after the Japanese attack on Pearl Harbor in December 1941 and the fall of Singapore in February 1942. But by June 1942 it was the Americans who had arrived in Fiji in force, taking over the command of defense and thereafter using Fiji as a rest and supply base. In Fiji during the war, many things occurred simultaneously, notably the erosion of British prestige in light of the demonstrated superior powers of the more boisterous, more egalitarian Americans in their rest-and-relaxation mode, as Brij Lal (1992) has detailed. But if a more serious threat to empire had to be named, it would surely not have been either Japan or the Americans, but rather, the Freedom Movement in India.

The Indians in Fiji avidly followed news of the Indian National Congress debates, Mahatma Gandhi's nonviolent activism, the failure of the Cripps Mission to India, the Quit India call, and the development (in Southeast

Asia) of Subhas Chandra Bose's Japan-allied Indian National Army. What these events meant for them was a matter of considerable controversy. In 1929 the leading Fiji Indian politician, Fiji-born Vishnu Deo, had articulated as a political formula self-rule for India and equal citizenship in Fiji. The colonial British in Fiji uncompromisingly resisted the latter and sought to divide voting rolls by "race" as they defined it and limit representation for Indians in government. This was a matter of empirewide policy and was resolved by the Colonial Office in London in favor of allowing racially de-limited voting systems, especially after whites in Kenya threatened another African breakaway (see Tinker 1976). A major Indo-Fijian boycott of the Fiji Legislative Council that began in 1929 failed in great bitterness (Gillion 1977; Kelly 1991; Kaplan and Kelly 1994).

As war reached Fiji, then, the capacity of the British to maintain their racial privileges through spectacle, awe, and invocation of common sense was eroding, and increasingly rigid color bars were sought instead. Even though Labour Party governments in London gave the Fiji Indian sugar growers the right to organize unions, the Colonial Sugar Refining Company preferred strikes to collective bargaining with ex-coolies, and at the outbreak of war, both the company and government sought opportunities to recoup lost ground in matters of labor and "racial" discipline.

With this background, I begin my description of what the Indo-Fijians did during the war with a simple contrast between their actions and those of the Japanese Hawaiians. Japanese Hawaiians fought; Indo-Fijians did not. In Hawai'i, after interning the suspected "subversives," the American military invited other Japanese to serve on an "Emergency Service Committee." That committee enthusiastically connected American military demands for ser-vice with Japanese Hawaiian demands for the chance to serve and prove loy-alty. Nisei in the U.S. Army had already proven themselves loyal by shedding blood and dying in Europe, and combat volunteers were sought; the U.S. Army called for only 1,500, and 9,507 volunteered.

In Fiji, however, the Defence Force disbanded its only Indian platoon in 1939, following conflicts over a novel and racially discriminatory wage scale that was to pay whites twice as much as nonwhites. The government set up a Central Indian War Committee to channel Indo-Fijians into war service; in its first meeting in May 1942, the committee unanimously passed resolutions expressing Indian willingness to serve, but only on equal terms with whites. The government then passed legislation enabling it to require compulsory service (a law it never put to use) and announced a plan for an Indian labor battalion to serve the war effort, at wages well below those paid to Europeans. The Governor refused requests to meet with the committee to discuss un-equal wage levels, and in November 1942 the committee, in a difficult and open debate, resolved to disband itself and leave government service up to the consciences of individual Indo-Fijians. The government asked for a thousand laborers, but even with the aid of some Indo-Fijian leaders, notably Vishnu Deo, only 331 men volunteered (Gillion 1977:177–78). Meanwhile, the Fiji Defence Force saw its only local action in the entire war in 1943 when it was called out to patrol the sugarcane fields during a strike of the cane growers (who were almost all Indo-Fijians). Ostensibly there to protect the few growers willing to cut their cane for the price offered (which was unchanged despite inflation of about 100 percent for other goods and services in the islands), the deployment was seen by most as a failed attempt at intimidation. A joke still remembered among the Indo-Fijians is that for each Indian willing to cut and sell his cane, five soldiers were there to guard him. Again, as in the case of the army recruitment effort, the racial schismogenesis was pronounced. The government manipulated law to discipline the Indo-Fijians and test them in the emergency, declaring sugar an "essential war commodity" in order to justify deploying the army during the strike.

AGAINST IDENTITY

As we approach my brief manifesto against identity fetishism in current scholarship, let us first examine another ethnographic contrast of the war and its implications for Indo-Fijians and for Japanese Hawaiians. The contrast of two generations among the Japanese Hawaiian labor immigrants was more clearly etched than it was among the South Asian labor immigrants to Fiji. This is only partly an accident of lexical elegance, that is, because the terminology, Issei and Nisei (Japan-born Issei versus Hawai'i-born, "second generation" Nisei) is simply more visible, exotic, and specific than the contrast in Fiji. In Fiji it was well known by the 1930s at least that the India-born could be distinguished from the Fiji-born. The Fiji-born consolidated in social institutions called Modern Youth clubs, some of which still carry on an attenuated social existence today. But let us take a closer look at the political assertion of the importance of the "Fiji-born" as a group and interest among Fiji's Indians.

As early as the 1920s the first formal organizations were established that asserted a generationally located agenda. A Young Men's Indian Association was organized, led by Fiji-born Chattur Singh, and in the 1930s Singh and others even organized a semisecret, short-lived New Youth Army, whose anonymous "commander in chief" launched newspaper attacks on Gujaratis immigrating to Fiji to be shopkeepers and moneylenders (Gillion 1977:118). As the politics of sugar-grower unionizing came to the fore and attention and controversy focused on efforts to organize a Farmers Union (Kisan Sangh), the interests of the Fiji-born were made a leading, visible campaign issue in the 1937 Legislative Council elections, when A. D. Patel, a Gujarat-born barrister sent to Fiji by Gandhi, was defeated by Fiji-born Chattur Singh. Singh favored restricting all further immigration to Fiji from India, in the interest of the Fiji-born; Patel opposed such restrictions in the larger interest of Indians in Fiji and the British Empire. The government used Singh to help justify the severe restrictions it instituted on further Indian immigration, which at this point in Fiji's history was mainly from Punjab and Gujarat. However, the division of Fiji-born versus India-born, or first versus second generation, was never the single most salient distinction in the political complex of the time. Other articulate interest groups were sugar growers versus town dwellers; Gujaratis (less than 5 percent of the Indo-Fijians but major providers of provisions on credit, a network of capitalists alternative to the white colonials) versus other Indians; "North Indians," the first 76 percent of the indentured laborers and their descendants (who had been out of indenture longer and were more likely to have their own lease-hold land) versus "South Indians" (more likely to be leasehold-less agricultural laborers, with their own social-political organization, the TISI Sangam); Arya Samajis (a Hindu reform society) versus Sanatan Dharmis (defenders of a devotional Hinduism portrayed as more traditional); and Hindus versus Muslims. Unstable alliances across these lines of contending interests came and went as the sugar industry was forced to accept the reality of unions, and as war approached.

North Indian, Arya Samaj leaders of the cane-growing areas of the main island were heavily involved in organizing the Farmers Union, which worked especially in the interests of leaseholding growers, and in the late 1930s and early 1940s even tried to "get the growers out of debt" by replacing the Gujarati credit network with a new system of credit-extending cooperative stores of their own. In the midst of both this project and the confrontations with the monopoly sugar buyer and miller, the Australia-based Colonial Sugar Refining Company, in 1940 the Fiji-born union leader B. D. Lakshman was soundly elected to an Indian seat on the Legislative Council. Meanwhile, as early as the 1920s, South Indians responded to pressures exerted by the Hindu reformist Arya Samaj to boycott Muslims, pressures for them to boycott indenture-line mates who shared the same language and region of origin, by sponsoring South Indian cultural organizations (Kelly 1991). And in June 1941 a new, second union of sugar farmers (the Great Union, or Maha Sangh) was formed, with A. D. Patel prominent among its leaders and, in the first instance, enrolling as members most of the South Indian sugar farmers (Gillion 1977:172).

The unions then competed to extract better terms from the sugar company for their members, leading to the bitter wartime strike of 1943, in which the company sought to break both unions, using government help. But before reconsidering these wartime events, let us return to the matter of the

political salience of the locally born "second generation." In the actual political complex of the late 1930s, it is not surprising that the leadership of the
Arya Samaj, the Farmers Union, and most other organizations included
both India-born and Fiji-born people, or that even the New Youth Army
included young immigrant Arya Samaj teachers as well as Fiji-born leaders.
Nor is it surprising that when social distinctions by birthplace were made,
as when the Fiji-born preponderance of Arya Samaj or Farmers Union leadership was contrasted to the immigrant leadership of the Great Union, their
importance was openly contested. In Fiji it was well known that the South
Indians, or Madrasis, had come last to the indenture lines; the Madras depot
only began sending South Indians to Fiji in 1903 and closed in 1916. Thus,
the India-born nature of most adult South Indians was hardly surprising,
and the claims to priority for the Fiji-born could easily be interpreted as
covert North Indian chauvinism.

In Hawai'i, by contrast, all immigration from Japan ceased after the
"Gentlemen's Agreement" to prohibit it in 1908 (excepted were returnees
and kin, the latter coming to include large numbers of "picture brides"; see
Okihiro 1991:37–38). An argument could therefore be made that the importance of a "second generation" was simply more likely on demographic lines.
I am skeptical that this is the whole story, especially since the actual demographics strongly suggest that a third generation (Sansei) is neglected in the
dual reckoning. There is also some merit to the most common explanation,
that the marked distinction of generations follows from the stresses that their
different life experiences put on the matter of "filial piety," the subordination
and loyalty to parents that was overturned especially during the war. Clearly
there were deep, specific cultural contradictions negotiated between these
generations. But the contrast with Fiji can help underline another irreducible dimension of the relevance of intergenerational politics.

In Fiji, voting was conducted by what came to be called "communal roll."
Elections with only "Indians" voting were held for specifically "Indian" seats
on the Legislative Council. Empirewide reform campaigns in the late 1920s
and early 1930s failed to persuade London to mandate "common roll" voting
for the colonies, that is, voting with one electorate without regard to race
among voters or candidates. Consequently, communal roll voting persisted,
especially in Fiji. In Hawai'i, none of the alien Issei could vote (until legislation in 1952 granted them naturalized U.S. citizenship), but adult Nisei,
locally born, were citizens with the right to vote on the same voting roll as
all others. It was no accident, then, that authorities in Hawai'i, tracking the
demographics, were insistent to the point of bombast about "Americanization," *long* before war with Japan became the primary issue, nor that the Nisei
were their specific target. Nor was it an accident that grave, ponderous
speeches about the necessity of Americanization came not at conventions for

all Japanese leaders but at conventions held specifically for Nisei leaders, for example at the Conference of New Americans inaugurated in 1927 (Okihiro 1991:142). It was a battle for specific hearts and minds, begun long before the military war with Japan, a conflict in which the war intervened decisively: the Japanese-language schools, entirely shut down after the Pearl Harbor attack, had at the time an enrollment of more than 80 percent of school-aged Japanese Hawaiians (Okihiro 1991:156). Especially *as* new Americans, the Nisei were quite forcibly distinguished from their parents, and the distinction between generations gained a prominence outweighing other real and possible lines of distinction among the Hawaiian Japanese: rural versus urban; English versus non–English speaking (among the Issei); non-Japanese versus Japanese speaking versus those sent to Japan for education (the *kibei*) (among the Nisei); plantation workers versus others; different types and periods of indentured labor (*gannenmono*, "first year" people, of the 1868 experiment versus *kanyaku imin*, or "government-contract migrants," of 1885–94 versus *jiyu imin*, "free migrants" brought by private emigration firms to 1908); Okinawan versus Japanese; and other distinctions according to region or prefecture of origin.

Can the concept of identity help us, as scholars of such complex political and cultural history? Or is it so flawed that it makes for sloppy synthesis of disparate projects of finding, using, making, preserving, or imposing orders of difference located quite variously in minds, bodies, and relations between and among them? It strikes me that, much like Pierre Bourdieu's elaborated conception of symbolic and cultural capital, the generalized conception of identity politics so pervasive in current scholarship is indeed fatally flawed. Of course, translations are always possible at some cost (as is argued by Latour 1988). But just as surely as one is reinscribing history in the language of the victors (as Walter Benjamin warned against), if one describes all social fields, relations, motivations, and events in a vast apparatus of metaphoric capitalism, so, also, one universalizes the subjectivity incited by the bourgeois Western, secularized-Christian form of self-determining when one seeks to capture all political positions, relations, movements, and outcomes as equivalent stories of identity and difference.

Three problems that arise from scholarly fetishism of identity are particularly relevant here. First, "identity" blurs the samenesses imposed on others with samenesses of selves, selves "imagined" (as we now like to reiterate) as deep with morally crucial and active parts (Christian or post-Christian, still confessing or witnessing). Second, homogenizing of "identity" underestimates the importance of specificities of discourses of race, especially regarding imputations about moral inferiority and capacity. Third, applied identity theories can sanitize the role of the will, both individual and collective, in actual political history. To understand all political movements and conflicts as assertions of and contests over identity requires a simplistic framework for recognizing motives and tracking success: as if it is always all about achieving a redemptive moral being.

In Fiji, when the government, "European" settlers, indigenes, and sugar company confronted the indentured laborers from the Calcutta depot, and later from the Madras depot, with the news that they were "Indians," they brought a substantive, social Indianness into consequential existence in a Fijian social field, an Indianness that was no substantial part of the lives of the recruits in various locales of northern and southern India before they were recruited. Before, and concurrent to, the stirrings in India of a middle-class public culture of Indian "national" interest and experience, with its emergent *self*-consciousness incited by "vernacular" and English-language print capitalism and motored by elite National Congress organizing, the indentured Indians brought overseas were taught something very different about being Indian in the British Empire. But this Indianness, in the imperial imagination, was not a matter of national memory and will, but of race. In my view, it does not help to blur this point by subsuming both as matters of "identity."[5] We cannot track the contradictions and political complexes of race and nation that are the legacy of European colonialism by way of a generalized notion of identity as the true currency of politics: this is precisely to generalize from the premises of political ordering of the post–World War II nation-state.

The apparently innocent conception of identities allows some to make race, class, and gender into a three-coordinate grid for all history. Meanwhile others can add more potential axes and at the same time deconstruct all political action, first by positing realization of some kind of identity as the goal of all political acts and then by demonstrating that all identities are nonfoundational, imagined, invented, made, contingent. I would trace the problem here back to the scholarly community's reliance on Anderson's emphasis on memory and modalities of homogenizing it in *Imagined Communities*.

Contrast this to the Renan argument that Anderson draws on: indeed, all foundations in territory, race, language, even the real past, claimed by the nation are invented, imagined, fictions that are useful. But Renan saw more than memory in what the nation really was—he also insisted on shared will. Nations exist with relations to the future as well as the past. Much here would seem too dangerous to touch, especially in view of the pathology we see intrinsic to shared will in a post-fascist, post-communist, post-totalitarian age. Shared will is too collective and mindless to be liberal, yet it is at least as obviously present in the actions of "our own" capitalist corporations as in the actions of any political nemesis. It is easier to make identity the homogenized name for the goal of all nations, and then of everything else as well, and just to skirt the issue of the will. But I think we learn much more if we do not always already know what people really want, if we seek to grasp irreductively what they do individually, and more importantly what they do collectively.

With this in mind, I propose that we banish the very concept of identity from its current fetishized place in our scholarly vocabulary. To the objection that it captures quite precisely a form of self-consciousness produced in many nation-states, I do not disagree. It is rather that it would be utopian to hope that we, the uneven "we" of transnational scholarship, can turn to using the word this specifically. It is harder work to limit the term than to banish it. I am skeptical that we can use "identity" to refer only to what the Americans, in Hawai'i, thought they had for themselves and sought with great ambivalence to incite in the Japanese Hawaiians. I am skeptical that we can avoid symmetrically projecting the concept onto the political interests and will of groups facing quite different situations, especially in situations of imposed racial difference with histories of discrimination built into contemporary institutions. I am skeptical that we can avoid calling identity what it was that scared a U.S. congressman from Georgia, who spoke against a Hawai'i statehood bill in 1947, arguing that "it makes citizens with equal rights with you and me of 180,000 Japanese. . . . It gives these people the same rights you and I have; we the descendants of those who created, fought and maintained this country" (quoted in Ogawa 1978:384). To say that this congressman was concerned about identity, either his own or the Japanese Hawaiians', does not clarify why he fulminates against the prospect of equal rights, about giving "these people the same rights you and I have," his sense that "you and I" are individuals with a depth of heritage and morality while "these people" are not merely distinct, but something else entirely. The problems of scholarly description that come up are actually quite productive, when we forbid ourselves the premise that all contemporary politics turn on a "need for a narrative of 'identity'" (Anderson 1991:205) or, worse, "the need, sometimes the demand, for *recognition*" (Taylor 1992:7).

SHEDDING BLOOD, SHEDDING RACE

John Dower, the historian of Japan and World War II, has argued eloquently that we have forgotten the degree to which World War II was regarded, by all sides, as a race war. Dower's observations of Japanese and American racial propaganda and stereotyping, coupled with the clear evidence I see in Fiji of increased colonial British determination to force racial distinctions into civil institutions, makes all the more interesting one of Partha Chatterjee's (1986) observations about Gandhi's form of nationalism. Gandhi was particularly insistent *not* to articulate an Indian national agenda on the basis of racial or cultural distinctiveness. Gandhi condemned not Western or Christian civilization but modern civilization. He sought an alternative form of self-rule that would be universally applicable; in Chatterjee's terms, he worked outside both the thematic and problematic of nationalist thought as we know it.

Yet there is one aspect of the practices of nationalism, emphasized but, I think, misunderstood by Benedict Anderson in his theory of nationalism, that Gandhi did embrace. For all his nonviolence, there was one situation of violence Gandhi celebrated, namely victimhood. The suffering of the victim could reach into the conscience of the oppressor, and it could inspire anyone with sympathy to comradery. For Gandhi, the pain of suffering people, notably including the shedding of blood, could reveal the truth. At least, it can resolve hybridity not arbitrarily but creatively, forcing one to accept or resist a kindred alignment, forcing one to move to one side or the other.[6] Anderson errs when he emphasizes patriotism as a force that can particularly and actually motivate people to martyrdom, when he names willingness to die for the nation "the central problem posed by nationalism" (1991:7). If we attend to the lessons of studies of battle, we learn it is rarely easy to motivate soldiers. It is not the abundance of martyrs but the value of stories of martyrs that is truly central here. Martyrdom stories signal an effort to force a social alignment, to force a decision about a social truth. Recently, science studies scholars Malcolm Ashmore, Derek Edwards, and Jonathan Potter (1994) have written about references to death as one of the classic resorts in arguments against relativism. The point, and it is a strong one, is that the political objection to relativism is not that relativism allows anything to be asserted, believed, or remembered, but that it allows anything to be denied or forgotten. For a left-wing version of this politics of shed blood, one is reminded of Walter Benjamin's image of the historian seizing the flash of memory—notably memory of past struggle and death—at the moment of present danger. Not even the dead are safe when only the victors tell the story.

Simply put, memories of blood shed, lives or limbs actually given over to a cause, can serve like investments in the cause, or better, gifts of meaning for which we are told we owe the return. When pushed to honor, or at least to respect the dead, our other proffered choice is exit—love it or leave it— a choice that is real only if the door is open. It is always very difficult to argue against death stories, and the fresher the blood and higher the body count, the more difficult this becomes. This can make martyrs tremendous political weapons, for left and right, colonial and democrat, silencer of racism in one place, licenser of racial pride in another.

During World War II the British in Fiji shaped the options for the Indo-Fijians in a way that sought to force them into their place, a racially subordinate place, but India's own emergent independence suggested alternative possibilities. Most Indo-Fijians sought to find their own way out of the colonial system. For all that many in Fiji now like to accuse the wartime Indo-

Fijians of shortsightedness, accounts of the final meeting of the Central Indian War Committee in November 1942, in the wake of the Governor's refusal to discuss deliberately discriminatory wages, indicate the opposite.[7] They show acutely self-conscious deliberation on the dilemmas in dealing with a violent, structurally racist state. Consider, for example, the arguments of Muhammad Tawahir Khan, who soon thereafter helped lead the unsuccessful efforts to recruit for the Indian "labor battalion," and of Battan Singh, in favor of adherence to the committee's May resolutions against discrimination:

> Muhammad Tawahir said Fiji is our country. When we are asking for our rights we should also be ready to assist Government. . . . I am now looking far ahead. Let the May resolutions remain as they are, and after the war we can put our claims before Government. Meanwhile, . . . show some self-sacrifice so that we may be able to say that although the Government acted unworthily, we assisted, disregarding the racial discrimination. Yes, the word "labour" is unpleasant. In the days of indenture we were called "coolies," even now the stigma pursues us. Even after enlistment in the army we shall remain Indian coolies. We should tell the Government that we want to get into the army to fight, not as coolies.
>
> Battan Singh said that a people without principles or which cannot hold to its decisions receive no respect. . . . [T]he Indian people of Fiji have presented their demand for equality. Disregarding this, to bring forward the question of a labour battalion appears very unwise. . . . We want to place these matters before the Government, so that in these days of difficulty, by abolishing discrimination, we may be given an opportunity to take a full part gladly, enthusiastically and realizing that we too are members of the British Government. If Government will heed our petition and accept the principle of equal rights, we are ready to offer our lives as a sacrifice.

Few Indo-Fijians took the lead of M. T. Khan. As already detailed, the committee disbanded, the battalion recruitment largely failed, and efforts to negotiate an equitable sugar contract fared even worse. If the Japanese Hawaiians, scapegoats for a new enemy, suddenly found that eager subordination was their only option, the Indo-Fijians knew that there was much to negotiate in a changing and collapsing empire and refused the only deliberately humiliating forms of self-sacrifice that they were offered. This left the theater of war to others, especially the "loyal" indigenous Fijians.

Always favored over the Indians by the British in Fiji, the indigenous Fijians largely took the opposite tack during World War II; while a few in the hills openly praised Hitler and Hirohito, large numbers joined the imperial army.[8] When it was clear that there would be no real fighting in Fiji, the Fijian chiefs petitioned for the chance for Fiji troops to fight elsewhere in the war, suggesting Egypt. The Americans found use for them as jungle scouts in the Pacific, thinking that they were trumping racial capacities of the Japanese as stealthy jungle war types by using the Fijians. Fijian leaders gained precisely what they sought: blood credentials. Ratu Sir Lala Sukuna,[9] the leading high chief of the indigenous Fijians of the time, could not have put it more explicitly when he was recruiting soldiers: "Fijians will never be recognized unless our blood is shed first" (quoted in Ravuvu 1974:15).

Ever since these events, this distinction of dying for empire has been used in Fiji to allege differences in racial character. The argument does not always shape events. Efforts to portray A. D. Patel as unpatriotic or cowardly neither deterred his efforts to constitute an independent Fiji with common roll nor undermined his support among Indo-Fijians, which in fact clearly increased as Fiji's independence was negotiated, at Indo-Fijian instigation, in the late 1960s (see B. Lal 1992:195–213). Indo-Fijian leaders gave in on common roll after Patel's death in 1969, agreeing to separate racial voting rolls in order to attain independence. Thus when Fiji's independence became real in 1970, the constitution insisted that races still existed in Fiji and had to vote separately. Since then parties have generally and increasingly followed racial lines, and the army has remained an enclave of indigenous Fijians. When political parties backed mostly by Indo-Fijian voters won Fiji's 1987 election, this army took over the country after only a month. The constitution that was then installed in 1990 returned to even more naked discrimination against Indo-Fijians in regard to voting rights. Quotidian forms of discrimination are also more open, and scholars as well as politicians debate Fiji's future.[10] Indo-Fijians still fight back, most notably through boycotts, a famous Gandhian tactic. But they cannot win arguments about blood and, indeed, generally do not try.

In Hawai'i, on the other hand, the terrors of the war rebounded extraordinarily. Well known are the Nisei soldiers, who under the motto "Go for Broke," lost life and limb and were decorated in great numbers. "We who are permitted to return," announced one returning Nisei soldier, "and you who are fortunate to be here have a challenge—an obligation to those who now peacefully sleep under the white crosses in Italy and France—to build a better Hawaii" (Okihiro 1991:274). During the war years, the first and only mainland authorities to intervene in favor of Japanese Hawaiian rights were the Labor Department and the Congress of Industrial Organizations.[11] Federal legislation passed during the war forbade racial inequalities in wages paid to workers in defense industries, and in the last years of the war, big labor and the Labor Department both began to protest the general suppression of labor unions in Hawai'i. In the immediate aftermath of the war, white leaders of the CIO-affiliated International Longshoremen's and Warehouse-men's Union (ILWU) organized the first significant multiracial unions in Hawai'i, led successful strikes, even organized a Democratic Party victory in one round of territorial legislature elections, only to be brought down as communists during the McCarthy era. More permanent change came after the Nisei veterans had completed their GI Bill educations.

The 1954 territorial legislature elections were the real watershed in Hawai'i. To fully understand these events, we need to consider changing world economic patterns. The emergence of U.S. economic and military su-periority is as irreducible as anything done by Indo-Fijians or Japanese Ha-waiians to a good account of Hawai'i's integration into the United States and Fiji's departure from a disintegrating British Empire. Similarly much in the postwar period merits more attention than we can give, notably the rise of tourism, and the trends in U.S. national and global postwar politics, from the New Deal to the Cold War. We focus here on only one theme, and if it is only part of the story, it is a crucial part. In 1954 Japanese Hawaiians were qualified to vote in larger numbers than ever before, and the traumatized Democratic Party was overhauled by an ambitious group of young Nisei and their political allies. They won and Hawai'i changed, not only from a terri-tory to a U.S. state in 1959, but from a territory that was a Republican stronghold grounded in the powers of the big planters dating back to pre-annexation days, into one of the strongest bastions of Democratic Party power in the United States. One of these Nisei politicians narrates the 1954 election events:

> The six of us running from the Fourth District campaigned as a team. Each of us had a particular issue—mine was education—on which we spent many after-midnight hours of study, but our central theme was progress, for all the people. We had played a small but vital part in the great war and now that it was won we were not about to go back to the plantation. We wanted our place in the sun, the right to participate in the decisions that affected us. Day after day, at rally after rally, we hammered home the point that there must be no more second-class citizens in the Hawaii of tomorrow. (Inouye 1978:392)

I quote from the memoirs of Daniel K. Inouye, a soldier who lost an arm to a German grenade, a politician who won his first election in this 1954 campaign and who is now one of the most senior U.S. senators. Republicans responded to the new campaign by sending what they called a "Truth Squad" to rebut the new Democrats' speeches at a public debate and radio broadcast. The Truth Squad stormed the stage and announced to the crowd and radio audience that they had evidence that "these so-called Democrats" were actually pawns of the ILWU and soft on communism. Inouye responded:

> I put the notes for my speech into my clenched teeth and tore them in two with my only hand. I said that in my view the danger to our democratic institutions was less from communism than from the social conditions on which communists fed and flourished—poverty, slums, inequality of opportunity. These were evils, the very real evils, that my fellow candidates and I were pledged to fight. If our opponents wanted to wage a shadow war, a smear campaign, that was their sad privilege.
>
> "But I cannot help wondering," I said, "whether the people of Hawaii will not think it strange that the only weapon in the Republican arsenal is to label as communists men so recently returned from defending liberty on the firing lines in Italy and France. Let me speak for those of us who didn't come back— I *know* I speak for my colleagues on this platform, and for good Democratic candidates everywhere in these Islands—when I say we bitterly resent having our loyalty and patriotism questioned by cynical political hacks who lack the courage to debate the real issues in this campaign." (393)

Inouye amplified the campaign by paralleling it with the war; he invoked the dead and made visible his loss. He inoculated himself against communism by way of the firing line against fascism. Loyalty is loyalty. Inouye could accept, and even promote, the simplest possible equations. You have it or you don't, you are in or you are out. But in or out of what? Inouye, Dan Aoki, Spark Matsunaga, the other Nisei politicians and their supporters were not just the mimic men of Naipaul's scorn. They didn't simply become Americans. They became New Deal Democrats in the new terrain of the Cold War and really did fight a good fight to remake Hawai'i, to the point, now, that their political machinery is almost as long in control there as the Congress Party in India.[12]

DIASPORA AND BLOOD POLITICS

Both the instituted racism of Fiji's economy and government and the backdrop of the collapsing Raj invited the Indo-Fijians during World War II to imagine themselves neither as locals nor as an inferior race, but rather as citizens: citizens of an emerging nation somewhere else. An Indo-Fijian newspaper started in 1944 chose to call itself *Pravasini*, "Foreign-dwelling." Despite the bitter ending of the 1943 cane strike, the leader of that strike, A. D. Patel, the barrister sent by Gandhi, defeated B. D. Lakshman in a 1944 election for the Legislative Council, and the campaign's very terms were revealing of the turn in Indo-Fijian attention. While the Japanese Hawaiians were anxious for news about Nisei soldiers, Patel and Lakshman argued not about the significance of being Fiji-born or the progress of the war, but about who would be "the Mahatma Gandhi of Fiji." Lakshman's advertisements and speeches pointed out that while a student in India he had once been imprisoned for civil disobedience, but to no avail. Then, while the ILWU was being pushed over the edge in the onset of the Cold War in Hawai'i, Indo-Fijians could happily celebrate India's independence. But they have never yet been able to kill off either their foreignness or their racial difference in Fiji. While Inouye hammered home his point, rally after rally, that "there must be no more second-class citizens in the Hawaii of tomorrow," and his Democratic Party made this new deal a reality for plantation-labor descendants there, A. D. Patel and other Indo-Fijian leaders worked for decades to get the new deal they wanted, independence for Fiji. But the Indo-Fijians had less foundation for righteous thunder. In contrast with Inouye's hammering insistence on rights, consider the call, also much applauded, made by a leading Indo-Fijian intellectual in March 1988, less than a year after Fiji's first coups in March 1987. Subramani was making the Inaugural Address at the TISI Sangam Education Conference: "It may be that we have become second class citizens but we should never allow ourselves to become second class people" (Subramani 1995:163). Subramani urged a revitalization of the Sangam educational mission, arguing that "excellence for our community is no longer a vague ideal but a real necessity" (164). Many have come to feel that exit is a necessity. Even when Fiji is democratic and at peace, local discrimination prompts Indo-Fijians to emigrate in large numbers to Australia, New Zealand, and North America. For them the global swirl is a refuge, and by and large they pursue better life chances in the transnational capitalist terrain insofar as they can, while in Fiji a basic racism persists, buttressed by two powerful blood arguments—blood of descent and blood of sacrifice.

Much in this ethnographic history is specific to Fiji and Hawai'i, two small remote places. Clearly, I am not claiming that the shedding of blood is either a necessary or sufficient condition for what I have called "shedding of race," or the erosion of civil barriers that were constituted by the discourse on race in colonial capitalist spaces. Comparison of Japanese Hawaiians with African Americans suggests to me that a new deal can be easier for a local majority, and that military service does not automatically overcome attribution of essential racial traits. (Neither should we underestimate what military service has contributed to the civil standing of African Americans or the continuing bite of racial discourse in Hawai'i.) The argument is not deterministic. I simply seek to point out that arguments about shed blood can be powerful tools for social movements out to make or unmake political limits.

To conclude, then, I present two more general considerations. First, war promotes the political absolutism of the nation-state, which is condensed in the very idea of identity. Second, and therefore, as we reckon the practicalities and political possibilities of global transnationality, we should attend to deployments of memories of blood and war. We already know that some in diasporic populations are avid participants, especially financially, in continuing bloodshed in homelands they have left behind. We know that others, notably refugees, by needs seek to mobilize their suffering and victimhood as grounds for political and social rights wherever they can find them. However, we need to be more attentive to the ways that blood arguments can be used both for and against diasporic populations—not merely the sons of the soil, blood of descent arguments, but also, and sometimes very potently, the ways that the rhetoric of blood shed, stories of blood sacrifices for nation can irrigate, ennoble, and even sanctify the projects of many interested claimants.

FOUR

"They Cannot Represent Themselves"

COLONIAL COMMUNITIES IN FIJI, 1936 TO 1947

In the twilight of empire, through the course of a world war, and in the midst of rapid industrial and social restructuring in the Fiji Islands between 1936 and 1947, some crucial decisions were made. They were made by British imperial officials, Australian capitalists, Fiji sugarcane growers, Fijian chiefs and commoners, and Fiji Indians of many religions, occupations, and aspirations. Initiatives were taken that renewed race and racial difference as Fiji's single most salient principle of political order. This chapter of historical ethnography will focus on obscure episodes in a chain of dramatic and extraordinarily complex events, episodes often passed over or briefly noted even in detailed histories of Fiji, in an effort to highlight moments of specific political will in action, their connections and their consequences. Why did the corporation that dominated Fiji's economy, its monopsony sugar miller, the Australia-based Colonial Sugar Refining Company (CSR), choose to lobby London to keep the price it was paid for sugar *low* throughout the war years? Why did Fiji's Central Indian War Committee vote in 1942 to disband rather than coordinate Fiji Indian service to the imperial war effort? And why did Ratu Sukuna, preeminent ethnic Fijian leader, seek and then repudiate an agreement to accept the 1943 sugar crop as a gift to Fiji from the sugar growers?

This chapter will also be oriented toward a specific issue in social theory, namely, how to study community. In this chapter as elsewhere in our work, we treat agency irreducibly, and we seek out not only resistance on the part of colonized people, but also their initiatives.[1] But here in relation to community, I want to thematize complexity as well as agency. I want to consider complexity, like agency, as a matter of fact and also as an issue for theory and method. In 1934 Gaston Bachelard announced a "new epistemological relationship between simple and composite ideas" (1984 [1934]:147). I will try to keep with Bachelard's advice—not to seek out the simple, but to make complexity intelligible—regarding both agency and complexity. Regarding agency, I hope to be irreductive, to trace interconnections of cause, concomitance, and consequence linking the three episodes of decision and action without in any way undermining the freedom of will each expressed. And regarding complexity, I think much is at stake. I hope, in fact, to open some grave doubts about apparently clear, simple concepts, or to put it more positively, to demonstrate the utility of a new approach to community and communalism. To name this new approach, this chapter will study "represented communities," especially the represented communities of colonial Fiji, communities constituted by specifically imperial institutions of representation. It will study the fates of these represented communities—"imagined communities" in a sense very different from Benedict Anderson's—and how they were affected by changing institutions of representation and by particular negotiations and decisions at crucial moments made by acknowledged, instituted community leadership. I will track, ethnographically, key moments in the racialization[2] of community in Fiji. And from this vantage, I will reflect on the problems posed by the emerging nation-state for the represented communities of empire and the problems these specifically colonial communities pose for postcolonial nation-states.

Back to Fiji and its empirical complexities, especially from 1936 to 1947. A world war impinged: after Japan attacked Singapore, Hawai'i, and the Philippines, it was young male Americans who came swarming into Fiji, undercutting British mana with a much less formal style of swagger. And meanwhile, another globally significant struggle impinged: the British Raj in India was collapsing. Long before 1936, Fiji government officials rewrote their sedition laws concerning journalism, originally limited to false reports, in order to be able to outlaw accounts of actual events and public speeches in India, when they were deemed likely to foment strife in Fiji. While Gandhi and the Indian National Congress were generally and, in a sense, correctly represented in Fiji's English-language media as threats to the very fabric of empire (let alone the fulminations when Subhas Chandra Bose began to build his nationalist army allied with Japan), Fiji's Hindi-language presses were mostly shut down during the war, for publishing news that threatened peace and good order, and Fiji Indians got their news about South Asia by mail and shortwave radio. And meanwhile, yet another very global struggle impinged: a succession of Labour Party and coalition governments in England forced the colonies of empire to allow the possibility of labor unions even among the colonized. In Fiji in the late 1930s, the first cane growers unions organized and demanded recognition from the Australian monopsony miller, CSR.

So what happened? In the midst of the war and all the rest, the ethnic Fijian chiefs decided in 1944 to overhaul the "Native Regulations" in their entirety, tying "their people," the indigenous or ethnic Fijians, more tightly then ever to their natal villages, while also packing boys off to war as scouts for the Americans at Guadalcanal in the Solomon Islands. The cane growers' unions, whose members were largely but not wholly Fiji Indians, successfully used a threat to strike in order to force CSR to negotiate with them. Then, after unsatisfactory negotiations in 1943, they did strike, in the midst of war, shutting down the mills for almost an entire growing season. Fiji's Defence Force was called into the fields to protect the few growers willing to cut cane, and this was its major local deployment of the entire war—a defense force largely without Fiji Indian members. In Legislative Council elections in the wake of the strike in 1944, the principal strike leader won the Indian seat for the district most deeply involved, despite being under virtual house arrest at the time (in the campaign in which both candidates were claimed to be "the Gandhi of Fiji"). Finally, in 1947, some Fiji Indian parade organizers vexed the government by requesting that the military band lead their parade to celebrate the birth of independent India. On Bharat Mata (Mother India) Day, January 26, 1947, they marched in fact behind banners of Mahatma Gandhi and Subhas Chandra Bose, larger than life. Generally, however, the colonywide political mood, postwars, was not simply triumphal. In a very angry debate in 1946, Fiji's Legislative Council affirmed that the Deed of Cession, an 1874 treaty between some ethnic Fijian chiefs and representatives of the British Crown, was the foundation of law and government in Fiji and alleged that this treaty required that indigenous Fijian interests should always be accorded paramountcy in the islands.

The rhetoric of the Deed of Cession Debate was insistently racialist, on every side but the Indian. While it was hardly the first debate to represent Fiji's history in terms of racial interests and positions, it is the landmark that scholars generally cite. The 1946 Deed of Cession Debate solidified the union of racial and political categories that has persisted in the islands through all constitutions to the present day—including the constitution that set law in independent Fiji from 1970 until it was overturned in 1987, along with a month-old Labour government, by the homogeneously ethnic Fijian military, and including all constitutions promulgated since, and even those proffered in the spirit of liberal reform. Fiji without race has become, at least for now, unimaginable. In quest of how it became so, we do well to examine the war years.

SETTING THE SCENE: THE "INDIANS" IN FIJI, 1936

In 1936 about 42 percent of Fiji's population were immigrants from South Asia and their descendants, the Fiji Indians or Indo-Fijians. By 1946 the Indo-Fijian population numbered 46 percent, and they had surpassed the indigenous or ethnic Fijians as the largest population group in the islands.[3] The Indo-Fijians, apart from much smaller, later chain migrations of free immigrants from Gujarat and Punjab, came to Fiji under indenture contracts mainly for sugar plantation work; they were called "coolies" but called themselves *girmitiyas*, from *girmit*, the Fiji Hindi version of "agreement," referring to the indenture contract. Fiji became a British colony in 1874 when leading ethnic Fijian chiefs signed the Deed of Cession. Within five years, the new British government had CSR signed up for state-of-the-art sugar milling, had arranged a trickle, fast becoming a stream of indentured labor from India, and had set in motion a plan that eventually reserved 83 percent of Fiji's land for perpetual ownership by ethnic Fijian kin groups (*mataqali*, "clans"). This reserve policy not only pleased and rewarded the government's chiefly allies, who largely controlled those kin groups and served the Governor's paternalistic interest in the ethnic Fijians (to the frustration first of white, or so-called "European," adventurers and, later, of Indo-Fijian settlers destined to lease but never as yet to own much land). It also met the requirements of a nervous CSR Company, cutting off all rivals from access to large blocks of land. Between 1879 and 1916, over sixty thousand South Asians came to Fiji to work five years under indenture; they were owed passage back to India after an additional five years "industrial residence," and about 40 percent did return. In the 1910s the indenture system was abolished, for Fiji and the rest of the British Empire, as a result of protests in India, abolished, in fact, to forestall Gandhi's first national *satyagraha* campaign.

The title of this chapter, "They Cannot Represent Themselves," is part of a sentence written by Karl Marx that Edward Said makes the frontispiece to *Orientalism*—"they must be represented" goes the rest. The very different meanings read into it by Marx and Said are now relevant to the history I am narrating. Said chooses to see in the line a succinct statement of the general thesis he elaborates concerning Orientalist discourse (1979:21). Said argues that the power of discourse emanating from the West, representing the East as its inferior antithesis, overwhelmed all other powers and depictions of things Asian, both for Westerners and for Asians themselves. He argues, in the sort of circuit sometimes admired in discourse theory, that "the idea of European identity as a superior one" is "precisely what made that culture hegemonic both in and outside Europe" (7). For Said, "represent" refers primarily to the process of constituting a sign or image capable of standing for someone or something, the constitution of representations in discourse that will not only refer to but also characterize their referent. The struggles that most interest Said are those over modes, relations, and forces, not of production but of this kind of representation, struggles to control signs and images. And the general, interesting allegation of *Orientalism* is that, at some point, Asia lost control over the means of its own representation.

As a colleague of mine once found out the hard way, representation also has another obvious nexus of sense and reference: attending a conference on "Representation and Power in Latin America," she was set to accuse the other scholars of shallow misunderstanding of the literature on representation, until she suddenly understood, just before her turn to speak: it was, of course, a conference on voting systems. When Marx wrote, in *The Eighteenth Brumaire of Louis Bonaparte,* "They cannot represent themselves; they must be represented," he was referring to peasant smallholders in rural France, isolated families often hostile to one another and without means of organizing or even communicating. They were the majority group, Marx argued, that Louis Bonaparte was, in effect, representing when his state served no better organized group, a majority incapable of expressing its collective interests by any direct means. Marx, far more than Said, was inquiring into concrete social relationships and institutional vehicles for effective collective assertion, especially group action out to control or influence the state, including but not limited to mechanisms for electing representatives.[4]

Attention to struggle over representation in both senses is crucial to understanding the situation of the Indo-Fijians in 1936 and thereafter. In the first place, the indentured laborers did not, generally, think of themselves as "Indians" before they got to Fiji. They did not truck and barter, at the outset, in any sort of representation of South Asian regional, cultural, or racial character. Texts built from 1970s interviews with surviving *girmitiyas* suggest that religious and even caste self-identification was uneven from estate to estate, collectively maintained some places and ignored or suppressed elsewhere (Ali 1979). And to put it most generally, they were simply not one people from one place. They were recruited from all over South Asia, the space inhabited by 400 million people, a significant proportion of the total population of the planet, the first three-quarters from a depot in Calcutta, roughly half drawn from what is now Uttar Pradesh (itself, of course, enormous), the last quarter from a Madras depot, mostly from South India. On arrival they spoke different languages and had different perceptions of propriety in marriage, food, and almost every other practicality of life, all of which had to begin to be calibrated first of all in the context of plantation lines. And this is not to speak of the free immigrants, the Gujaratis and Punjabis. These "Indians" were not only not "Indians" in self-conception on arrival; they learned additional, new dimensions of social connection and difference from the experience of indenture itself, not only North Indian versus South Indian, but indentured versus free, and status groups set by year and, more especially, ship of arrival. *"Jahazi bhais,"* ship brothers and sisters, had social relationships persisting long after *girmit* itself. And, of course, the ongoing process of social and cultural calibration and organization, especially when it intertwined in high-charged countercolonial politics, led to its own points of difference and conflict, especially when efforts to organize so-called Hinduism by the Arya Samaj were contested by proponents of a Sanatan Dharm, when a Fiji Muslim League emerged, when Ahmadiyya missionaries debated the Arya Samaj and were challenged by defenders of Sunni Islam, and so on. In short, we should banish any premise, no matter how weak or residual, that these people arrived in Fiji with a shared heritage, a unitary collective tradition setting a baseline for their group existence.

What first constituted their group existence was precisely indenture itself. In the social system of plantation Fiji, they were very totally situated as a specific sort of Oriental. What was neither uneven nor optional for them was being a "coolie" to European eyes and under European control. As I have argued elsewhere, the highly elaborated narratives of indenture as a dirty trick, recruiters as liars, and so on, clearly reflect on this hidden transformation of standing, just as the self-designation as *girmitiya* both referred to it and contested it (indexing a self made by indenture, but as a contracting agent, not beast-of-burden essence). *Girmitiya* (and Indian National Congress) dislike for the representation "coolie" was clear to CSR and to the Fiji government in the 1910s, as each searched for schemes to continue some form of "assisted labor emigration" to Fiji. In 1915 a circular to District Commissioners explicitly forbade use of the term. But with the end of indenture, there was much more to struggle over.

To make long stories short, in 1921 the Fiji government promised the *girmitiyas* and their descendants elected representation to Fiji's Legislative Council, part of a complicated, ill-fated strategy to encourage more labor immigration, and by 1929 London forced them to live up to their promise. But by then the nascent, and short-lived, Fiji Indian National Congress articulated a different political goal: so-called "common roll," representation to Legislative Council from a single voting roll regardless of race. Boycotts of Legislative Council eventually failed, destroying both the Fiji Indian National Congress and, in a sense, the Fiji Arya Samaj in the process (see Kelly 1991). In light of precedents elsewhere, London eventually backed racially defined "communal rolls." As the Indo-Fijians kept electing representatives the colonials found too "radical," controversy erupted in Fiji over whether to abolish democracy there altogether, to develop an entirely appointed Legislative Council. (It was always, already majority official, not elected.) When Fiji's governor first proposed this change in London in 1933, he was told by the Colonial Office that the initiative had to appear to come from the elected members, not the government—here the government could not represent the resident Europeans; they had to represent themselves, in order to lose the privilege—and in fact, dispute among the elected Europeans as well as Indian protests were crucial to the failure of the plan. In 1936 London announced the compromise. It trimmed the elected representation of "Europeans" to three seats, equal to the elected Indian representation, but added two appointed unofficial Europeans and two appointed Indians—they could no longer simply represent themselves but would also be represented—while the Fijians would continue, as before, to be represented by five nominees agreed upon between the Governor and the Great Council of Chiefs.

All of this enables us to more precisely compare these 1936 Indo-Fijians and Marx's French peasants, as we turn to the question of the restructuring of the sugar industry. The allegedly Oriental, allegedly "peasant" ex-indentured laborers and their descendants in Fiji lived lives in many ways similar to Marx's French peasants, isolated families on scattered bits of land, largely bereft of collective institutions, let alone leverage against the rest of the colonial society. In sharp contrast to the ethnic Fijians, among and for whom elaborate colonial codifications of customary law buttressed hierarchy and reconstituted chiefs into virtual aristocrats, the Fiji Indians could not arrange government support even for egalitarian *panchayats* to settle local disputes over debt or marriage arrangements. But here, we touch the key difference: the sheer fear, among the colonial "Europeans," that the Indians would develop leverage. Much unlike the French peasants, the Indians had become "peasants" only very recently, by CSR corporate policy: after Indian strikes in 1920 and 1921 established clearly their lack of interest in working for European bosses from plantation lines, CSR determined that it could profit by leasing the Indians small farms and controlling the harvesting rules and cane price, that it could profit far more, in fact, than it did from plantations (less overhead and less expensive discipline). Extraordinary steps were taken to guarantee that no individual Indian could lease more than ten acres, to guarantee that leased land would be entirely devoted to cane production, and, originally, to ensure that company officials (originally called overseers) would organize and oversee the schedule of cane cutting and delivery to the mills.

Without a full résumé of the electoral history of France, the comparison is incomplete, but the general outline is, I think, clear: like the French peasants, the scattered smallholding Fiji Indians faced barriers to organizing themselves. Perhaps unlike them, this was in large part due to deliberate, dovetailed corporate and government policies. Given electoral rights, they demonstrated a proclivity to elect representatives that government and company found regrettably "extremist," leading to reforms in which they were again represented, as well as representing themselves. Into this situation, then, came the interfering hand of London Labour and coalition governments, forcing open the door to trade unions. With the aid of a memorandum from his favorite Indian leader (one he was quick to appoint to Legislative Council in 1936) and a letter including thinly veiled threats from CSR's attorney in Fiji (also later appointed to Legislative Council), Fiji's governor was able in 1933 to stall the instruction for legalization of labor unions on the ground that Fiji had no working class, the Indians largely being peasant proprietors. But in 1937 Fiji's new governor was much more sympathetic to Labour, and in any case was still under instructions to reconsider the matter "if and when there is any indication that wage laborers in the Colony are disposed to form associations for the protection of their legitimate interests" (Secretary of State to Fiji Governor, March 7, 1933). The stage was set, as storms of war also gathered, for the labor confrontations.

THE LOW PRICE OF CANE

Despite the emphatic wording of the London instruction, "any indication" and so on, Fiji's government did not in fact pass a law making cane growers' unions unambiguously legal, even in restraint of trade, until 1941, after two rounds of threatened strikes had finally forced CSR to officially recognize the first and then largest union. However, the government's unwillingness to intervene against the strikes helped push the company to recognition.

We could animate the company, here, and claim that by 1943 it desperately wanted revenge. But such emotive depiction of its interests would underestimate the structural interests it sought to preserve and sustain. Of course, for CSR officials negotiating with union leaders, the world tipped. In 1941 Fiji's new Industrial Relations Officer (IRO) (the title preferred over "Secretary of Labour") was only cautiously optimistic:

> It is very difficult for men who were long associated with the indenture system to come round to the idea that the labourer or grower whom they have known as a "coolie" can be successfully reasoned with round a table. The success of the Company's recent venture into the field of collective bargaining ought to have opened its eyes very wide, but the "coolie" tradition dies hard.

The growers' unions had originally brought the company to the bargaining table by establishing real leverage. Cane growers elected the cutting gang leaders who coordinated the cutting with company overseers (soon to be retitled "field officers"), traditionally by receiving and carrying out their instructions. The first farmers' union, the Kisan Sangh, organized a network of candidates and won enough elections to interpose its authority between the company and the growers, instantly making its strike threats palpable. A decade before, when first confronted with the Labour government's instructions to legalize trade unions, Fiji's Colonial Secretary had minuted that the new law "would be a proverbial lever in the hands of a few well-known agitators." By 1941 it was clear exactly how the lever could be operated.

Even before it passed its Industrial Associations Ordinance making trade unions legal, the Fiji government (now under yet another, less Labour-friendly new governor) took a different step to change the rules in the sugar industry. In November 1940 the Governor proclaimed sugar "an essential wartime commodity," creating new grounds for interference, not against restraint of trade but against efforts to hinder the war effort. As the 1943 cutting strike developed, the government put union leaders under virtual house arrest, sentenced one to jail with hard labor, banned public meetings in specified cane-growing areas, as "likely to promote disaffection," and eventually sent in the army in a failed attempt to encourage individual growers to cut by offering "protection" against intimidation.

Most accounts of the cane strike of 1943 doubt its wisdom and emphasize its extremism. No doubt, the sharpness of confrontation was ratcheted up by competition for growers' support between two rival growers' unions. And the strike, together with the absence of Indo-Fijians in the army, is frequently cited by ethnic Fijian nationalists (of course, projecting the "geobody" of the nation-state back in time) as evidence of lack of Indian loyalty to Fiji and even as evidence of racial selfishness (e.g., Ravuvu 1991). But the deliberation of CSR in provoking the strike—and of its effort, coordinated with government, to mark it as a matter of loyalty—is more rarely noted.

Starting in 1939, the Ministry of Food in London became the sole legal buyer of sugar in the British Empire. Other goods and services in Fiji suffered a vast inflation over the course of the war, by 1943 close to, or more likely over, 100 percent in total, due both to supply bottlenecks and American demand. However, up until 1943 the price of sugar had gone up less than 12 percent. In March, before the beginning of the cutting season, the Kisan Sangh asked CSR to raise the price it paid for cane by 50 percent, was told that the increase had to come from London, and in April asked the government to petition London for a price increase. In the months that followed, both the Kisan Sangh and the newer Maha Sangh (Great Union) asked the company for a rise in price and asked the government for beneficial interventions. And consistently, in both Fiji and London, CSR spokesmen argued for keeping the price low, rejecting even the Secretary of State's suggestion of an explicitly temporary rise in the form of a "bonus." The strike continued through many months of highly stressed dialogue, leading eventually to the dramatic intervention of the ethnic Fijian chief Ratu Sukuna, to be detailed below. But CSR bent very little and ultimately considered itself a major victor, despite the fact that it lost most of a year's income, failed to disgrace the union leadership, and angered many previous supporters in government, especially when it punitively refused to keep the mills running when growers gave in and sought to deliver their cane at the end of the season.

In fact, CSR declared victory precisely because it had kept the price it received for cane low. The price paid to growers was set in a fixed proportion to the price CSR received. While its books, and thus its profits, were opaque to the Fiji government, it is certain that the profits would have gone up with the price. But CSR greatly feared delivering any reward to union action. And in fact, it explained its reasoning quite clearly, if partly implicitly, in its letter of May 29, 1943, officially refusing the Kisan Sangh's request for a price rise. CSR did not mention that two days later it would officially ask Fiji's Colonial Secretary not to request a price increase. It argued, instead, in social and moral terms:

> The increased costs and difficulties referred to are war burdens which the Company also had to bear and for which it cannot be held responsible.
>
> We can only carry on hoping that conditions will revert to normal and that the growers and Indian community realize that Fiji is dependent on the Sugar Industry's successful continuance.

There is that word, "community." It is used, as I have already noted, when the colonial Europeans are most attentive to their manners. If the first paragraph was doubly hypocritical, since CSR was entirely responsible for refusing to request and then refusing to accept offered price increases, and thus did not have to bear war burdens it chose to force onto others, the second paragraph clearly names their motive: "hoping that conditions will revert to normal." What, exactly, was normal, as CSR saw things? The letter concluded:

> It therefore behooves them to carry on during these abnormal times the proper cultivation and harvesting of their cane crops to the best of their ability.

Who, exactly, is "them"? The growers, or the Indian community? To CSR they were essentially the same thing. The Indian community was not well served by agitators, especially in abnormal times. The Indians needed to understand that they, and all of Fiji, were dependent on the sugar industry, and thus on CSR, that they had a duty, especially in abnormal times, to cultivate and harvest cane properly—"to the best of their ability." As far as CSR was concerned, the combination of dependency, and dreams of things reverted to normal, should have been sufficient, should have behooved them into service. The last thing "they" needed was representations of things organized differently, let alone representation, as in collective bargaining.

In fact, CSR had prospered for decades by avoiding bargaining in any form, as much as possible. It had settled the last major strike, in 1921, essentially by arranging the small-farming new deal. Even then, an official in India reviewing events in Fiji had commented archly on Fiji's solution to 1910s wartime and postwar inflation. Rather than raise wages and cane prices, CSR and official Fiji devised a scheme to provide household goods to Indians at reduced prices. "Living out of the world, they seem to think that they are unaffected by world causes," the Raj official wrote (quoted in Gillion 1977:61). CSR's pricing policies were consistent, also, in the reverse situation. When the world price of sugar sank steeply during the 1930s depression (the effect somewhat mitigated, also, by an Imperial Preference pricing system that softened the blow), CSR trimmed its large profit margin far more than it lowered its payment to the cane growers. It deliberately lessened the impact of the depression on its relation to the growers, again in expectation of return to the highly profitable "normal."

We are circling in, here, on the significance of "community." I want to complete this brief look at economic crisis and restructuring by noting something odd and fundamental about the arguments that were carried on, in 1943, on behalf of as well as against the growers. At exceptional moments, union representatives and even government officials, especially the Industrial Relations Officer, suggested that efforts at real equity would require CSR to open its books. The IRO once even argued that the growers, like CSR, were capitalists investing and sharing risk in sugar production and deserved a return proportionate to their investment. But the more common calculus of equity was very different: it measured growers' incomes against a normal standard of living—and not just any standard of living. For decades, by 1943, the government of Fiji had run regular, increasingly standardized commissions of inquiry into the standard of living "for Indians" in Fiji. Arguments would then routinely follow, over whether enough kerosene, ghee, and clothing was included in the budget, how many children was appropriate, whether the government had any notion of how extraordinarily expensive an Indian wedding routinely was in 1940s Fiji (roughly equal in cost, it was said, to a year's farm income). Massive inflation gave the Indian growers' arguments bite not merely because they were paid little and basically impoverished, but rather more because their communal "standard of living" had been highly normativized by company and government for a generation.

Of course, not every "Indian" in Fiji accepted it, and there were many modes of resistance, many kinds of initiative taken as well. (Not least, during the war, were lucrative enterprises working for or selling to Americans, legally and illegally.) But from their days as "coolies" to their days merely as

"Indians" and *kisan*—"farmers," "peasants," or "cane growers"—the "Indian community" was offered a highly normativized place in Fiji. Institutions were designed to maintain that (basically very low) place. And it is a place that still perdures for many Indo-Fijians. But there have also been a variety of efforts to contest those arrangements, across decades of Fiji history, efforts that came generally to be known as "the Indian problem," a problem that emerged in many new forms, as segments of this increasingly racialized mass have sought and found new ways to represent themselves. In Fiji touchy, self-interested, but morally thematized contestation has itself long been regarded as an Indian racial trait.

So, what does this have to do with Indian communalism, or "imagined communities," more generally? We turn to theory, before returning to Fiji.

COMMUNITY, IDENTITY, COMMUNALISM

There are no simple phenomena; every phenomenon is a fabric of relations. There is no such thing as a simple *nature*, a simple substance; a substance is a web of attributes. And there is no such thing as a simple idea. . . . Simple ideas are working hypotheses or concepts, which must undergo revision before they can assume their proper epistemological role. Simple ideas are not the ultimate basis of knowledge; after a complete theory is available, it will be apparent that simple ideas are in fact simplifications of more complex ideas. . . .

In short, the only way to form a correct idea of the simple is first to study the complex in depth. (Bachelard 1984 [1934]:147–48, 152)

Bachelard makes a very general point about theory development in science with a specific example in physics. The first atomic spectrum studied by physicists was that of hydrogen, not just because its lines were most clearly organized into distinct series, but also because the hydrogen atom, a single electron revolving around a single proton, was thought particularly simple. To make a long story short, this approach not only led the original equation for the "Balmer series" to omit a necessary term—the square of the atomic number, which for hydrogen was one—but also confused physicists about the crucial significance of the outer electron, there being only one in hydrogen. Spectra data were far better, though less elegantly resolved after two further steps. First, the hydrogen spectrum was reconsidered in comparison to what were, falsely, considered "hydrogenoid" degenerations of other atoms (other atoms stripped to a single electron). Then, finally, the spectrum of hydrogen was itself reconsidered as a special case, "as in fact a degenerate alkaline spectrum," leading to new, successful predictions and observations about the fine structure of lines in the hydrogen case. "In order to give a detailed account of the spectroscopic data, the more complicated spectrum (here that of the alkaline metals) had to be treated first. . . . No one would ever have looked for the doubling of lines in the hydrogen spectrum had such doubling not already been found in the alkaline spectrum" (Bachelard 1984 [1934]:154).

Bachelard himself generalizes this as a story about theory building. The apparently adequate mathematical description of the hydrogen spectrum prompted more exact observation of other spectra, leading to additions, corrections, and complications of the theory.

> Yet these corrections, essentially empirical in origin, appeared to leave the functional role of the various terms in the formula intact, so that the rational basis of the theory still seemed valid. The empirical results could be explained, it was believed, as *perturbations* of a general law. Two-stage processes of this sort are actually rather common in the history of science. In the first, more feverish stage, the general law is established. This is followed by a second, more relaxed stage, in which various complexities, at first ignored, are interpreted as perturbations of the simple, general law. This second stage generally lasts for some time. The whole process is a fundamental feature of a characteristic psychological structure, in which there is a sharp division between the clarity of theory and the inevitable murkiness of reality, between what is lawful behavior and what is irregular, and indeed, as is all too readily assumed, between what is rational and what is irrational. (149–50)

Eventually, Bachelard then observes (in a line much noted, especially when this text is read as a prefiguration of Kuhn's philosophy of science, which it is not), "If enough perturbations accumulate, it may become necessary to take a fresh look at a complex problem" (150). And at that point, what was once thought simple, and was theretofore modular, is itself better understood as one of many outcomes of more complex processes. The superficial clarity of isolation and privilege gives way to the descriptive precision of real comparative perspective, when cases are grasped as related outcomes rather than measured by degrees of modularity and irregularity.

I am not a physicist nor a historian of the physics of the early twentieth century. But regardless of the adequacy and limits of Bachelard's description of theory building in the history of physics, I think his depiction applies extremely aptly to discussions of nation, community, and identity of the last two decades. The general law has been provided by texts such as Benedict Anderson's *Imagined Communities*. By now, we are very long into the "more relaxed stage" in which an army of young and old scholars seeks to render actual national and communal histories, and a variety of political struggles, "as perturbations of the simple, general law." In general form (though admittedly with many more exceptions than I will note) the scholars seek to add to, correct, and complicate the general modernization model that gives us the nation, a specific kind of "imagined community" characterized by its sense of "deep, horizontal comradeship," as the modern successor to hierarchical, traditional social and political orders.[5] But perturbations are accumulating.[6] Most salient here, much criticism has been directed at the image of "Third World" nationalists simply "pirating" a Western model and at the lack of analysis of colonial social relations, especially in the first version of Anderson's argument (Anderson tries to patch the leak with an added chapter in his second edition). Some of the most articulate critics have been from South Asia, especially Partha Chatterjee and Dipesh Chakrabarty of the Subaltern Studies school of historians; while Chakrabarty has challenged generally the problems posed both by English exceptionalism and Europe-focused universalisms for writing South Asian history, Chatterjee has sought various ways to calibrate the actual history of nationalist and other communal political discourse in India with the categories of the European Enlightenment and the experiences of empire.

I think, in short, that we are at the point where the "imagined community" model is breaking down under the weight of all these additions, corrections, complications, and on top of them the various outright challenges—that the time has come to reconfigure the place and relations of the allegedly simple unit at the core. As many have pointed out, Anderson's nations as "imagined communities" are actually historicizations of Enlightenment political philosophies (liberal, secular, egalitarian, and democratic), made real in connection with state and market means of maintaining boundaries, linguistic and territorial, and homogenizing within them. As we have emphasized, a particular synthesis of such themes, heavy on egalitarian, quiescent symmetries of self-determination, was instituted globally via the UN at the conclusion of World War II. Much of what became historical reality was prefigured when Enlightenment philosophy was still only radical political discourse, notably, the evolutionary story reproduced in the tradition to modernity scenario and the claim to uniquely universalistic and therefore normative standing. But can this Enlightenment itself be contextualized, or are we doomed, together with philosophers from Kant to Lyotard, to reproduce its own Europe-focused story of evolving universals?

It would be easy to add that much of Enlightenment philosophy never made it to our reality, and that reality also includes much never imagined by Kant and company. I want instead to add more vectors to the imagining of community, in hopes of rediscovering the Andersonian nation as an extraordinary, special case, and a case not only of Enlightenment but also of imperial imagination, the single "community" imagining itself to monopolize a social space, representing itself to itself and others. I want to place the emergence of, and insistence on the superiority of, that form of community in a particular moment of service to imperial diaspora: in short, to reconceive, and recognize, the UN model nation-state as a motivated degeneration (in the above sense) of imperial complexity. Rather than simply placing the UN model nation-states at the top of a time line, could we develop an understanding of their consolidation concomitant with the other political phenomena of their imperial, global time?

I am not suggesting that I can even outline such a whole approach here, let alone document the equivalent to the doubled lines in the spectrum that it might reveal. The point is that complex cases reveal things about apparently simpler ones. Bachelard describes it, again, via his atomic spectra case. The so-called "hydrogenoid" atomic spectra helped clarify the simpler case of hydrogen, but failed to help as one moved up the periodic table; the spectrum of iron, for example, was still completely indecipherable. "How does a scientist react to such a failure? By declaring that reality is hopelessly complex and fundamentally irrational? . . . The scientist's response is rather to pursue his education in the theoretical and experimental study of complex phenomena" (Bachelard 1984 [1934]:155). So here we are: Are we undertaking merely a regional study, measuring regional cases for deviations from universalistic norms? Should we, for example, presume complexities observed to reflect some kind of aggravated turbulence in societies festering in a liminal evolutionary space, communalism somewhere in between wholly insular traditionalism and a catholic, cosmopolitan modernism? Or should we presume, instead, that the more complex political histories of community imagining that we study are both coeval (in Fabian's sense) with the self-horizontalizing and homogenizing imagined communities of the New World "creole pioneers" and the European liberals, and not only coeval, but somehow connected. We know, in fact, that they are connected. We know, empirically, that personnel circulated through empire and back to metropole. We know, even, that the canon of English literature was first shaped as curriculum for India (Viswanathan 1989).

I wish we were nearing the last gasp of the project of studying the world as a series of only partially successful efforts to live up to the norms of Europe. But the more I hear scholars theorize about identity, the more I doubt we are. I won't repeat here our polemic against scholarly fetishism of identity (see chapters 2 and 3). Let us simply note, from what I have introduced already about the history of Fiji, that there is something very uneven about the way the Fiji's whites were "European" and "British," on the one hand, and the way the ex-*girmitiyas* were "Indian," on the other. Not only were the categories very different in the economic nature, rank, and limit they implied, "Indian," the successor to "coolie," being the much more restrictive, but they were both imputations from the "European" side. Next, I think our scholarship makes a grave error, in effect following the Saidian model, when it presumes that the goal of these freshly minted "Indians" must be to represent themselves in the symbolic, semiotic sense, to constitute an identity for themselves, rather than, for example, to seek leverage and varieties of alternative, the paths that really scared the "Europeans." The "Indian problem" was often reported as Indians seeking to take over in Fiji, unwilling to stay in their place. But it would be more accurate, I think, to argue that in many ways they were highly ambivalent. More positive constructions of Indianness were explored, from Sanatan Dharm to Ghadr Party, from Bose's militant nationalism to Gandhi's devotional universalism. Attending to these is important, as I have tried to in my study of the failure of the Arya Samaj to organize the Fiji Hindus into a fascist-style Aryan brotherhood capable of global rivalry with the British (Kelly 1991). But if we really want to study the whole politics of imagined community, we should also study attempts to evade its impositions, even initiatives out to deny it, such as the quest for common roll voting and, as a 1929 Fiji Indian National Congress broadside put it, "EQUAL CITIZENSHIP IN EMPIRE." If I sense a constant across the history of "the Indian problem" dialogics in Fiji, it is efforts to move away from a colonial hierarchy of peoples, efforts in the first place not to be the "Indians" of the British imagination. We have to capture the agency of people not rising to the bait of identity, especially imposed or proffered ones, if we really want to understand the whole range of identity and imagined community politics.

Against the Saidian model of European kidnapping of others' powers to represent themselves, with its implicit utopia of restoration (redemption?), I am suggesting that we follow Bachelard's method. Rather than anticipating globalization of the power for groups to be self-defining—one can see how tightly, and simply, the Saidian model of colonial history can fit with Anderson's story of modernization—let us seek complexities to the powers and history of representation, especially in the connections between representation's two senses, in the actual history of colonial and postcolonial societies.

Brackette Williams has developed a general model of a different special case in the imagination of community, a general model of ethnic competitions in colonies with plantation economies. It is a very perceptive model, I think, especially if we take it not as more normative or generalizable than the nationalism of "deep, horizontal comradeship" filling the territorial space, but rather as a coeval, and connected, social history. Observing that explantation colonies in the Caribbean have not developed unified, unitary national communities, Williams argues that the social disciplines of the plantation era amply explain it. The plantation owners and operators were never a majority, nor particularly self-identified with Guyana, Trinidad, or the like, but lived and thought in the terms of an essential global imperium—global, yet loyal to a nation elsewhere. The peoples of their colonies were typified first of all as types of labor, in fact brought in as such (for Guyana and Trinidad, first African slaves, then South Asian "coolies"), and then were encouraged, in effect, to compete for second rank in the locale, according to their imperial loyalty, service, and, on an imperial scale, their relative degree of civilization. And the more these terms of competition are challenged, the more the images of group character harden into accounts of group racial nature. Britishness, here, was not simply superior, but was rather, out of the picture, centered elsewhere, and the coach and judge, rather than a player, in the imperial competition.

Applying this model to Fiji is very fruitful, interestingly complicated by the fact that the competition in Fiji, unlike Guyana, Trinidad, or Mauritius, was and is constituted not especially by contending groups of "marooned" plantation labor, but rather between plantation descendants and indigenes. Again, to be clear, I am not suggesting that it should replace the Anderson model as the simplex to build from, but rather that we need an interconnected sense of various kinds of sites, operating in one imperial network. The history of community imagination in India, then, could be a site for a third, distinct historical model of "communal" politics—or more appropriately, the site of many, connected with many different moments and arrangements of non-European and European empire—all the more important because, clearly now for more than a century, its communalisms have been exported out into the labor diaspora realms. In lieu of any précis of what such ideal typical models might look like, clearly beyond me here, allow me a coda: my initial feeling of sheer shock, and continuing disquiet, when reading Partha Chatterjee's praise in *The Nation and Its Fragments* for the concept of community and for *jatis* as communities of struggle, his praise for minorities empowering themselves with claims to historically organic, particularistic rights and interests. Where Chatterjee seeks a way to a politics outside of both Western individualism and the stereotype of a harmonic, totalizing Hindu caste hierarchy, his sense of mission for struggling communalists sounds to me astonishingly like the way Fijian chiefs justify their claim both to represent all Fijians and in effect to rule Fiji, land and state. I strongly suspect that there is more to the image of *jatis* as communities of struggle than I could initially see, something kindred to the "communalism" often taken as a long-established feature of Indian society, and something for which I suggest that we still need more precise articulations.

But, in sum, I am not trying to replace Anderson's territory-filling horizontal communities with Brackette Williams's communities imagined by others, especially as workers and subjects, let alone with a model of a premodern versus a modern type of community or communalism. Quite the contrary: the point is rather that many kinds of imagined communities were and still are concurrently sustained, and that what sustains them is not only ideas or representations in an exclusively semiotic sense, but definite structures of legal identification and representation. While it is wiser, as has been endlessly reiterated in Anderson's wake, to depict communities, national and otherwise, as imagined rather than actually organically primordial, this insight does not explain the mechanisms that make some "imaginaries" more foundational than others, nor how alternative representations gain the substance to change things. Actual regimes of representation, routines legal and otherwise, constitute the communities represented. The legal regimes of empire connected concurrently some highly different regimes of community representation, regimes that differed for motivated, traceable reasons. And the possibility of borrowing alternatives across the connections was one major source of vulnerability to the colonial status quo. But the whole point about such "pirating," whether of the homogenous, horizontal nation, or of labor unions, or indeed of Aryan countercolonialism, is that new difficulties arise for those trying to adapt the borrowed form of community representation to another part of the imperial legal structure. It strikes me that many of the problems faced by the ex-*girmitiyas* and their descendants in Fiji followed from the fact that the tools they imported for community representation, as means to deal with "the Indian problem," the means to initiative, were tooled in fact for different political purposes, even when they were already colonial-era hybrids. What nation, exactly, was a Fiji Indian National Congress working to forge? How, exactly, was an Arya Samaj to address the reality of South Indian descended people in Fiji (Dravidians?), let alone Muslims of more than one form of commitment? As events moved fast in India, what was in the interests of the so-called "Indians" of Fiji?

THE RACE WAR AND THE CENTRAL INDIAN WAR COMMITTEE

In chapter 3 I argued, following Dower (1986), that both sides in the Pacific theater in World War II represented the war as a race war, and in contrast that Gandhi's nationalism was unique for its insistent universalism, its denial of the salience of a racial or even cultural difference as the foundation for the need for *swaraj*. While the Europeans and the Americans sought to determine who, white or yellow, would dominate the Pacific, the Indo-Fijians, watching and listening to Gandhi and others, and observing also the coming regional war, faced a dilemma: Should they fight for the British Empire, and for the "United Nations" (aka Allies) more generally, in the Pacific?

This dilemma is interesting enough: an inescapable moment for agency. As discussed in chapter 3, the Indo-Fijians overwhelmingly (but highly individually, that is part of the point now to be made) chose not to volunteer to fight. Their history contrasted very neatly with that of the Japanese ex-indentured laborers and their descendants in the U.S. territory of Hawai'i, who chose overwhelmingly to force their way into the world war on the American side and after the war parlayed their proven patriotism into domination of Hawai'i's state government as Hawai'i became a U.S. state. Other differences between Fiji and Hawai'i are also extremely important to explaining these contrasting cases.[7] But no doubt the blood sacrifices of war were a crucial moment in the social trajectory of the Japanese Hawaiians, establishing their right to American citizenship, just as the Indo-Fijian refusal of wartime service and sacrifice was a crucial moment in their more complex civil history.

This dilemma is interesting enough, but I doubt you will now be surprised to learn that the Fiji Europeans used the occasion to raise the stakes. Fiji discharged the only "Indian" platoon in its Defence Force in November 1941. This was a month before the Japanese attacked Pearl Harbor and three months before the fall of Singapore. But it was more than two years after the Working Committee of the Indian National Congress in India had asked the British government to declare freedom and democracy war goals, and to promise both for India. Upon refusal, the Congress Working Committee in India decided flatly not to support the war, and Congress ministries in India resigned in protest (Chandra 1989:250). The Indian platoon in Fiji was almost discharged even before these events in India. On September 8, 1939, a week after the Nazi invasion of Poland, Fiji mobilized its Defence Force and changed its system of wages (N.B., this was years before the first confrontation between CSR and the Kisan Sangh over cane prices). Theretofore, soldiers had served voluntarily and were paid "capitation grants" according to efficiency ratings without regard to race. On September 8, new regular wages were announced, four shillings a day for European privates and two shillings a day for non-Europeans. Even before the Congress Working Committee in India succeeded in temporarily coordinating the vast differences of views and strategies of Gandhi and Bose and posed its challenge to Britain, Fiji felt crisis when the Indian platoon members refused to accept their pay.

The Commandant of the Fiji Defence Force asked in 1939 for every member of the Indian platoon to be dismissed. The platoon had only been constituted in 1934 to help celebrate a royal visit—the Colonial Secretary's original vision had been a line of red turbans to complement the dramatic jagged-edged black-and-white uniforms of the Armed Native Constabulary, but the turban thing never worked out, something to do with religion—and to reward "moderate" politicians, on the heels of a very successful boy scout enterprise. The Commandant minuted that this platoon, awkwardly attached to an otherwise European battalion, "had always been a cause of difficulty and dissatisfaction, and it is obvious that this is an attempt to take advantage of the state of war to air Indian political grievances." The Governor refused to dismiss them and in fact praised the European second lieutenant who persuaded them to accept the non-European pay. Little thereafter happened in Fiji, despite events in India and Europe, until the soldiers asked again, in late 1941, for permission to make the case for equal pay. Thereafter, each member of the Indian platoon was separately asked to accept non-European pay, refused, and was dismissed, with the entire support of a new governor.

And then came Pearl Harbor and the fall of Singapore. Fiji did not immediately or vastly enlarge its Defence Force. Instead, it made quick and major deals with the Americans. Relief came first in the American victories at Midway and in the Coral Sea, May and June 1942, and simultaneously in the physical arrival of Americans to new bases in Fiji starting in May 1942. On June 30, 1942, the Americans took over command of the Fiji Defence Force. The sense of war changed, then, quickly and radically. No longer threatened, Fiji's war experience increasingly focused on foreign news and American comings and goings. By September the indigenous Fijian Great Council of Chiefs grew worried that the chance for glory in war would pass them by, and they informed the Governor of their unanimous wish for indigenous Fijian soldiers to be sent to fight in Africa or Egypt.

In May 1942, then, coincident with the American arrival and victories, and a year before the onset of the major cane strike, the government sponsored the founding of a Central Indian War Committee. Its membership was composed of prominent Indians from a variety of other organizations, the qualitative mode of representation classically preferred for colonial commissions and committees. But it was not destined to become a vehicle for transmission and ramification of the government's will. At its first meeting, it called for equal pay for equal work and an end to discriminatory government policies. Fiji's governor refused to reply directly, but letters from the Colonial Secretary and announcements in the *Fiji Royal Gazette* made it clear that wage and rate policies were not going to change and that the Governor would not attend the committee's November meeting to discuss any policies. In August in India, Gandhi, Nehru, and other Congress leaders were imprisoned. The same month, Fiji's government also ignored a resolution from a meeting of the Mazdur Sangh (Laborers Union) calling for wage raises in line with rising prices of government-controlled commodities. And finally, also in August, Fiji's Legislative Council approved the introduction of compulsory national service in a military labor corps, a labor corps to support especially the American military installations and projects. The government never in fact attempted compulsory recruiting but gave itself the power to.

The government wanted the Central Indian War Committee to sponsor and recruit a voluntary labor corps, in effect to organize the Indians again as enlisted labor, at fixed low rates of pay that it refused to negotiate. The November 1942 meeting of the Central Indian War Committee was a heated debate of the explosive issues it faced, leading to two resolutions. Later accusations that "the Indians" acted rashly, lacking foresight into how their actions would be perceived, are belied by the available transcript of this extraordinary debate. Speakers taking many views—from support for the labor battalion to quest for enlistment in the army, from a search for new negotiations with the government to a flat boycott of the labor battalion and war effort—implored others to think of the past and future. In chapter 3 I quoted from this transcript, Muhammad Tawahir Khan arguing, "Fiji is our country. . . . I am now looking far ahead," calling for enlistment and self-sacrifice on the offered terms, while most others, for example, Battan Singh, declared Fiji's Indians "ready to offer our lives as a sacrifice," but only if the British accepted equal rights, "sacrificing life itself for the Government" but only without racial discrimination. The committee did not resolve many sharp differences of opinion among its members, but it did fashion a strange consensus that I hope we are in a better position to appreciate than most Fiji scholars have been. Concluding the meeting, two resolutions were passed unanimously. The first declared the government proposals for a labor corps unacceptable but refused to organize any obstruction to voluntary government recruiting efforts. The second dissolved the Central Indian War Committee.

The result was not precisely a boycott or a strike against the war. In fact, not only K. B. Singh, the government's favorite appointed member of Legislative Council, but also M. T. Khan, one of the organizers and leaders of the Kisan Sangh, toured on the government's behalf after the meeting, recruiting for the labor corps, Singh in military uniform, a lieutenant. Only 331 Indo-Fijians could be enticed to enlist. But there was no active opposition. The Central Indian War Committee had not condemned the war effort, as the Congress Working Committee had in India. The few who worked in government had not resigned. Instead, in the face of flat government refusal to discuss equity, in the face of a government using the war emergency to introduce new, newly naked codes of racial difference in wages, they had simply refused to represent themselves, if representing themselves meant accepting and extending the organization of a fixed racial position.

SUKUNA'S CHOICE

So now we return to the cane fields and the events of the next year: the decision of CSR to hold back price increases and the decisions of the unions to strike. The growers' unions, unlike the Central Indian War Committee, were ready, willing, and anxious to represent themselves.[8] Against them CSR operated with a very large measure of government support until CSR grew too vindictive at the very end.

Over the course of the strike, many initiatives were launched by both governments and unions, most of which reached dead ends sooner or later. As the milling season passed its peak, CSR and Fiji's governor rebuffed offers of compromise prices from leaders of both unions. On October 22, 1943, Fiji's Supreme Court overturned convictions of union leaders A. D. Patel and Swami Rudrananda for interfering in an essential war service, finding after all that sugar production was not an essential war service; the Governor then had Defence Regulation 22 revised, making it a crime "to endeavor to induce any person not to cultivate or not to harvest any crop which has been declared by order of the Governor to be essential for the prosecution of the war or essential to the life of the community." The same day, he declared sugarcane, copra, rubber, and "vegetables and fruits" to be such crops. On December 13, the Secretary of State suggested secretly that the Fiji government institute "as soon as may be practicable a system of price fixing for cane." But the Governor cabled back secretly, asking to defer such legislation, and then a few days later, in Legislative Council, told the Indian representatives that they should tell their constituents to harvest and plant, to work "with zeal," and to "await patiently and lawfully the decisions which the Secretary of State is now deliberating and accept them loyally in the confidence that they will be based on full consideration of your welfare." And on December 26, when A. D. Patel specifically suggested a government-appointed price-fixing board for future years' crops as a part of a solution to the crisis, the Governor had his adviser Ratu Sukuna, foremost among the indigenous Fijian chiefs, write to Patel in reply that "no guarantee that such legislation will in fact be introduced can be given by His Excellency until the Secretary of State's decision is known." Similarly, the Governor instructed the mid-December session of the Legislative Council to vote down Indian motions in council to declare a Commission of Enquiry mediation a failure and to bring in an outside expert—even though the Governor had, in fact, abandoned his commission's report and was already arranging for a tour by a sugar expert from the Imperial College of Tropical Agriculture.

We don't need simply to infer from this that the Governor was willing to go to great lengths to avoid any appearance of victory for the strike leaders. He told the Secretary of State as much, in a secret cable of January 5, 1944: "All my advisers are agreed that Patel and Swami should now be left to sink in the quicksands that are forming round them and that our line for present should be to concentrate on assurances that you are giving urgent and careful consideration to whole problem. . . ." That Patel would, in mere months, be elected to Legislative Council as "the Gandhi of Fiji" surely frustrated this governor; that Patel would have been the closest thing to a consensus leader of the Indo-Fijians for decades, until his death while negotiating Fiji's independence in 1969, would likely have amazed him. But what amazes me, and I think could have changed Fiji's history radically, is what Patel tried to do, at this moment in the endgame of Fiji's bitter wartime strike. He tried to involve the indigenous Fijian leadership, to find a way to ally their mana with the growers against the colonial capitalists.

In the Legislative Council session in mid-December, the indigenous Fijian chiefs had spoken about the cane conflicts for the first time, and they spoke most forcefully. For them, the war was everything, the global rise of labor unions was invisible, and labor rights mattered little. Ratu Tuivanuavou had spoken straight to the point when in the debate he observed that he was "a product of the communal system, a system in which compulsory controlled production is often brought to bear where the interest of the State is at stake" (quoted in Scarr 1980:134). Before we go on, a digression on ethnic Fijian polity, economy, and discourse: In Ratu Tuivanuavou's remark, we can observe in condensation the colonial amalgam of indigenous and British customary hierarchies, chiefly and British interests that, by the 1940s, was well routinized in the "native" parts of Fiji. "Communalism" in Fiji referred and still refers to the principle seen as the foundation of Fijian culture and economy, a theme of commitment to group over individual, organized as hierarchical reciprocity between chiefs and people, expressed in service to chiefs and their custodial care in return. Indians, in contrast, were economic individuals from the *girmit* onward and, more often than Europeans, have been the bad example cited in Fijian critiques of selfishness, acquisitiveness, absence of loving and giving spirit, and its just deserts. (Thus, for another reason, it is hard to speak with analytic clarity about communalism in Fiji, as in India.) Employing classic sociological and anthropological vocabulary with increasing facility over the course of the twentieth century, the Fijian chiefs insisted that their economy and society were founded on gifts and their binding ties, obligatory gifts set by status, and not commodities transacted freely. And, as here, duties to the colonial state, including taxes and other services, were also entailed: after all, the mythology had complexly developed, British sovereignty was founded on a gift from the chiefs, in the Deed of Cession, a gift binding the British to put first their custodial duty toward ethnic Fijians. It is this idea that the 1946 Deed of Cession Debate, after the war, established as virtually constitutional law in Fiji.

Returning to the war years: while this political discourse on communalism and cession had not yet been wholly, officially, and unambiguously embraced by the Fiji government's Europeans before 1946, in one dimension especially it circulated widely between ethnic Europeans and ethnic Fijians: rhetoric about loyalty and affection. They had it for each other, and part of "the Indian problem" was the way the Indians lacked it. By 1942 the rhetoric of loyalty, with an implication of hierarchical duty, was in turn entwined with the war effort. On July 23, 1942—a few weeks after the Americans had already taken over command—a new governor arrived for Fiji, a former governor of Uganda, Major General Sir Philip Mitchell. And as he was ritually "installed" as governor by Fijian chiefs, this governor (the one who refused to reply directly to the resolutions of the May meeting of the Central Indian War Committee, both the committee and its meeting preceding his arrival) made a speech translated by Sukuna, especially its crucial point: "I have come to wage war; loyalty does not consist of lip service but of action" (quoted in Scarr 1980:130–31).

By December 1943, then, the Central Indian War Committee was long gone, the continuing strike had covered almost the entire milling season, and ethnic Fijian military recruiting efforts, led by Sukuna following Mitchell's request for a thousand Fijian soldiers, had gathered over five thousand ethnic Fijian volunteers. Picking up the action again, the chiefs spoke up in Legislative Council. The Governor and other Europeans had hoped that the Indians would be chastened to hear the strong accusations of disloyalty and lack of patriotism leveled at them by the Fijian chiefs, whose votes the government had relied on to crush the Indian legislative motions. The tone of the accusations was damning: Sukuna accused the Indians of the "lowest effort in Empire" in support of the war, citing army enlistment as well as the harvest boycott "when the enemy was at the gate." Relying on a classic imperial analogy, but ignoring power positions, Sukuna compared the Indians to Nero (as the Governor reported his words in a cable to the Secretary of State):

> They had played hymn of hate while Rome was burning. When you had community of that kind in war it was not an occasion for conciliation or talking. Government should use powers to requisition cane and Fijians would harvest it.

Chief Edward Cakobau used the Governor's own legal language, calling cane "essential to life of community," and also urged the Governor to consider having Fijians cut the cane.

Whether chastened or not—as we have seen, the questions about patriotism and duty were much more clearly understood and were much more fraught with contradictions for the Indo-Fijians, than the others in Fiji, then and now, appreciate—hearing these speeches, Patel and Rudrananda saw an opportunity. If the ethnic Fijians wanted to be involved, then get them involved. Sukuna's biographer Scarr recounts events as follows:

> As he [Sukuna] told it, he had barely escaped from the Legislative Council Chamber on this occasion [the Nero speech] than he had an approach from S. B. Patel [a long-standing friend], as a result of which he drove round with him to Nadi and talked with A. D. Patel and the other strike leader, Swami Rudrananda. . . . As S. B. Patel remembers it, the initiative had first come from Ratu Sukuna. What followed was an exchange by word and letter in

which A. D. Patel and the Swami offered first a return to cane cutting, against agreement that the cane should be delivered to government rather than the mistrusted CSR Co., at a price to be dictated by government's conscience. (Scarr 1980:132–33)

On December 26, Sukuna, Swami Rudrananda, A. D. Patel, and S. B. Patel (a barrister like A. D. Patel sent by Gandhi to Fiji, but who was not directly affiliated with any union) signed a memorandum to Governor Mitchell, here reproduced in whole:

> After considering the interest of growers, the sugar-industry and the economic welfare of the colony, We, the undersigned agree that it is in the best interests of all parties concerned to settle the present dispute over the price of cane immediately in the manner following, that is to say:—
>
> I. The Growers would offer their cane to the Government who will be responsible to the growers for the payment of a fair price.
>
> II. The Government should appoint as early as possible Price Fixing Board to determine price of sugar cane from year to year.
>
> These are the broad principles on which the dispute can be settled. If these two principles are acceptable to His Excellency, the details of the settlement may be discussed with His Excellency by us and may be agreed on.

Sukuna, with no particular interest in maintaining the "normal" structure of the industry, was quite willing to have government take responsibility for both order and fairness within it. But his position changed after he brought the memorandum to the Governor, and in the week following he became Mitchell's representative in a final negotiation with the Patels and Rudrananda. Mitchell later informed the Secretary of State that Sukuna had been "unwise" in signing the declaration, which Sukuna had viewed as an unconditional surrender. Anxious to dispel the impression that he had "overawed" Sukuna into a recantation, Mitchell even suggested vaguely that it all "sounded like an old trick."

In fact, as Mitchell was aware, the offer *was* a surrender, but a conditional one, conditional on the government taking responsibility for fairness that the government did not want to take (even while Mitchell sat on the Secretary of State's urging that he set up "as soon as may be practicable a system of price fixing for cane"). A quick exchange of long letters between Sukuna and the growers' leaders followed. The growers' leaders agreed to the price as specified by current contract procedures, as long as it was government and not CSR company buying the cane. Then, when this was refused, they offered the cane to the government as a gift, if the government would only pay cutters' wages, so long as it was the government and not the company that was the official recipient.

This point, exactly, is the one I refer to by the title, Sukuna's choice. Sukuna, the great communalist, turned down this offer of a very large, very important gift. So thoroughly had he become the Governor's mouthpiece, that Sukuna responded to the gift offer by breaking off the negotiation, writing that he found the offer "very disappointing, for I was under the impression that you wanted normal activities to be resumed." Forcing the Indian growers to accept the "normal" system had thus become the wartime government's, as well as the company's, guiding principle, and Sukuna also chose to adopt this normality, which could only maintain itself by rigidifying racial differences and barriers, rather than to seek a new constitution by gift.

On one major theme Sukuna was consistent: haranguing the Indo-Fijians for lack of loyalty and patriotism. This theme of the Nero speech was repeated when Sukuna addressed a meeting of growers, chaired by Patel, on January 6, 1944. As Scarr summarizes it, "His theme was the Indians' lack of patriotism and the advisability of their doing the one thing they were normally prepared to do, cut cane" (1980:133). There's that word "normal" again. As Sukuna (or perhaps Scarr) saw it, there was only one thing "normal" for "the Indians" to be doing in Fiji. In any case, at the same meeting, Patel led the growers to resolve to plant the 1944 crop, to leave it to the conscience of individual growers whether to harvest any of their 1943 crop, and to rely on the Governor's assurance that he and others in the imperial government "would do their best to raise the standard of living of cane growers in Fiji." The growing trickle of growers abandoning the boycott became a rush overnight, but only days later CSR closed its mills, leaving 39 percent of the crop green in the fields. The government offered to arrange a subsidy with London to inspire the company to keep its mills open, but CSR refused. While this and other vindictive CSR moves lost the company much support in government, no one in government ever argued that this Australian company had a patriotic duty to provide services essential to the economy and "the life of the community."

Patel later told a minor British official, Sykes, that he had told the growers to plant and cut on January 6 because "there was nothing else he could tell them." And Sukuna was consistent, as just noted, in emphasizing the theme of loyalty. But what intrigues me in this endgame is especially Sukuna's room to move and his abrupt change of course. Scarr claims that Sukuna supported all the deals offered by A. D. Patel and Swami Rudrananda, including the gift offer, that he "urged government to accept these formulae in the belief they were face-savers for leaders who were losing control of their followers" (133). But, then, Scarr also reports on the same page that the Governor was "at war with the Colonial Office" over "the ruling artificial low price of sugar," and that it was a war he had "no chance of winning"—both claims flatly not true. As we have seen, on January 5 the Governor himself alleged to the Secretary of State that "all" his advisers agreed that no action should be taken to intervene on price issues until Patel and the Swami had sunk in the quicksand forming around them. This "all" would surely have included Sukuna. In sum, there is a certain mystery about just when and why Sukuna turned from his support of grower delivery of cane to the government. But there is no doubt that he personally spurned the gift.

Marcel Mauss's *The Gift* (1967) concludes with the image of gifts as an alternative to war with "Others." Peace, he concludes, could be made if one could find a way to give without sacrificing one's self to others. In fact, Mauss has trouble in his analysis with gifts within hierarchical relationships; for example, he ransacks *śāstra* pathetically for proof that Brahmans owed a return on the gifts they received. The gift Patel and Swami Rudrananda had offered was in fact thoroughly attuned to the hierarchical nature of so-called "communal" exchanges in Fijian society.[9] Far from a gift that thereby avoided submission to the will of the recipient, the growers' leaders sought precisely to submit unambiguously to governmental will and sought thereby to bind the government into taking responsibility, unambiguously, for the price of cane. Especially within the logic of colonial-Fijian communalism, this would have implied a great custodial duty for the government.

My point is certainly not that Ratu Sukuna was some kind of hypocrite, violating the ethics of his own communal system. He had no duty to accept this proffered gift, no traditional exchange relationship with either cane growers or "Indians," either in his station as a chief or even as a servant to the Governor. The status quo ante was clearly that the cane growers were bound by their contracts with CSR, not by routines of gift exchange with ethnic Fijians or the government. My point is rather that this was an opportunity to change that. Sukuna either began or joined an initiative that could have been rendered an incipient "Indian" submission to government sovereignty, the beginning of a new cycle explicitly requiring and, with proper returns, engendering trust before calculation. Instead—whether in fact he was "overawed" by Governor "come to fight" (but not army commander) Mitchell, whether he independently decided that it was some kind of trick by people in fact ineluctably disloyal, or even if he simply obeyed the Governor and carried out his will—Sukuna allowed to pass the chance to create a binding tie of submission, in favor of more total humiliation and exclusion. In 1942 collected Indo-Fijian leaders determined themselves unwilling to be the collective "Indian" instrument ramifying the Governor's will and carrying out his racially hierarchical war plan. They chose not to represent themselves as agents of government. At the outset of 1944, many of the same individuals, now as cane growers' leaders, sought alliance with government against the monopsony company literally at any price, and the government chose not to represent them. And Sukuna, who had a choice, either willed or allowed them to remain outside the binding structures of rank and respect that integrated the rest of Fiji.

RACE

If you look in the index of R. R. Nayacakalou's monograph about leadership in Fiji (cf. note 9), you find something extremely typical of books mainly about ethnic Fijians written in the 1950s and since. The "Indians" do come up but always connected to one topic. The only index entry for "Indians" is "Indian domination, threat of." Nayacakalou summarizes the 1963 situation as follows:

> Although in many situations members of each community are brought into close contact, relatively few lasting relationships develop. There is very little intermarriage and, because of differences in language, religion, and culture, it seems unlikely to increase in the foreseeable future. The overview, then, is that of two different racial groups living side by side, one growing faster numerically and economically than the other, their relations uneasy, and no immediate prospect of any long-term alleviation of the unease. There are very strong demands by Fijians for leadership which will guide them back to a pre-eminent position, and continuously affirm their political demands at the national level. (1975:7)

By 1963, and in fact much earlier, the communities are clearly separate races, with few expecting the boundary between "Fijian" and "Indian" to be blurred, softened, or cross-cut by deeper forces. The temporary successes of the Labour Party in 1987 and 1999, and still perduring reactions against them, are stories still to come, in chapters 5 and 6. I will finish, here, with the sad complexity of communities that are also races, but not always all in competition, expressed in the Deed of Cession Debate in 1946.

It was a large jump in logic from Indian unwillingness to be "normal," when "normal" meant one step past "coolie," to the idea of Indian plans for "domination." In 1946 that jump was fostered, I think, by the astonishing events still under way in India, by fear of what truer democracy would have to imply for Fiji, and by awareness both of the utility of the synergistic loyalty binding Fijians to their chiefs and the chiefs to the empire, and by awareness of the utility of an outside threat against which to locate that loyalty's necessity. In short, an Indian threat made both chiefs and empire necessary, and the "Indian"-elected leaders had the extraordinary problem of seeking effective countervailing forces or arguments, while being themselves constantly scrutinized as the living representatives of the threat.

The debate began when elected European A. A. Ragg moved that "the time had arrived . . . to emphasize the terms of the Deed of Cession to assure that the interests of the Fijian race are safeguarded and a guarantee given that Fiji is to be preserved and kept as a Fijian country for all time."[10] He explained his reasoning through an analysis of Fiji's races, asking what "prescriptive rights" each race was "entitled."

> The Indians are an alien race which, due to heredity, customs, religion and environment, has not assimilated and will not assimilate with the Fijians. . . . These factors in the situation constitute a distinct menace to the Fijian race. . . . The Fijians . . . placed their fate fully and freely in the hands of the British Crown: they are loyal to the crown. . . . The Indians . . . even attempted to use the war as a bargaining instrument to further their demands.

The Indians objected to the racial analysis, especially to the claim that Europeans were trustees of the Fijians under the Deed of Cession, while the Indians were not, since it was the Crown, not a race, that accepted the gift of sovereignty. "Sir, we Indians can also lay a claim because we belong to the British Empire also," concluded Vishnu Deo. In contrast, accepting the racial categories, A. D. Patel eloquently argued that the Fijians in fact had an unacknowledged debt to the Indians, that it was in fact Europeans who came and colonized, and that Indian labor in the Fijians' stead had saved Fijians from the fate of other indigenous peoples. "As a matter of fact, if anything, the coming of my people to this country gave the Fijians their honour, their prestige, nay indeed their very soul." These arguments had some effect. A compromise new wording was worked out, in exchange for a unanimous vote for the new motion: "That in the opinion of this Council the Government and the non-Fijian inhabitants of this Colony stand by the terms of the Deed of Cession and shall consider that document as a Charter of the Fijian people." The Indians were included, but only as non-Fijian inhabitants, specifically to avow that the deed was a charter, a charter privileging one of Fiji's "peoples." Three days later the Fijian Affairs Board, with no need to compromise with Indian members, passed much stronger resolutions, "that this Board views with alarm: (a) the inroads now being made by the Indians of the Colony into the Fijian life, (b) the influence which the Indians are attempting on the everyday life of the Fijians," and so on.

Up to the administration of Philip Mitchell, the war governor, there was much ambivalence in Fiji's administration concerning how far the government should support indigenous Fijian "communalism," especially because it seemed unlikely to lead to economic development. A coordinated issue was the degree to which a separate ethnic Fijian polity within the polity should be maintained. Many steps had been taken over the first decades of the twentieth century to wear down the bureaucratic barriers doubling personnel in each district, separating "Native Affairs" or, later, "Fijian Affairs" from the rest. Even in 1940 Sukuna fought a losing battle against reforms that firmly put the Rokos, often elderly and experienced officers in the sheerly indigenous part of the government hierarchy, under the authority of District Commissioners and even District Officers, who were then all Europeans and often very young "cadets." Further, the rowdy and powerful young Americans, so unlike the British, were willing (and indeed eager) to do things like drink home-brewed alcoholic beverages with ethnic Fijians and Indo-Fijians. They radically upset those concerned with rank and propriety, in a colony where the only legal places for non-Europeans to drink were special bars for those with permits. By 1944 Sukuna and others had persuaded Mitchell to take concrete steps to protect indigenous Fijians from such disorder, to side more firmly with communalism and separation for the Fijian Affairs bureaucracy. In 1944 government reforms reconstituted Fijian Affairs as a separate branch of government, and with its new designation, this bureaucracy regulated ethnic Fijian life with new vigor. For example, starting in 1944, in the name of village-oriented development, it was made explicitly illegal for Fijian commoners to remain more than seven days in an industrial or closely settled area outside their village (B. Lal 1992:137–38). It was this purifying bureaucracy, then, that protested as sinister all Indian "inroads" and attempts to "influence" the everyday life of the Fijians.

Indigenous Fijian communalists did not attempt to be sheerly insular, at least until 1987. In the colonial era, they nurtured their self-submission to the British Empire and had to be coaxed with many concrete legal protections before they agreed to allow Fiji independence in 1970. But that also is another story, one for chapter 5. Here I merely observe that they, like the Fiji Europeans, found racial exclusivism very useful and very righteous in the wake of their experiences from 1936 to 1946, much against more global trends against racism and colonialism itself, following shock at the Holocaust, shock and awe at the potential and reality of nuclear weapons, and the normativization of the nation-state in the new United Nations utopia.

It is possible to render this segment of Fiji's history as inevitable tragedy, only if we simply accept as unproblematic the colonial notion that Fiji's history is, in the main, the story of interaction between three collective, distinct, contending groups. In fact, in crucial ways it does not matter, once we have made this choice, whether we call the groups races, or ethnicities, or interest groups, or, to deploy currently favored vocabulary, subject positions or identities, or the polite term, communities. It, of course, makes a general tragic sort of sense that "the Indians" drifted out of sympathy with the imperial cause and were more interested in the end of the Raj than the struggle with Japan, especially after it quickly became clear that Fiji would not be invaded except by Americans on R and R, that "the Indians" took every sensible step to free Fiji from imperial government and imperial capitalist monopolies, only to find themselves accused of disloyalty to the islands, while the imperials, in the endgame, handed over control of land and state to their loyal Fijian, and especially chiefly Fijian, allies. But there is more to it than inevitably self-advocating and competing groups. In fact, Fiji still suffers the legacy of official choices in the war years, to seek to support normality and community in a rapidly changing world.

Top, Kisan Sangh leadership at Drasa Tramline, Lautoka, May 1941, the month CSR officially recognized the union. Ayodhya Prasad, M. T. Khan, and B. D. Lakshman are third through fifth from the left, front row. *Bottom,* Sugarcane for the Lautoka mill, September 1954. Photograph by Rob Wright.

Maha Sangh leaders Swami Rudrananda and A. D. Patel, second and third from left, at the Ramakrishna Ashram, Nadi, early 1940s.

Celebration of Bharat Mata (Mother India) Day in Ba, Fiji, January 26, 1947. Marchers hold pictures of Subhas Chandra Bose and Mahatma Gandhi. This photo is one of a set purchased in Ba by District Officer H. G. R. McAlpine from photographer Ram Garib.

Top, Arms drill, September 1949. Photograph by Rob Wright. *Bottom*, Guard of honor at opening of Legislative Council, October 1947. The soldiers are all ethnic Fijians. Photograph by Rob Wright.

Top, Vishnu Deo in his Legislative Council campaign office, August 1950. Photograph by Rob Wright. *Left*, Ragg poster on taxi, August 1950. Photograph by Rob Wright.

Queen Elizabeth II is given a chiefly ceremony of welcome on arrival in Suva, December 1953. Photograph by Rob Wright.

In absence of the Governor, Ratu Sukuna delivered the Cession Day address, Levuka, October 10, 1954. Photograph by Rob Wright.

Top, A. D. Patel and Swami Rudrananda at the Swami's house in the 1960s. *Bottom*, Ratu Sukuna receives a whale's tooth during a Lau Provincial Council meeting, August 1955. Photograph by Rob Wright.

FIVE

"Blood on the Grass and Dogs Will Speak"

RITUAL POLITICS AND THE NATION IN INDEPENDENT FIJI

If nation-states require narratives, stories of their past, present, and future, then surely rituals are quintessential moments of power in which such narratives are made and sustained, contested and overthrown, accommodated or transformed. Examining ritual efforts that failed to make a national community, rituals whose narratives failed to convince, this chapter considers the ritual requirements of nationhood.

In Fiji, from independence in 1970 to the present, there have been national rituals. But these national rituals have been an uneasy articulation of ethnic Fijian and Indo-Fijian "customary" ceremony. This chapter considers two ritual projects: the official national rituals of newly independent Fiji in the 1970s and 1980s and an alternative series of rituals conducted by a visionary mystic Fiji citizen, who in the same decades sought to create a unified Fiji through media, prophecy, and his own forms of national ritual.

AN UNUSUAL RITUAL: THE OPENING OF THE *SYRIA MONUMENT*

The rituals of Harigyan Samalia, an Indo-Fijian eccentric visionary mystic, will serve as our point of entry into these questions of ritual and nations.[1]

In 1984 Samalia organized the building of the *Syria Monument,* a large stone structure erected at the bridge that spans the Rewa River and connects the town of Nausori to Fiji's capital city, Suva. The monument commemorates the *Syria,* a "coolie" ship carrying new Indian laborers to Fiji's plantations, which was wrecked on a Fiji reef in 1884, and the help given to the drowning Indians by Fijians who swam out to rescue them. The opening of the monument was attended by several members of Parliament; the guest of honor was Ratu Sir George Cakobau, a high-ranking Fijian chief who was a former governor-general of Fiji. Throughout the course of the ceremony, Samalia made speeches of welcome in English, Hindi, and Fijian. The chief guest was garlanded; his wife was presented with a bouquet of flowers. Samalia then unveiled the monument and gave out medals and certificates to elderly Indo-Fijian survivors of the indenture era and to ethnic Fijians who were descendants of those who swam out to save the drowning people.

But the opening of the *Syria Monument* was far from a typical national ritual in Fiji. The monument is not a civic municipal project. It was not sponsored by a government ministry. It is the work of one person (and his organization, the India Fiji Girmit Council), who raised the funds, mobilized the support, and organized the rituals to inaugurate the monument—and Samalia was not a typical person. Neither a politician nor a civic official, he was in the 1980s a keeper and maker of historical record, an advocate for (but not typical of) Indo-Fijians, and a prophet and visionary. Shortly before he inaugurated the *Syria Monument*, he had visited the people of Drauniivi village to bring them a message from their ancestor Navosavakadua, a nineteenth-century Fijian prophet-leader of the Tuka movement (often described as a "millenarian movement" or "cargo cult"—see Burridge 1969; Worsley 1968; Kaplan 1990b, 1995a). In Drauniivi, Samalia was received with Fijian ceremonies normally reserved for a Fijian chief. He gave the people of Drauniivi a blue flag with a lamp on it, which he told them was Navosavakadua's flag. The lamp is, however, of the type lit by Hindus for the festival of Diwali. The same flag flew along with flags of Fiji and India at the opening of the *Syria Monument*. At the opening and in Drauniivi, Samalia appeared in an unusual white uniform with a blue sash emblazoned with the lamp, the white uniform itself a variation on the uniform of governor-generals in the colonial era.

Most importantly, the "opening" of the *Syria Monument* unveiled key aspects of Samalia's cosmological vision. He said that the figurehead mounted atop the monument was the actual figurehead from the original *Syria* ship (in fact, it is not). He claimed that the figurehead represents both the Hindu goddess Lakshmi and the Fijian ancestor goddess Adi Sovanatabua, who will bring all the world's wealth to Fiji. He believed, as he wrote in the text that became visible when the monument was unveiled, that "Fiji is the fatherland and India the motherland of the world" and, as he has proclaimed elsewhere, that Fiji is destined to be the home of the returning Messiah, the King of Kings.

This was not an ordinary or typical view in Fiji, among Hindu or Muslim Indo-Fijians or Methodist ethnic Fijians. Indeed, most people in Fiji do not believe in Samalia's prophecies or share his cosmology. One of the issues to be explored in this chapter is how, given his eccentricity, Samalia managed to pull off his rituals to the extent he did. The chapter also inquires into the reason he felt he needed to do these rituals, to claim that Fiji is the fatherland and India the motherland of the world, that Hindu and Fijian goddesses are one and the same. The answers to these questions lead us squarely to the issue of ritual and "the nation" in postcolonial Fiji, for Samalia sought to address, in his own eccentric way, a much more general failure of ethnic Fijians and Indo-Fijians to form a coherent national narrative, in politics, myth, or ritual—the failure that led to the military coups of 1987. Here it is worth noting that Samalia prophesied the coups in 1984, saying that after the 1987 elections there would be a cloud of blood in Suva. Few took him too seriously because he also prophesied that flowers would sing and dogs would talk.

NATIONS, NARRATIVE, AND RITUAL

Monuments and flags, rituals seeking to constitute or enact narratives of past, present, and future of a people, these are the stuff of the making of nations, the tangible vehicles for personal experience of the nation as a real ity. As anthropologists make explicit the fact that for a very long time we have been studying complex situations of change, contact, and history making, we have started to analyze what is meant by "the nation" and to question whether the nation is an ideal, homogeneous, or inevitable form of polity (see Foster 1991). Current positions are divided on whether there is some single defining characteristic to all nations or whether the rubric itself links fundamentally disparate sorts of polities (and here, mindful of Chatterjee 1986, I don't intend to suggest that there exists an ideal [Western] sort of nation and then other sinister or ineffectual variants upon it). My sense is simply that in a complex, dynamic, colonial, and postcolonial world, plural and competing forms of organization are juxtaposed under the single rubric. This is most powerfully obvious if we attend to the different narratives that make these nations real: we find nations self-represented, for example, in narratives of egalitarian antimonarchical revolt, in narratives of anticolonial movement, and—in the Republic of Fiji circa 1987—in narratives of the divine right of kings (see also Rutz 1995).

At least since Geertz's (1973a) epistemological musing on culture and ethnography—that anthropologists tell versions of the stories people tell about themselves—anthropologists have found it highly productive to conceive of their project as seeking out a play of narratives or representations. This approach intersects with literary critical consideration of texts and context (Bhabha 1990; Eagleton, Jameson, and Said 1990; R. Williams 1977) and with study of "mentalities" (e.g., Darnton 1984). It can be traced into the "invention of tradition" literature, too. But these studies leave ambiguous what is real, whether representations make their own reality or have a social structural (as for Geertz) or political economic (as for Williams) ground. In fact, scholars committed to such groundings have given us some of the most influential conceptions of the play and power of representations, notably Hobsbawm and Ranger's (1983) invented traditions and Benedict Anderson's (1983) imagined communities. Whether national narratives are conceived, following Durkheim, to be real collective representations that make polities, or whether, following Marx, they are conceived as tales of elites, mystifying underlying power relations, in all, some sort of narrative—historical, cosmological, whatever—is crucial. But if we don't accept a Parsonian separation of culture from social structure or a Marxist separation of imagined communities, invented traditions from "relations" of production, we need to understand how and by what agency and power proliferating narratives and other representations are ordered and limited.

I would not want to imply, as does certain of the invention of tradition literature, that a universal underlying maximizing interest constructs ideologies. Instead, we shall presume that subjectivities and interests are themselves established by routinized systems of representation (Sahlins 1976), and further that agency and relations of production, of kinship, and of political and social order in general use and remake available, culturally constituted materials. By this approach, the existence of one system or order—a social structure, an economy, or a totalizing cultural system—is not a given. Routinization and establishment of system in economic or other social relations is instead a historically observable and variable phenomenon. Rather than being given, structures are established.

In Fiji, as elsewhere, no narrative is eternal or uncontested. And if narratives of nations are plural and competing, the question becomes: how are they established and routinized? Or, to add some agency to the question, how do persons, groups, and/or classes make real their versions and visions of a nation? How do they constitute a nation? One way is through ritual. As I have been studying the painful and peculiar transition of Fiji from colony to nation, I have been especially interested in the role of ritual.[2]

By this approach, ritual is not superficial or "symbolic," just as narratives are not superstructural frosting on a political-economic cake. Instead, I take ritual to be those powerful moments in which people make things happen by appealing to some force, some defining cosmology (fate, history, manifest destiny, the gods, a constitution, dialectical materialism), which is claimed to be beyond the individual him- or herself. Nor are rituals static and repetitive, traditional and unchanging. People are constantly creating new rituals. By so doing, they create and implement narratives to control or empower, to contest the old or envision the new (or even envision the old anew). Nor must rituals be the tools only of elites, nor always the collective expression of shared sentiment, nor necessarily the enactment of revolutionary anticipations. As Tambiah has noted, rituals may take "opposite turnings: to the right when they begin to lose their semantic component and come to serve mainly the pragmatic interests of authority, privilege and sheer conservatism; and to the left when committed believers . . . strive to infuse purified meaning into traditional forms, as often happens during the effervescence of religious revival and reform" (1985:166). To illustrate this ritual dynamism, I think we can tell the story of Fiji's political history best if we pay attention to the ways in which ethnic Fijians and Indo-Fijians have used ritual to make and unmake their nation.

Thus, this chapter will continue with a discussion of the articulation of indigenous Fijian chiefly ritual and colonial British rituals that shaped the colonial order. I will argue that the power of Fijian chiefs and colonial British authorities depended on a narrative of indigenous loyalty and aristocratic chiefly right, enacted in ritual. I then turn to the ritual history of Fiji Indians, a history of resistance and social transformation through ritual. Next a section on independent Fiji from 1970 to the present discusses unsuccessful attempts to create national rituals that incorporated British, Fijian, and Indian ceremony. Here I argue that rather than creating a whole and convincing narrative, such rituals merely juxtaposed segments from the various ritual practices. In a sense, Indo-Fijian ritual was merely "tagged onto" an already whole Fijian-colonial ritual practice, parallel with the way the Indo-Fijians were given a marginal political place in an ethnic Fijian postcolonial political hegemony. The contradictions of 1970s national ritual are thrown into relief when compared with Samalia's attempts to create cohesive and coherent national rituals. Samalia's rituals proposed a narrative in which world history has ordained the coming together of Indians and Fijians in Fiji, so that God can come to earth again. The chapter concludes with an analysis of the failure of Samalia's vision—not through internal illogic, but through the more powerful appeal of other narratives to the people of Fiji, especially to Christian-chiefly ethnic Fijians. In conclusion, I return to the broader theoretical question of the ritual requirements of nationhood.

RITUAL AND COLONIAL FIJI

Nineteenth-century indigenous Fijian kingdoms and the British Empire had a lot in common. Both were ritual polities. Both were ruled by high chiefs who were also gods, or at least very close to gods, in the case of Queen Victoria, head of the Church of England. Most important, both were very hierarchical. The British Empire's local and ongoing practice was a series of "routines and rituals of rule" (Corrigan and Sayer 1985): celebrations of the sovereign's birthday, the launching of ships and opening of monuments, village inspections, sanitation projects, the exchange and filing of sacred documents, daily teatimes (see, for example, Thomas 1990). Fijian chiefly power and British colonial power both relied on narratives, stories mapping time, space, and asymmetry of power between rulers and ruled. In their indigenous rituals and myths, Fijians told a story of the relationship between people of the land and chiefs, between indigenous, original Fijians and stranger, powerful Fijian chiefs who arrived later, to rule rightfully but never to own the land (Hocart 1969; Sahlins 1985). In their myths and rituals, the British told a story of a British Christian duty to civilize and protect "primitive," "uncivilized" indigenous people and of the desire of the uncivilized to be ruled by the civilized, so that they might advance eventually up an evolutionary ladder (see France 1969; Gordon 1879b; Macnaught 1982).

Perhaps the first ritual political step in the making of colonial Fiji was the acceptance of Christianity by Fijian chief King Cakobau in 1854 (on Fijian Christianity, see Kaplan 1990a; Toren 1988). But if the entry of the chiefs into Christian ritual space and time opened the way, the most important ritual in the making of colonial Fiji was "cession" in 1874, the formal signing of a treaty (the Deed of Cession) that created this new polity, "Fiji," a "colony," where before it had not existed. Colonial historians carefully chronicled the moments when thirteen high chiefs, from the eastern and coastal kingdoms of Fiji, signed the document ceding the islands to Queen Victoria and her heirs and when the Union Jack was raised thereafter.[3] They celebrated the occasion annually.

From the British point of view, they were there to rule, settle, and protect. The first colonial governor was a paternalist, amateur anthropologist, and reader of Lewis Henry Morgan determined to protect the Christian Fijians from settler exploitation. He set in motion projects to reserve 83 percent of Fiji's land for Fijians, which endures to this day, and a program of "indirect rule" that used local traditional chiefs as colonial officials. He created a new advisory council called the Great Council of Chiefs, to inform him on Fijian tradition and to endorse his decisions about it. From a Fijian point of view, Fijians as a whole were constituted as people of the land (*taukei*) in relation to British chiefs (*turaga*) in the signing of the document, but perhaps the relation was most powerfully sealed not long after in a famous moment when King Cakobau of Bau made an offering of yams and kava root to the first colonial governor (Legge 1958:206). Cession was known to Fijians as "the raising of the flag" (*vakarewa na kuila*) by the British. In oral and written histories, ethnic Fijians refer to it as a founding moment, the moment of the assertion of power on the part of the new rulers. And, in a happy coincidence, unusual in colonial encounters, the British did carry out one thing the Fijians expected: they came to rule but not to seize the land (or at least no more than that which had already come into European settler and missionary hands; ultimately 17 percent of Fiji's land has come to be held by the Crown [now nationally owned] or privately).

The relationship between these leading Fijian chiefs and the British administration was a relatively happy one (see Rutz 1995 on recent versions of ethnic Fijian "royalist" political rhetorics). From the beginning of the colony, the British presented their authority in ways that incorporated and appropriated Fijian chiefly ceremony. Certain Fijians were participants in this appropriation, for example, Cakobau's conversion or the signing of the Deed of Cession.[4] In the early decades of this century, British and Fijian officials of the Native Administration would carefully codify ritual acknowledgment of rank due to officials and to traditional chiefs. They also decided who was not entitled to rituals of respect. Thus, for example, in 1917 G. V. Maxwell, a British official, and Ratu Lala Sukuna, Fijian high chief and colonial official, lectured a Fijian commoner called Apolosi Nawai for accepting whales' teeth in a ritual to which he wasn't entitled. Apolosi was an innovator who founded a Fijian-run produce company (see Macnaught 1982). Colonial officials hated him; one called him the "Rasputin of the Pacific" (Luke 1945). Maxwell told Apolosi that the rituals of *tama* (salutation of a chief) and *qaloqalovi* (presentation of whales' teeth to the arriving chief) could "properly be performed only in respect of the Governor [the *British* governor], the Vunivalu, and certain other high chiefs."[5] Combining Fijian "custom" with British etiquette made public ceremony in colonial Fiji a truly weighty matter for the British.[6] For example, among the bright-red confidential records were numerous and voluminous files concerned with the visits of royalty and colonial and foreign dignitaries; everything was confidential, from security arrangements to floral arrangements. On these occasions, a careful calculus of status, self-representation, and welcome was observed. Only royalty and high colonial officials were entitled to "Fijian ceremonies of welcome." Then there was the question of which Fijians would get the honor of performing them. Colonial officials minuted one another on issues of suitability, and they consulted Fijian colleagues on "tradition." The Fijian officials they consulted frequently manipulated their participation toward their own dynastic and colonial interests, a story in itself.

A similar correspondence exists concerning the bestowal of local honors. Fiji already could make recommendations to the British queen and prime minister for the bestowal of knighthoods and the like, but in addition, the colonial administration decided in 1930 to begin to issue local honors, medals, and certificates to especially loyal, heroic, and meritorious members of the colony. Medals were ordered from the mint, and when their ribbons were not the right color, they were sent back. An interesting point to note concerning the local honors is that not until 1956 was a Fiji Indian honored. Even more interesting, the administration slipped up in actually presenting

him his medal. They were so used to issuing the medals at the annual meetings of the Fijian Great Council of Chiefs that they made no provision for a
special presentation for the Fiji Indian dairy farmer. In sum, colonial ritual
in Fiji told the story of a British and Fijian relationship of British and Fijian
aristocratic duty and the loyalty and service of indigenous commoners.
Where, we may ask, did disloyal Fijians and the Fiji Indians stand, ritually?

DISLOYAL FIJIANS AND FIJI INDIANS: RESISTANCE
THROUGH RITUALS

Much of Fiji's history was made in dramatic anticolonial ritual politics,
whether indigenous Fijian political-religious movements such as those led
by Navosavakadua or by Apolosi Nawai, or the Fiji Indian rituals of reversal
of indenture days and their Gandhian devotional politics of the post-
indenture years, which created a total transformation in their status and in
the organization of Fiji's capitalism. Strikingly, Fijian and Fiji Indian anticolonial movements were highly separate phenomena. No common cause was
struck between hinterland Fijians and the indentured and post-indenture
Indians. (It is equally striking that the far less successful Fijian movements
have attracted the majority of anthropological interest as "millenarian" or
"cargo" movements, while Fiji Indian rituals have only recently been discussed [see Brown 1984; Kelly 1988b].)

As to disloyal Fijians: during the 1870s through the 1890s, Navosavakadua, an oracle priest, called upon Fijian gods and the Christian God to organize claims to autonomy by peoples of the northeast of Viti Levu island.
Their local mobilization, the Tuka movement, directed earliest against eastern coastal chiefs and then against the colonial government those chiefs came
to serve, became a British symbol of danger and disaffection. Colonial officials wrote a new law to deport Navosavakadua and his people. Later, during
the 1910s through the 1940s, Apolosi Nawai attempted to found a produce
company that would cut out white intermediaries. He, too, claimed both Fijian and Christian sources of power and was seen as equally heathen and
backsliding by colonial officials. Both Navosavakadua and Apolosi challenged
the colonial-chiefly narrative of Christianity and the colonial civilizing mission, a historical moment of transformation from darkness to light. Both
were portrayed as unnatural, heathen, and backsliding (Kaplan 1989). From
a Fijian perspective, both spoke to a different story of power and time: the
power of indigenes, the first, original people, as opposed to the power of
the later, stranger kings (Kaplan 1990b, 1995a).[7] But while these movements
offered powerful explanatory cosmologies for some Fijians, they did not replace the colonial-chiefly hierarchies and the colonial narratives told in
Methodist churches and colonial-chiefly rituals. Navosavakadua was de-

ported in handcuffs; Apolosi Nawai was summoned to be lectured by G. V. Maxwell and later exiled as well.[8]

Among the Fiji Indians, ritual practice changed dramatically from indenture, which began in 1878, to post-indenture days, following 1919 (see Kelly 1988b, 1991). Indenture itself was experienced by many in terms of the story of Ram, a Hindu god and king, exiled and oppressed by demons who stole his wife Sita. Far from India, laboring in oppressive conditions, constrained by the plantation system from constituting stable families, religious practice stressed the *bhakti* (devotional) version of Hinduism. In indenture days, the Hindu festival of Holi was the primary celebration. Holi, a ritual of inversion, dramatized the harsh hierarchies of the plantation system. With sprays of bloodred fluid, women bespattered men, and "coolie" laborers marked the oppressive *sardars* and overseers. Troubles were cast into the bonfires that burned away evil and saved the virtuous. Similarly, Ram Lilas, dramas of the story of Ram, climaxed in the burning of huge effigies, effigies of the demon Ravan, who tormented Ram. Read in colonial context, it was the immorality of the indenture system that was burned with the demonic image. Accounts of the Fiji indenture system (phrased as "a sorrowful story of Ram"; see Sanadhya 1991 [1914]) were crucial in the Indian nationalists' successful campaign to end by 1919 indenture of Indians throughout the empire.

In post-indenture Fiji, devotional Hinduism continued to orient political and economic activities. Strikes of the 1920s were headed by holy men who led the Fiji Indians to refuse to work on plantations. The strikes drove the plantation system out of Fiji and forced change of the land-tenure rules to a system in which Fiji Indians rented land from Fijians and grew sugarcane, which they then sold to the mills. Ramayan *mandalis* (neighborhood associations that met to chant the Ramayan, the text that chronicles the story of Ram) were closely related to cane-harvesting groups as this new system of independent smallholding farmers was arranged with the government and sugar company. In efforts for community uplift, groups built schools and temples. In the sixty years following the end of indenture, the Fiji Indians became the rural backbone of Fiji's sugarcane economy and the urban middle class (Kelly 1988b).

By the 1970s public celebration of Holi had diminished. Instead, the festival of Diwali was the principal Hindu ritual. In India, Diwali celebrates households and prosperity, focused on Lakshmi, the goddess of wealth. In Fiji, Diwali was celebrated also as the night of the god Ram's return from exile. Families lit up their houses with beautiful little lamps and distributed sweets. In urban areas, there were joyous displays of neon. Up until 1987 Diwali in Fiji celebrated the Hindu devotion that uplifted a community (Kelly 1988b).

But while Fiji Indian ritual politics ended indenture and built a relatively prosperous largely Hindu community, it failed to break British political and legislative dominance. Marches and assemblies mirroring nationalist rallies in India were held to protest British rule in India. Fiji Indians looked forward to India's independence. The British colonial officials in Fiji were terrified of these events and sent spies to report on them. Moreover, the colonial British in Fiji could not see which way the wind was blowing. They truly never believed that one day India would be free. But by 1947, the Fiji Indians were celebrating India's impending independence. On Bharat Mata (Mother India) Day, January, 26, 1947, a parade in Ba carried banners portraying Mahatma Gandhi and Subhas Chandra Bose (leader of the separatist Indian army during World War II, who for a time sought to ally with the Japanese rather than fight for the imperial British; see Gordon 1989). In the face of this challenge to their dominance, the colonial British developed a new rhetorical strategy (Kelly 1988a). Beginning in the 1920s, in response to Fiji Indian demands for electoral representation and independence, the British began to phrase their rights to colonial domination in terms of their duty to protect indigenous Fijian interests. In this strategy of divide and rule, the British drew upon old themes, of Fijian "primitiveness" and hence vulnerability, Fijian loyalty, and Fijian "customary" specialness. These differences sowed the seeds for the racial–political divisions that would plague independent Fiji.

NATIONAL RITUAL IN INDEPENDENT FIJI

Fiji's independence was a contested matter, insisted upon by Indo-Fijians, feared by ethnic Fijians. Yet, after World War II, it became clear that a Labour government in Britain and a world insistence on decolonizing would create an independent Fiji. Constituted from the beginning as a community of diverse groups, independent Fiji did not institute an electoral system based on common roll (one person, one vote). Instead, independent Fiji's constitution created an elaborate system requiring that each citizen register as a Fijian, Indian, or General Elector (*race* is the local term). In its ritual self-definition, Fijian independence was celebrated as the making of a nation dependent on three communities. Ratu Sukuna, the famous Fijian high chief and colonial official, used the image of a three-legged stool to symbolize Fijian, Indian, and European interdependence (Sukuna 1983).

Fiji's 1970 independence ceremonies were specifically designed to stress this image of the three-legged stool, but they had a second message as well: to emphasize continuing links to the British Commonwealth. The national independence ceremonies centered on the capital city, Suva, and were planned by a committee consisting of British colonial officials and appointed European, Fijian, and Indian prominent persons. Prince Charles was the guest of honor who presided over the weeklong ceremonies in the capital while smaller celebrations were held in towns and outlying areas. In representing Fiji through new national rituals, for the first time Indian rituals were included as part of official ceremonial. In fact, there was a full-scale, self-conscious attempt to give equal time to Fijian and Indian ceremonies and entertainment. (British forms of ceremonies and entertainment got their full share, too.) Fijian ceremonies of welcome to a high chief were performed for Prince Charles, and then, as a South Asian Hindu practice, he was garlanded and given *arti*, the circling of a tray of incense in front of him, an Indian way of welcoming a stranger or worshiping a god. In addition to a plethora of British ceremonial (flower shows, review of troops, youth rallies, and such), traditional dances, songs, and entertainments were performed by ethnic Fijians, Indo-Fijians, and members of some of Fiji's other, smaller ethnic communities. Even the amounts budgeted by the central planning committee for Fijian and Indian ceremonies were roughly equal (*Fiji Times*, 10/10/70).

The importance and novelty of this balanced self-presentation was displayed in Prince Charles's carefully scripted remarks of thanks, which were prepared for him with significant help from the independence celebration local committee. He addressed his remarks to the "chiefs and peoples" of Fiji, a neat rhetorical trick that maintained respect for indigenous Fijian aristocracy but indicated that not all Fiji citizens were indigenous Fijians. As reported in the October 10, 1970, *Fiji Times*, his remarks continued:

> Thank you for such a magnificent and touching welcome, and thank you also for the welcome that the Indian community have given me. I am told that it is a departure from tradition for a welcome of this kind to be combined with Fijian ceremonies, but this is a true indication of the future potential of this multiracial society and I wish all its people success beyond measure.
>
> One of the characteristics of the people of Fiji, which many remark upon, is their loyalty and affection for the Crown.
>
> Her Majesty the Queen greatly appreciates this, as have all previous sovereigns since Queen Victoria. . . .
>
> [He concluded with] May God bless you all.

In intention, at least, independent Fiji's ritual was meant to create a nation that was a three-legged stool, drawing on Fijian, British, and Indian ceremonial to create a harmonious, balanced nation. Not surprisingly, these new national ceremonies did not draw on Fijian or Fiji Indian rituals of resistance. Instead, they looked to a theme common in both cultures, especially respect for a visitor, treated as though he or she is a god.

But, in so doing, the new ceremonies of Fiji as nation managed to subsume, to submerge, the narrative of the three-legged stool, of balance among communities, into another narrative: the long-standing, powerful British colonial-Fijian story of the stranger king. Notice that independence itself was dramatized—not as egalitarian democratic overthrow of monarch or colonial hierarchy, but as an enduring hierarchical relationship between royalty and people. (The British flag was tactfully lowered one evening, and the new Fijian flag raised the next day.) Prince Charles's own presence, and his words—to the chiefs and peoples of Fiji—recreated the articulation between British and Fijian aristocratic projects. Note also that however well Indian ceremonies of respect for visitors fit in, however much attention was paid to equal time for the three communities, there was a crucial way in which Indo-Fijians were left out of the story of the independence celebrations. The Indo-Fijians have no chiefs. They have no aristocracy. They have no stranger kings. To the degree that the new rituals of nationhood continued to define power in Fiji in terms of chiefs and people, then only the ethnic Fijian community could offer those leaders with the right to power. So, the story told in Fiji's independence rituals was twofold: on the one hand, the explicitly intended narrative of the three-legged stool; on the other hand, the powerful, inescapable colonial-Fijian narrative of hierarchical relations and ethnic Fijian privilege. This uneasy juxtaposition of narratives was continued in the public rituals—and the political rhetoric—of independent Fiji throughout the 1970s and early 1980s.[9]

Thus, Fiji failed to live out the vision of communal diversity and interdependence proposed in the independence rituals. Ritual emphasis on "racial" distinctions and chiefly privilege were mirrored in political discourse. Each election from 1970 on became more "racially" polarized. Fijian chiefly leaders, in particular, came to emphasize pro-indigenous Fijian rhetoric to maintain their position in the ethnic Fijian voting constituency in a rapidly changing nation. Indeed, ultimately independent Fiji's constitution itself had enshrined the "racial" categories of "Europeans," "Indians," and "Fijians," failing to weave a convincing narrative of interdependence, and the constitution gave disproportionate representation to ethnic Fijians in both the House of Representatives and the Senate. In the House, although there were more Indo-Fijians than ethnic Fijians in the population, the two groups received equal numbers of representatives. In the Senate, the Fijian Great Council of Chiefs had special rights to appoint members, and these members had the power to veto legislation that might affect ethnic Fijian affairs and land rights. In the ritual sphere as the years passed, the balance sought in the independence rituals diminished. Ongoing public ritual (for example, welcomes to visiting ambassadors or the opening of public buildings) became uneasy amalgams of lengthy Fijian chiefly rituals of welcome, the briefer presentation of flowers by a small girl (a feature of colonial British ceremony), and the Indian ceremonies of garlanding and *arti*. In percentage of time, personnel, and emphasis, ethnic Fijian ceremonies dominated "national" rituals.

In such Fijian-ritual preeminence lay the expectation that ethnic Fijians had ritual political preeminence in the nation. From independence in 1970 until 1987, Fiji's national leaders were high chiefs, ethnic Fijian paramountcy firmly established. Fijian chiefly ritual, used in Fijian national ritual, constituted a Fiji from the top down, a continuant of chiefly-Christian-colonial synthesis. Fiji was said to be a "three-legged stool," but it was to be the seat of power of ethnic Fijian chiefs. This confident synthesis was challenged by the Fiji Labour Party, a coalition of Indo–Fijians and ethnic Fijians seeking to define the nation as political-economic and democratic, enacting a theory of polity and power not based on divine kings, but on individuals, common roll electoral politics, and labor. The incipient crisis long threatening the "South Seas Paradise" crystallized in the military coups of 1987.

In 1987 the new Fiji Labour Party, headed by a Fijian commoner, Timoci Bavadra, joined together with the National Federation Party, the party of the Indo-Fijians, to achieve a parliamentary majority. The head of the Labour Party, this Fijian commoner, became prime minister, replacing Ratu Sir Kamisese Mara, the Fijian chief who had been prime minister since independence—but not for long. In less than a month, an ethnic Fijian lieutenant colonel, third in command of Fiji's almost completely ethnic Fijian army, staged a military coup. He led armed men into Parliament, took the prime minister and his cabinet prisoner, and took over government and media. Although the prime minister and cabinet were released unharmed, the colonel handed over power to the Fijian chiefs who had lost the election and handed over the authority to endorse a new constitution to the Fijian Great Council of Chiefs (see Howard 1991; Kaplan 1988a; Kelly 1988a; B. Lal 1988). Ritually speaking, as well as politically, concerns of ethnic Fijians became concerns of the nation as a whole. Chiefly succession disputes had an impact on national political issues. Celebration of the Sabbath, on Sundays, which is important to Christian ethnic Fijians, was made mandatory law for all of Fiji's population, including the roughly 50 percent Hindus and Muslims. In public ritual following the coups, the Indian component of garlanding and *arti* was dropped out. Press releases from the colonel's ministry of information described only ethnic Fijian participation in ceremonies of welcome to ambassadors. I found only one account of a public ceremony of welcome that included an Indian garlanding. In addition to simply ignoring Indian ritual, there were also attempts to eradicate it, including the burning of four Indo-Fijian religious buildings, two temples, a mosque, and a Sikh Gurudwara, by a Fijian Methodist youth fellowship group in 1989 (see also Kelly 1995a).

Now we step back in time, back from the coups of 1987, to the 1970s and early 1980s.

THE ALTERNATIVE VISION OF HARIGYAN SAMALIA

In the 1970s and 1980s, in the face of the dominant Fijian chiefly national ritual discourse (but curiously intertwined with it), Harigyan Samalia propounded his own vision of what a united Fiji might be, through newspaper articles and public rituals. What was extraordinary about Samalia was the way he drew eclectically upon a range of opposed narratives, communities, and ritual practices: the dominant Fijian-colonial chiefly ritual and the history of Fijian anticolonial ritual, the pro-colonial Indian Alliance and the history of Fiji Indian anticolonial rituals of resistance as well. He did all this to develop a cosmology that would include both Fijians and Indians, and all their gods.

As I have described earlier in this chapter, Samalia was a well-known eccentric who in the 1980s was head of the India Fiji Girmit Council, a group dedicated to preserving the history of Fiji Indians. Samalia also had close ties to ethnic Fijians. He claimed to have been raised in the Lau Group of islands, a primarily ethnic Fijian area, and spoke fluent Fijian. He was also one of the few Indo-Fijians to serve in the Fijian army. In 1984 he lived in an ethnic Fijian squatter settlement in Suva. He was a welcome figure in the ranks of the Indian Alliance (a small group of Indo-Fijian politicians who collaborated with the chiefly Fijian party), participating in events sponsored by the Alliance Party and receiving perks, such as representing Fiji at a conference on world peace in India. His name seems to have been adapted from the name of one of the coolie ships, the *Somalia;* he may have been born on it. His first name means "knower of Hari," that is, knower of Krishna, but he also stressed its similarity in sound to Harijan, Gandhi's name for the "untouchables," meaning "children of god."

As a visionary mystic with no single "natural" constituency in Fiji for his idiosyncratic positions, Samalia's notoriety came largely from his skill in using public media. Through this means he gained a hearing in several communities, though no sustained following resulted from his attempt to unite ethnic Fijians and Indo-Fijians with one cosmological history.

In 1983 he ran a paid advertisement in the *Fiji Times* (the quoted text reproduces his spelling, abbreviations, and syntax; my additions are in square brackets):

WARNING TO THE WORLD

Adolf Hitler is from Fiji, (Lord Krishna) na gone turaga ko Ratu Navosavakadua [Sir Navosavakadua the child chief], King of Fiji, King of Kings will be inform of Fijian, and will command the World.

[Samalia explains the reason for this ad. It is the text of a telegram to the mayor of Bonn, West Germany, concerning the removal of the name of Adolf Hitler from a still-extant West German honors list.]

S. Harigyan Samalia Junior Counsellor delegated by the Supreme Counsellor on Earth 10/10/83. Fiji Times Newspaper p. 2.

Fiji is a small Jerusalem in the South Pacific, Rarama kei vuravura [Fijian for "light of the world"], light of the world, ramnick deep [Hindi for "the place where the serpent Kaliya was thrown by the Hindu god Krishna"].

New book of god will be written in Fiji, the place of the living God, Fiji Fatherland will announce one religious body and the world will obey. India Motherland of the world will become a great empire. And coming of great man Netaji Subhas Chandra Bose.

Phone.

P.O. Box 3883 Samabula, Suva

When Samalia calls himself the "junior counsellor on earth," he means he is the prophet of the senior counsellor, who is the King of Kings, who has been incarnated in forms including Krishna, Jesus, Navosavakadua, Subhas Chandra Bose, and Hitler. Navosavakadua, as I have explained, was the important indigenous Fijian leader of an anticolonial ritual-political movement, who lived at Drauniivi. Subhas Chandra Bose was the Indian nationalist who formed an Indian army contingent to fight for Japan in World War II, an important hero to Indian nationalists in India and Fiji, who was pictured on banners along with Gandhi in the Fiji Indian celebration of Indian independence in 1947. Hitler, to Samalia, is not the Hitler of the concentration camps. He is seen simply as the enemy of Britain in colonial days. (It is not uncommon to read of anticolonial movements in the Pacific or other parts of the British Empire that used images of the German kaiser during World War I, or of Hitler, or of the Japanese emperor during World War II, because they were thought of as being in opposition to the British Empire. See, for example, Dower 1986.) Samalia believes that Fiji is a sacred center, a little Jerusalem, product of India and Fiji. It is a little Jerusalem because, like Jerusalem, which is a holy city to multiple religions, he believes that Fiji is going to be the site of the return of the King of Kings. I interviewed Samalia in 1984, and he explained the relationships (I quote from my notes from this conversation):

The King of Kings began as Krishna of the Mahabharata, who, when he had finished his work in India, disappeared and changed his form. He sent a snake to Fiji [Degei, the Fijian ancestor god who takes the form of a snake], then went to Fiji himself and became incarnated as Navosavakadua; there he performed miracles and was deported. . . . Navosa said to the people of Drauniivi, "Don't worry if I am gone for long. My flag will be raised." He pushed two stones into the ground, saying, "When the stones rise, it will be time." Those stones are now two feet above the ground. Then he went to Germany and became Hitler, he shaped the world; it was growing fast at that time. At another time he was incarnated as Jesus Christ. He returns each time in different forms. His next incarnation will be as a Fijian to found the new Kingdom on Mago Island in the Lau Group. The living God will arise from earth, flowers will sing, dogs will speak like humans.

Thus, the King of Kings has been incarnated as Krishna, Jesus, Navosavakadua, and Hitler. Samalia concentrates on the Navosavakadua story in part because I asked him, in part because he was then in the process of announcing Navosavakadua's imminent return.[10]

In March 1984 Samalia visited Drauniivi, Navosavakadua's village in the 1880s, where he announced Navosavakadua's imminent return. People in Drauniivi described the visit to me. He wrote in advance to tell them to build a flagpole. When he arrived, they performed Fijian ceremonies of welcome for him, including *qaloqalovi*. Their choir sang a hymn and they all prayed. Then he said, "I am going to raise the flag." He raised the flag in the center of the village, and one of my friends in Drauniivi told me:

> Many people said it was the Girmit [indenture] flag, the flag of an association or whatever, we don't know. But we just know, the lamp on it is bringing light to us . . . because of the lamp the light of God is with us.

In his speech at Drauniivi, Samalia told the people of his vision of India the motherland and Fiji the fatherland. He said that a red cloud in Suva portended bloodshed, that Prime Minister Ratu Mara's government would be changed, that Fijians would lose their land, that there would be blood on the grass.[11] About two thousand people attended the meeting, according to newspaper reports, more according to informants who were there.

At Drauniivi, Samalia, claiming to speak for Navosavakadua, raised a flag. This action evoked the way the British ritually constituted their rule when they raised their flag in 1874, and it recalls the anticolonial flag raisings of Navosavakadua and of Apolosi Nawai. Remarkably, Samalia, an Indo-Fijian, received the Fijian chiefly ritual of welcome from ethnic Fijians. Note that the rituals of welcome he received included *qaloqalovi*, the ceremony G. V. Maxwell had sought to regulate and restrict. We should also note his white uniform with gloves and a blue sash with the pink lamp of the India Fiji Girmit Council on it. The white uniform is part of the British ritual apparatus, reminiscent of the uniform of the governor-general. But the lamp, the same lamp that appears on his flag, is a picture of a Diwali lamp, lit at the yearly Hindu festival, symbol of Indo-Fijian devotion and prosperity. Samalia drew eclectically upon British, ethnic Fijian, and Indo-Fijian rituals. But there was a meaning to the seemingly disparate juxtapositions. He had an underlying purpose, a story to tell.

That story was told most clearly by his work to establish the *Syria Monument*. Not all of Samalia's attempts to make a nation ritually were held on the fringes of political life, in the hinterlands at Drauniivi, or at the Girmit Council. He used newspapers and he used the *Syria Monument* to make his most public statements. As noted at the beginning of this chapter, the monument was built at Nausori, across the bridge from Fiji's capital city of Suva. Samalia convened the small crowd of politicians and dignitaries for the ritual under the patronage of Ratu Sir George Cakobau, former governor-general of Fiji and Vunivalu of Bau (and a descendant of King Cakobau). The occasion was the commemoration of the wreck of the "coolie" ship the *Syria* and the memorialization of Fijians who came to the aid of the drowning Indians. (No mention was made of Fijians who looted the ship.) Samalia unveiled a monument, which portrayed the female figurehead of the *Syria* and identified her as both Lakshmi (Hindu goddess) and Adi Sovanatabua (Fijian ancestral deity). Elderly Indo-Fijian survivors of *girmit* and ethnic Fijians representing the kin groups who came to the aid of the ship were given medals and certificates (on the model of the colonial medals and certificates noted earlier). The certificates were headed: "India Fiji Bond of Relationship Syria Ship History," followed by a brief account of the shipwreck. The certificates mention India the motherland and Fiji the fatherland, but there is no mention of Navosavakadua or Hitler. Ratu Sukuna, the revered Fijian colonial official, is quoted instead. But it is worth noting that Samalia still signed himself "Junior Counsellor delegated by the Supreme Counsellor on Earth and President General of India Fiji Girmit Council," and it was by that authority that the certificates and medals were issued and the ritual was performed.[12]

In this ritual, like his others, Samalia strove desperately to create a narrative of mutual cooperation, interdependence, and goodwill between Fijians and Indians, invoking in the rhetoric of Fiji the fatherland and India the motherland the gendered relations of marriage.[13] In this narrative, the presence of Indians in Fiji is not a historical accident or a jarring difficulty. Instead, Samalia turns historical contingency into historical necessity: in his narrative, the presence of Indians in Fiji is blessed and desirable. It is the necessary condition for the return of God to earth and the founding of the new Jerusalem. The wreck of the *Syria* becomes proof of this interdependence.[14]

But Samalia's narrative, his vision, failed to unite, to persuade, to create a nation of Fiji. Like most Hindu Indo-Fijians, he argued that there is only one god, a rhetorical stance that some ethnic Fijians will accept, especially

in public ritual contexts. However, he believed that the one god had multiple
manifestations or avatars (thus Jesus and Krishna, let alone Navosavakadua
and Hitler). Here he lost most ethnic Fijians, who strongly believe that the
one god must be named Jesus Christ. In speaking to ethnic Fijians of Navosavakadua, Samalia lost his Indo-Fijian audience and got a polite but baffled
hearing from only some ethnic Fijians. In fact, the Indo-Fijian audience was
unconvinced by his insistence on tying together India and Fiji. Historically,
ethnic Fijians and Indo-Fijians have not frequently united, neither in political movements nor, more individually, in marriage. Thus the Fiji fatherland–
India motherland imagery did not engage the Indo-Fijians. They were looking to a wider world—specifically, planning to emigrate in many cases. The
joining of India and Fiji seemed the opposite of inevitable to them. Finally,
the most demure of his rituals, with the most public potential, the *Syria Monument* affair—with its theme that cooperation, interdependence, and mutual
service will lead to new prosperity—did not stand a chance against the forces
interested in ethnic Fijian political paramountcy. He did not offer anything
more concrete than a prospect of divine intervention to justify his alternative
to the stronger assertion of ethnic Fijian political paramountcy. While ethnic
Fijians readily accept arguments about impending benevolent divine intervention on their behalf, Samalia's vision of divinity contradicted the Christian version of the stranger-king narrative, the narrative of the relation of
aristocracy and people, by not finishing with a privileged outcome for the
"special" Fijian people. In his vision, Indo-Fijians still would own what they
own and the nation would be permanently plural and (in his marriage imagery) even more mixed.

At the meeting in Drauniivi, Samalia appears to have spoken freely about
his apprehensions concerning "racial" tension in Fiji. In 1984 he was one of
the few people openly speaking about impending violence, and certainly the
most fearless. In fact, he predicted the coups when he told me in 1984 that

> 1987 would be the most dangerous election. The military was advancing. Fiji-
> ans were fighting with themselves. Chiefs failed to control the people, they
> were criticizing Indians. Chiefs used to command the Kai Colo [literally "hill
> people," here used to mean commoners and Fijians from the west of Viti
> Levu], but now the educated Kai Colo spoke back to the chiefs. Fijians newly
> in power thought they knew what to do, but Indians and Europeans too had
> sacrificed and should be respected. That was why he founded the Girmit or-
> ganization so that Fijians would realize the truth about Indian sacrifices for
> Fiji. (From my field notes)

Samalia described contradictions in racial relations in Fiji that he sought to
resolve in his cosmological narrative. Only a visionary mystic such as he

could speak so clearly of these contradictions. He identified with both Indo-Fijians and ethnic Fijians and longed desperately to create a synthesis. He wanted ethnic Fijians to recognize and acknowledge the contributions of Indians to the making of Fiji.[15] But he did not seem to believe that they could or would do this, and thus instead saw a "cloud of blood in Suva" or "blood on the grass." Shrinking from this vision, ultimately reassured by belief in divinity in the world, he predicted that the coming crisis would give rise to the return of the syncretistic King of Kings, and dogs would speak and flowers would sing.

When the crisis Samalia foresaw came to pass, it was not his syncretistic King of Kings who came back to rule Fiji and the world. Instead, the ethnic Fijians who took power to prevent change in Fiji used chiefly Christianity as their main cosmological narrative. The colonel who seized power was a Methodist lay preacher and insisted on national observance of the Sunday Sabbath. In explaining his motives for the coups, he cited Saint Paul to prove that it was wrong that a commoner Fijian or an Indo-Fijian become prime minister: only chiefs should rule. And it was Methodist youth groups that burned temples and mosques. The new political order would dip as well into powerful ritual from Fijian nineteenth-century warfare, notably in an incident in which a *lovo* (earth oven for cooking cannibal victims) was dug and the Labour Party leader threatened with it. Most powerful of all was the endorsement of Fiji's first postcoups, anti–Indo-Fijian constitution by the Bosevakaturaga, the Fijian Great Council of Chiefs. In this replication of the rituals of cession and of independence, the authority of aristocracy to grant law and rights was reaffirmed, denying even the limited democracy in the alternative narrative of the three-legged stool. (The similar role played by the Great Council following the 2000 coup will be discussed in chapter 6.)

Thus, the national rituals of the 1970s awkwardly juxtaposed Fijian, British, and Indian ceremonial, creating no convincing narrative of mutual substance, history, or interdependence. Samalia's rituals, newspaper ads, and speeches created a powerful synthetic narrative, but it too failed to convince—or to create—Fiji citizens. Both were supplanted by the powerful Fijian-colonial Christian synthesis of aristocracy and people, bound in loyalty, propounded by the leader of the coups and the chiefs whom the coups reinstated.

THE RITUAL REQUIREMENTS OF NATIONS

In conclusion, I return to the ritual requirements of nations. I have tried to stress in this chapter the practical nature of rituals and the power of rituals in political order and change. Rituals are unavoidable and central in social life, including the making of those polities, those social groups, that seem to us so real, so given, so pragmatic, those entities called nations. In fact, I agree with those who argue that nations require narratives, and I am suggesting that they also require rituals that enshrine particular narratives as the real or true ones. To clarify these points, and to suggest what I see demonstrated by this review of failed national rituals in Fiji, I return to two basic problems about nations raised earlier: first, is there an essential form to "the nation," and second, what is the ground of "the nation," and where do rituals fit in?

Current anthropological debates seem to split between a camp seeking to find the general or universal features that all nations have in common and others skeptical of finding an essential, common content to all nations and nationalism (see Foster 1991). On this question I side generally with the second camp. I do not think that nations and nationalisms are always egalitarian and democratic; the current Republic of Fiji is a clear instance of a nationalism insistent upon hierarchy and aristocracy. I also don't agree that nations and nationalism require fixed boundaries, or "entitivity," fixed individualism of nation and of citizen as some have argued (see Handler and Segal 1993). Again, Fiji's current republic is a clear counterexample: the corporality of the nation depends upon hierarchical connections between chiefs and people(s); it depends upon the denial of autonomous individuality to its version of "the people."

We might look instead to studies of nations that emphasize cultural difference. Kapferer (1988), for example, locates differences between nations in different "ontologies," then organizes the ontologies in a Dumontian typology, principally hierarchical group versus egalitarian individualist. Whether or not such typology is intrinsically constraining, the idea of an underlying ontology makes real contest difficult to understand. A theory that is alive to difference is far more convincing if we can also understand the real contests and history in the making of nations. In Fiji it is precisely the problem which or what ontology will become the basis of national order. The potential limitation of a cultural approach is that it will reify or essentialize such outcomes. Further, even focus on struggle within a social-cultural universe might be misleading, involving the error Wolf (1982) identifies as the projection of bounded nation-society-cultureness onto parts of a world manifold.

Let us suppose instead that it is a world-level condition of possibility that makes nations the issue, that capitalist postcoloniality is the problem Fiji and other "new" nations struggle to deal with, that in a post-imperial "United Nations" world, bounded national order is forced upon all places that wish to be players on a world stage. Quite concretely, in Fiji's case, post–World War II United Nations resolutions and British Labour government platforms mandating decolonization made a partly reluctant population of Fiji into an independent nation.[16] To fill such a space, narratives are proposed that connect people to their rulers as one people, versus outside others, which create an "us versus them." National rituals are the place where these narratives of social contract are made real. These narratives get made, ritually, when individuals or groups propose versions of relationships, group order, and history, past, present, and future, which they claim are not simply their own view or in their own interest, but instead are given, cosmologically, by gods, by tradition, or by principles of some sort.

Is the political-economic order of the capitalist "world system" the grounding of all nation-states, then? Surely there is no question that the world system creates pressures and limits. But the question can be rephrased: do these pressures and limits have intrinsic priority over other structures and systems, "ontologies," and the like? The tendency in "invented tradition" and "imagined community" literature is to envision the representation of tradition and nation functionally, serving interests of implicitly or explicitly political economic agents. Sahlins (1976) offers the best case against universalizing the capitalist senses of utility, money, and self-interest, but he grounds the alternative in totalized and totalizing cultural systems. I am not saying that cultures, ontologies, or nations are or are not totalized or totalizing systems, but that they are sometimes. That kind of systematicity is made and remade practically, when self-reproducing agents, relationships, and subjectivities fit together coherently. The important point to draw from Wolf's (1982) study of the world system is that it is not totalizing, but rather a loose integration of highly various modes, relations, and forces of production. Sahlins (1988) clarifies this point, demonstrating that a plurality of cosmologies drive, expand, and sometimes limit world relations of commodity production and exchange. So, if the world system decrees a nation-state form to regimes of law and order, it hasn't actually determined much about the content of those nation-states.

In the wake of collapsed colonial politics in independent Fiji, the chiefs sought to sustain their privileges while the Indo-Fijians pressed for democracy. Nation-states mediate the interests of such groups with frameworks of law and administrative regulation. But what sort of regulation is routine? Should there be elections, and who should vote? Should land and/or labor be for sale, and under what conditions and restrictions? In Fiji, land reservation and even the overturning of elections have been justified by a narrative of Fijian autochthony and paramountcy. Myths may or may not ever have been social charters, but national narratives are charters for routine regulation. But what, in turn, routinizes such a national narrative? Surely, it is ritual. Here Durkheim has his moment, even though the world system also gets its due.

Since independence in 1970, nation-state rituals in Fiji tried to balance democracy and ethnic Fijian paramountcy with the uneasy amalgams of balanced ethnic Fijian and Indo-Fijian customary ceremony. These rituals did not routinize a coherent narrative of political ranks and rights in Fiji. The two messages in the rituals—that Fiji was a plural democracy and that its chiefs had customary prerogatives—failed to clarify how far any nonchiefly political authority could go. Thus, for instance, while the operations of the Native Land Trust Board regulating ethnic Fijian land rights were effectively routinized,[17] the elections were always a crisis. Elections, the constitutive political rituals of many nations, were in Fiji in 1977,[18] 1987, 1992, and 1999 contested in form as much as in substance. In the 1990s, even within the chiefs' new political party, established to contest the 1992 elections under the chiefs' new constitution, there were controversies about how districts should be bounded and how candidates should be selected. (Samalia founded an unsuccessful party of his own.[19]) Chapter 6 will discuss coup leader Rabuka's choice in 1997 to support a new constitution and the fate of the 1999 election held under it. Since independence, Fiji's chartering narrative has been contested, its official rituals have failed to settle the crucial questions, and, as a result, "the nation" is a contested idea, not an experienced reality.

Fiji is hardly the only place in the world where "the nation" is contested. I would suggest that the world is full of people and groups of people—such as Samalia, or Rabuka, or the colonial British, or the Fiji Labour Party—playing, with deadly seriousness, with elements and possibilities concerning order and cosmology, past and future, trying to make up nations and national narratives and routinize them through ritual. The narrative succeeding in Fiji today, unfortunately, is one justifying violence, division, and inequality.

SIX

Constituting Fiji

COMMUNITIES, THE NATION-
STATE, AND THE COUP OF 2000

On July 13, 2000, fifty-five days after
they took over Parliament and made hostages of the Prime Minister Mahendra Chaudhry and his ministers, coup leaders George Speight (also known
as Ilikini Naitini) and Ilisoni Ligairi sat behind a *tanoa* (kava bowl) together
with many of their followers. The eighteen men who were still their hostages,
including Chaudhry, sat before them. Speight and Ligairi had already negotiated the release of these remaining hostages, amnesty for themselves, and a
promise from Fiji's military that Fiji's constitution would be entirely redrafted to better secure ethnic Fijian paramountcy. And as Speight and Ligairi sat behind the *tanoa* full of *yaqona* (kava), the Great Council of Chiefs
was in session a few miles away, at an army barracks. Despite much countervailing pressure from local and global civic groups, foreign governments and
national and international trade unions, Fiji's Great Council of Chiefs was
prepared to elect Speight's nominees for president and vice president of Fiji.
But they sent a delegation of high chiefs led by Adi Samanunu Talakuli Cakobau (descendant of the Cakobau) and Ratu Inoke Takiveikata (the Turaga
na Qaranivalu, paramount of Naitasiri, Speight's province) to tell Speight
that they would not vote in the new president until he released his hostages.
Speight and his group were in fact under pressure as well because his
agreement with the military that guaranteed his success, the Muanikau Accord, specified that he must release the hostages on the day the Great Council met or else he would forfeit his amnesty. Yet Speight did not release the
hostages before conducting a final ritual, what ethnic Fijians call a *soro*, a
ritual of apology.

Isireli Vuibau, a Labour Party member of Parliament and fellow hostage,
acted as *matanivanua*, "herald" or "talking chief," for deposed Prime Minis-

143

ter Chaudhry. Vuibau accepted the apology. The first bowl of *yaqona* was passed to Chaudhry and Chaudhry drank it, a culminating moment in a *soro*. The Turaga na Qaranivalu, a Speight supporter, stayed "to make sure that the ceremony was completed," reported a radio station FM 96 reporter, Malakai Veisamasama. Veisamasama was allowed to be present at the ritual and described it as "moving." Then the hostages were released. Tears were flowing from both hostage takers and hostages, Veisamasama reported; Chaudhry hugged Speight and then he and the other seventeen were finally let out to the waiting Red Cross vans. "Civilian" supporters of Speight formed a line to the truck and waved good-bye to their hostages. Then the Great Council voted in Speight and Ligairi's candidates for highest offices and announced their support for a massive agenda of new laws establishing special rights and privileges, loan programs, set asides and abatements from taxation for ethnic Fijians.

In Fiji in July 2000, the "Interim Military Government" (a government allegedly established to stop this coup) made clear the hierarchy it envisioned between itself and the entirety of what it described persistently as "civilian" government, in the final clause of its decree (Immunity Decree, decree no. 18 of 2000) granting the Speight group its amnesty: "This Decree shall not be amended or repealed by Parliament or any other Decree." This elevation of the military voice to highest authority has an interesting parallel in the Speight group's elevation of the Fijian ritual of forgiveness. In July 2000 the Speight group tried to use Fijian *soro* rituals to absolve themselves of responsibility for overturning a democratically elected government and abrogating Fiji's constitution. And after fifty-five days of captivity, Fiji's first Indo-Fijian prime minister had a traditional Fijian ritual of forgiveness placed between him and his freedom. Ritually, nothing could be clearer about the nature of the nation envisioned. An ethnic Fijian tradition can suffice to excuse crimes—in Fijian villages, *soros* are often used to settle grievances over assaults, crimes against property, even rapes. The *soro* to Chaudhry not only ratified an amnesty granted by martial law decree, but also recognized him and his rights only within the framework of ethnic Fijian definitions of redress.

In this 2000 coup, Fiji again tests the limits of the nation-state as a political form. Fiji's chiefs and peoples, to borrow Prince Charles's phrase, did not invent the nation-state, but with the rest of the world have had their political horizons defined by it in the post–World War II, United Nations era. In this era of globalization and democratization, the characteristics of a proper nation-state are thought by many to be well established. When Bill Clinton went to Russia in 1998 to thwart a movement there to default on government debts, he spoke publicly and laid out a clear vision:

Russians will define Russia's future, but there are clear lessons, I would argue, from international experience. Here's what I think they are. . . .

To create jobs, growth and higher income, a nation must convince its own citizens and foreigners that they can safely invest. . . .

These are the imperatives of the global marketplace, and you can see them repeated over and over and over again. You can also see the cost of ignoring them in nation after nation after nation.

Increasingly, no nation, rich or poor, democratic or authoritarian, can escape the fundamental economic imperatives of the global market. . . . You will do very well if you just get your fair share of investment. To get your fair share of investment, you have to play by the rules that everyone else has to play by. (Quoted in *New York Times*, 9/2/98, A8)

Russians would define Russia's future, but investors were very clear about what they had better define if they wanted to prosper:

Again, experience teaches what works: Fair taxes and fair enforcement; easier transferability of land; strong intellectual property rights to encourage innovation; independent courts enforcing the law consistently and upholding contract rights; strong banks that safeguard savings; securities markets that protect investors; social spending that promotes hope and opportunity and a safety net for those who, in any given time in an open-market economy, will be dislocated, and vigilance against hidden ties between government and business interests that are inappropriate. (A8)

The gap between Clinton's vision of the world's rules for nation-states, on the one hand, and the power of the Fiji military, the premises of Fiji's Great Council of Chiefs, and the wishes of Fiji's Taukei, on the other hand, is the problematic to be investigated in this final chapter. The 1990s and the year 2000 are different from the 1940s or even independence in 1970 because both Fiji and the world are past the beginning of the era of nation-states and confront a more complex history than they used to. And in that history, considered dialogically, it is worth our attention how Fiji resists (not necessarily admirably) the Clintonian exigencies (not necessarily admirable) of nation as state, state as nation. We learn much about Fiji considering this history, and we also learn something about the nation-state in actuality. How has Fiji been constituted, and reconstituted, both before it was a nation-state and as a nation-state both before and after its coups?

L et us recall how the history of sovereignty in Fiji segments. Multiethnic Fiji, a British colony beginning in 1874, became an independent member of the British Commonwealth in 1970, until a military coup in May 1987 overturned the British-written constitution, or more precisely, until a second coup in September 1987 declared the existence of a Republic of Fiji. After a very long sequence of debates over new constitutions, a new constitution was promulgated in 1990 by the postcoups Interim Government and another was adopted in 1997. In 2000 this constitution has been suspended, martial law declared, and a new government imposed in the wake of another coup.

This chapter reviews the history of dialogues that constitute Fiji from four points of view: as a divergence from a normative model of "imagined community," as a history of struggle to protect indigenous rights and interests in opposition both to colonizers and labor diaspora peoples, as a history of struggle to establish civil rights for colonized people and civil rights for different ostensible "races" in a colonial and postcolonial society, and, most importantly, as a history of actually existing social contracts, focusing on constitutional struggles and their narratives.

FOUR POINTS OF VIEW

I. "This Historic Failure of the Nation to Come to Its Own"

The phrase is Ranajit Guha's; he calls it "the central problematic of the historiography of colonial India" (1982:7). The issue, as urgent for Fiji as for India, is the nonemergence of a national "imagined community" commensurate to the postcolonial nation-state. In Fiji there is little or no superordinate sense of citizenship, let alone a cultural homogenization of the population of the "new nation." More than one constitution hailed as a model for plural or multicultural societies has been abrogated violently.

In post-1970, independent Fiji we have something not readily addressed by Anderson's "imagined communities" model, not envisioned by Woodrow Wilson or Harry Truman: a nation-state with population evenly split between two ethnic groups, with support for the two major political parties increasingly correlate with ethnic boundaries in each successive election. In 1987 the new Labour Party succeeded in recruiting enough voters among the ethnic Fijians to win the elections, in coalition with the National Federation Party, the party that had long represented the Indo-Fijians. Out of fear of violence, the Labour Coalition named ethnic Fijians to the post of prime minister and many other cabinet positions. A month later it was victim of a coup d'état anyway, explicitly justified to protect the ethnic Fijian interests, led by an army that, since its inception in colonial days, has been made up almost entirely of ethnic Fijians. In the years following, government was dominated by a new political party, the SVT, founded since these coups, explicitly declaring itself the party of ethnic Fijian interests. The colonel who led the coups became the leader of the SVT and became prime minister for almost a decade.

A sad story, but a surprising one? Let us recall Brackette Williams's general model of plantation colonies (1989, 1990). She argues that national communities or identities have generally failed to cohere in Guyana, Trinidad, Mauritius, and elsewhere because the British not only held themselves aloof as the highest-ranking, most civilized "race" or ethnic group, but also staged elaborate contests for who, among scrupulously separated "races" or ethnic groups in their colonies, would rank second, according to civic virtues and contributions to the empire. The end of empire, then, simply uncapped these contests, with the new state at stake but victory chimerical, since the contest itself was, by then, ramified throughout all public institutions and state apparatuses. In such contexts, "print capitalism," democratic rules, and "party" politics lead not to national consensus but ethnic schismogenesis. The model fits Fiji's history well. But a puzzle still remains. In Fiji, one group almost always wins, and it is the more illiberal group, the one calling for instituted ethnic privileges rather than universal standards, for uneven "communal" reserves in land ownership, education, employment, and electoral representation. Why then, at a most illiberal moment, the first coup against the 1987 elected Labour Coalition government, were so many liberals and radicals elsewhere around the world applauding so vigorously? Why, for example, did the *Christian Science Monitor* print a hagiographic interview with the "gentleman" coup leader (10/1/87:12)? How, following the year 2000 coup attempt against the 1999 elected Labour government, Fiji's third coup in fourteen years, could the *New York Times* still connect Fiji and "Eden," tell a tale of paradise threatened, and in its first detailed account, emphasize the charm of the insurgency, the pig roasts and hymn singing on the lawn of the captured Parliament buildings?

II. Indigenous Rights, or, The Pacific Romance

In Fiji "race" has a far longer and deeper history than "nation" in routines of social usage and clarity in reference. The half of Fiji's current population called "ethnic Fijians," "indigenous Fijians," and often just plain "Fijians" are the descendants of the people already resident in the islands when various kinds of colonizing "Europeans" (another routinized race name in Fiji) came in the nineteenth century. Until recent decades they were also commonly known, in law as well as in general usage, as "the natives," as in the still-existing Native Land Trust Board or the Native Administration, renamed the Fijian Administration in the twentieth century. The "Europeans" have always been a very small minority in Fiji. The "Indo-Fijians," also known as "Indian Fijians," "Fiji Indians," or just "the Indians," are Fiji's other race, in multiple senses of "other," even in the days of migration from South Asia, when the British called them "coolies."

One would never guess, judging from the library shelves, that the Indo-

Fijians outnumbered the ethnic Fijians for much of this century.[1] The vast majority of literature on Fiji has focused on the Fiji of and for (ethnic) Fijians. And while swaying palm trees are the Edenic yet sensual icon of this "Pacific Romance," its cardinal rule, from trashy novels through scholarship of the driest rectitude, has long been deep sympathy with the indigenes as protagonists: vulnerable, threatened, innocent, and struggling. The Pacific Romance was and still is a potent force in regional politics, constituting not merely the foundations of global understanding of the Pacific social scene, but granting the Pacific a special spot in the global imaginary: a paradise preserve for the world-weary. The imagery is remarkably enduring even as it changes, now increasingly framed in an ecological rather than a social-evolutionary nostalgia. As the coup leaders of 1987 were acutely aware, this insatiable global appetite for stories of paradise could be mobilized to support even a military coup, if only the story was narrated correctly: friendly, peace-loving, naive locals struggling to defend their way of life against rapacious, tricky interlopers (Kelly 1988a).

And without doubt, Fiji's history is one of our planet's most inspirational, if one is actively seeking a story of a "primitive," atechnological culture defending its Herderian soul against a hurricane modernity. Fijian society, like many other Pacific societies, was strongly hierarchical in the early and middle nineteenth century. But unlike many, perhaps most other Pacific sites (Hawaii and New Zealand being opposite examples), the chiefs of Fiji did not sell off or otherwise give up most of their land to encroaching outsider Europeans. Or as local rhetoric would summarize it, they did not betray the land. Fijian chiefs have continued to this day to be influential political agents in the islands, increasingly entwined in colonial and postcolonial bureaucracy. Reconstituting themselves as a local aristocracy within the empire, they became simultaneously the bulwark defenders of indigenous Fijian custom and most loyal servants of empire, whether it was rallying military service, from World War II to UN peacekeeping in the Sinai, or simply rallying to the flag more generally, as when Fiji was the only "black" nation not to observe a boycott of the Commonwealth Games in an apartheid protest. As Henry Rutz (1995) has summarized very cogently, the most significant local political conflicts among and about ethnic Fijian interests since Fiji's independence in 1970 have concerned not the general propriety of hierarchy and privileges of chiefship within the Fijian community, nor the propriety of ethnic Fijian paramountcy in Fiji's civil order, but rather three different contending visions of the foundations of Fijian culture and the character of the threats to it: whether, in a royalist vision, the Fijian chiefs are constituted by their aristocratic standing, as revealed by their relations with the British Crown, and should be supported as such in their people's truest interests, or whether, in fact, some of them have betrayed the land through corruption, by

Westernization or otherwise, and are now a threat or fetter on ethnic Fijian interests, or third, a fundamentalist Christian vision, that they rule as special servants of Jehovah and should be led to express His will more effectively (cf. Toren 1988; Kaplan 1990a). As Rutz shows, the 1987 coup leadership deployed all three of these narratives at various moments in local contestation over the meanings of the 1987 coups, while simplifying matters for more romantic outside audiences. And at the same time, in 1987 a Taukei movement first arose, a romance within a romance, a self-proclaiming insurgency via rallies, marches, and mock rituals, alleging to speak directly for the *taukei*, the people of the land or owners of the land, the peoples who would otherwise install their chiefs and then follow their lead. We will see these three narratives, and self-proclaiming spokespeople for the *taukei*, again when we review the coup of 2000.

III. Civil Rights

"We Indians in Fiji ask for a fair field and no favour," argued so-called "radical" politician Vishnu Deo in a famous 1929 speech that ended, at least in its broadside version, with his call for **EQUAL CITIZENSHIP THROUGH-OUT THE BRITISH EMPIRE AND FREEDOM IN INDIA** (capitalization and emphasis in original, copy in Colonial Secretary's Office [CSO] 6141/29). "We do not wish to impose our civilization. We do not wish to deprive the Native of his right and liberties which unfortunately he is not allowed to enjoy. We want to see British justice meted out to all her citizens." The issues, as far as Vishnu Deo and other leaders of the Fiji Indian National Congress were concerned, were neither local nor concerned with Fiji as a "nation" or "state." The main issues were citizenship in an empire, nationalism in India, and truly global civil proprieties: "We ask for that equality and brotherhood and loving co-operation which it is meet that the sons of men should extend to each other all over the globe wherever they are thrown together," Deo orated.

The Indians were indeed thrown to Fiji, or more precisely imported as "labour units" (as the *Fiji Times and Herald* reported, with actual numerical allocations, but no names, each time a coolie ship came in: "Lever's Pacific Plantations, Ltd., Rabi, 10, C. G. Craft, Tuvanita, 12" and so on. [7/18/12]). They were there, from the late 1870s on, precisely to make viable the plantations that would enable the colony to pay for itself, without forcing the indigenous Fijians into the market. In the words of Fiji's influential second governor Thurston in 1883, the Indians were to be "a working population and nothing more" (CSO 1380/93). The various permutations taken by their desires for more became known to successive generations of colonial Europeans and Fijians as "the Indian problem." But it was not merely a local problem. All over the British Empire, and in other European empires as well, political controversies emerged over the civil rights of migrants of various origins, classes, and races, and more complexly, the rights of their (sometimes "mixed-race") descendants. One test case was Kenya, where white planters sought to deny ex-indentured Indians electoral rights. Here Winston Churchill, then Secretary of State for the Colonies, argued for "equal rights for civilized men." By Churchill's plan, Indians and others—but not Europeans (in all cases, men only)—would have to pass tests of economic means and English literacy, in practice maintaining "European" numerical dominance of the polls and, simultaneously, channeling the colonized elite into Westernization and loyal participation in empire (Tinker 1976:56–57). But as discussed in chapter 4, the issue was resolved in Kenya in favor of permanent racial or "communal" electoral rolls. For Fiji, this invigorated Vishnu Deo's enemies and doomed the efforts of the Fiji Indian National Congress to establish a unified "common roll" electoral system.

Race gained absolute primacy in the delimitation of democratic spaces in Fiji and in the imagination of "community," as in "communal roll." That primacy was maintained throughout the constitutional conferences leading to Fiji's independence in 1970. Indo-Fijian politicians, themselves the prime movers in local calls for independence, were repeatedly faced with dilemmas in constitution building. The British, almost as anxious for disentanglement as the Indo-Fijians were for independence, were happy to arrange independence at the price of instituting privileges for their more reluctant allies, the indigenous Fijians and especially their chiefs. In the end, at Fiji's independence in 1970 the bicameral Parliament was constituted largely on "communal" lines.

Thus citizens registered themselves "racially" as "Fijian," "Indian," or "General Elector" (all others, including Europeans, people of Chinese and Japanese descent and other Pacific Islanders, especially Rotumans). In the 52-member House of Representatives there were 22 Fijians, 22 Indians, and 10 General Electors. Of the Fijian and Indian members, 12 were elected by communal rolls (e.g., Indians in 12 districts voting for 12 Indians, Fijians for 12 Fijians), and 10 were elected from "national" (mixed) rolls where everyone in a particular district elected a Fijian and an Indian. General Electors elected 3 representatives from General Elector rolls, and 7 were elected by mixed rolls. The principle of communal roll sustained the primacy of race, and the Indo-Fijians, then 51 percent of the population, were granted only 40 percent of the legislative seats, not a small change in a democracy. And more significant was the brake on democratic expression constituted in the other deliberative body, the Senate. The 22 senators were all appointed, 7 by the governing party and 6 by the opposition, but, also, 8 more by nomination from the Great Council of Chiefs, and 1 from the Council of Rotuma. Thus, regardless of what party coalition could gain control of the House by electoral means, their gain in the Senate would be a grand total of one seat. As long as the chiefs remained united in support of a party that at least could claim status as opposition, they had control of at least one chamber of the legislature. But as things unfolded, these provisions were not seen as enough. This already Fijian-weighted constitution was the one overturned by the 1987 coups, when Fiji's ethnic Fijian-dominated army took Fiji out of the Commonwealth, on behalf of the interest group the British had always deemed their most loyal local allies.

One can cast almost every political event in Fiji's twentieth-century history within the story of a struggle to create egalitarian citizenship and equal civil rights. But do civil rights really constitute the civil space? "Fair field and no favour" is very persuasive, but freedom for India espoused an additional will—a will to bound and constitute a field. And in Fiji, the Pacific Romance narrative of indigenous rights has always posed a powerful challenge to democratic discourse. How can we capture an actual history of these social and political fields, in which various claims to right are made and contested, in which contrastive ethnicities are distilled? What, in particular, is the role of discourses of race in the actual constitution of colonial social fields? And what changes with decolonization?

We are interested in finding a means to greater clarity here. Thus we do not want to presume any of the following: either that nations or nation-states are normal or normative, or that nationalism is normal or pathological; that indigenous peoples are virtuous victims, or backward peoples in need of development, or obstacles to true civility; that civil rights and common roll democracy are the end of history, the true universal measure of political virtue for our times, or the most pernicious expression of Kantian or (as many Fijians would have it) colonial hegemony. We would rather leave all that up to you. Okay, we are skeptical of the Pacific Romance and sympathetic to discourse on civil rights. But most of all, we seek a way to investigate the real dynamics of Fiji's constitution as a nation-state that does not require us to follow only one of these positions. Therefore we will inquire into this constitutive process from a fourth perspective.

IV. A History of Contracts and Contract Narratives

Apart from law professors, economists, and liberal political philosophers, most social scientists would probably associate the idea of contracts with the over-narrow social theories of law professors, economists, and liberal political philosophers. The idea seems suspended uselessly between the historical fantasies of the social contract philosophers and classical political economists, on the one hand, and the quotidian grind of actual jurisprudence, on the other, capable of dragging the worst of both realms into any analysis. Social theory seems to have abandoned, and even largely forgotten, the ambition that the likes of Marcel Mauss had for conceptions of contract in the unification of social and political theory, forgotten in particular that Mauss saw both gift and commodity transactions as species of contract. This essay is an experiment in the renewal of that ambition, seeking a method out of the impasses of identity theory toward something more dialogical, equally irreductive, and more privileging of instituted, routinized practices: the quest for a history of actually constitutive arrangements, and of their routinization, even institutionalization in practice and memory, that is, a history of contracts and their narratives, a quest for conditions of possibility for any assertion of rights, community, or nation.

In what follows, then, we will examine actual deals made in specific places and times, with major implications for the parties involved and others, and also narratives of deals, purposefully told and widely known stories about crucial deals past, especially those invoked in political struggle. Tracking routinizations as well as negotiations, we hope to suggest an account of actually existing social contracts and their consequences, from which we expect more insight into Fiji and its real political dilemmas, and the actual history of global-local linkage, than could follow from any general theory of identity, resistance, locality, or ethnicity. In particular, we will reconsider the nationstate not merely as the context within which social contracts are negotiated, but as an object negotiated. We will reconsider global and local relations similarly, not only as a context for but also an object of dialogical process. The global consolidation of the nation-state form will be considered not merely in terms of global models available for pirating, or merely global forces impinging, but also in terms of active efforts to ally local and global forces, agencies, and interests toward the constitution of very different social contracts for Fiji, efforts in effect to make Fiji a more normative nation-state, and very successful efforts to sustain its differences.

A final preliminary note about contracts: to understand negotiations over Fiji as a nation-state, we will have to understand the deals already in place when decolonization began. Especially when we inquire into colonial deals and narratives about them, the reality of varying degrees of erudition among "Europeans" and others about contracts in law, and about political philosophies of social contract, cannot simply be set aside. It is worth remembering how radical, and contested, were Rousseau's assertions of a citizen's point of view, and his connection of justice and real freedom to actual social contracts. It is worth remembering Henry Maine's disparagement of Rousseau in *Ancient Law*. Maine was not only a scholar but a major legislator for the Raj, and when he insisted on a sequence of social orders of customary law leaving contract for the last, most modern, Western, free, and civil stage, he licensed and helped maintain an empire that conceived itself to be reaching beyond the realm of contract. It is worth remembering the declarations of Maine's blunter, more ambitious predecessor in projects of Raj law-giving, the Whig Thomas Babington Macaulay, who once insisted that "the right to exercise paternal authority" followed from the fact that it was by force, "not by free stipulation with the governed, that England rules India; nor is England bound by any contract whatsoever," and that seeking the free stipulation of the governed "would inevitably destroy our empire" (1860a:389–90).[2] Remembering such insistence on asymmetries will help us, in fact, to understand how colonials understood the arrangements they regarded as both constitutive and binding, and vigorously implemented and enforced.

RACE AND THE CONTRACTS THAT CONSTITUTED INDENTURE

"It is now recognized that the Indian is the best worker obtainable for the planters," reported the *Cyclopedia of Fiji* of 1907 (25). This encyclopedia was published in Sydney by "The Cyclopedia Company of Fiji." It was supported by paid advertising and by the "patronage" of the Governor and government of Fiji and was "assisted in the preparation" by Fiji's newspapers and "various gentlemen," including officers of church, government, and the Colonial Sugar Refining Company. For this encyclopedia to give us a first glimpse of both crucial deals and memories of them, its reason for being should be made clear. In addition to the hundred-plus pages of hagiographic who's who it provides concerning Fiji's leading "European" residents, the bulk of the work was a 190-page overview of the islands and their prospects, with the theme of opportunities for new settlers predominant.

> That Fiji, with its equable and healthy climate, its cheap labour, and its numerous areas of the highest class of agricultural lands, offers exceptional inducements to settlers possessing a sufficiency of capital for a start, and not entirely ignorant of the conditions of tropical culture, becomes patent to anyone with the slightest knowledge of this promising colony, practically yet to be exploited. (181)

Pacific Romance? The first sentence of the "Publishers' note," on the back of the title page, could not be more direct: "The history of the settlement and colonization of Fiji is one of the romances of the nineteenth century." And in keeping with this theme, the story of the Colonial Sugar Refining Company, in particular, was one of struggling heroes:

> It must not for an instant be imagined that the Colonial Sugar Refining Co. has had an easy field to furrow. In its early days it was confronted with difficulties which would have daunted a combination of men who did not possess

such absolute faith in the resources of the place and who were not endowed
with such indomitable courage and energy. Needless to say, the labour question soon arose to face the efforts of the managers of the company. (169)

The labor question, for which "the Indian" has become the answer, is separated in the *Cyclopedia* scrupulously from the question of employment, which
is something white people might take up. However hard the early days were,
in 1907 "there is little branded 'C.S.R.' that does not denote stability" (172).
"In its relations with its employees the Company is most liberal" (172), protecting their future welfare, for example, with a Benefit Society and a Provi-
dent Fund. Also avidly scientific, "the Company is indeed one of the most
progressive institutions of its kind in the world" (172). Romance, science,
progress, stability, benefits, and palm trees, too. What a deal.

The Company's indentured laborers came under contracts too, but a
different sort. Recruiters, operating mainly in small cities and towns across
South Asia, persuaded young men and women, usually already far from their
homes and usually already looking for work for wages, to enter a linked system of depots and closed rail cars that quickly delivered them before a magistrate for swearing to contract, and then shipped them off, via Calcutta or
Madras, to agricultural work somewhere else in the British Empire. By contract, they were required to work six days a week for five years, on threat of
penal sanctions including but not limited to extension of the five-year term.
For Fiji, forty women were required by quota to accompany each one hundred men, and a free return passage to India was offered after completion of
the five years of indenture and an additional five years' "industrious residence" in the colony.

There was no *Cyclopedia* for enticing destitute rural Indians to agree to
indenture. We get a picture of the negotiation between workers and employers in Totaram Sanadhya's *My Twenty-one Years in the Fiji Islands*, a polemic
against indenture ghostwritten by Gandhian journalist Benarsidas Chaturvedi and published in India in 1914:

> When I . . . never found work, I used to think . . . that I should do any kind
> of work. . . . One day when I was in a market near Kotwali, engaged in this
> worrying about finances, a man I didn't know came up to me and asked, "Do
> you want employment?" I said "Yes." Then he said, "Good, I can get you a
> very good job." . . . This recruiter fooled me and brought me to his house.
> Once there I saw about 100 men sitting in one line and about 60 women in
> another. Some people were cooking with damp wood and getting tired blowing
> and blowing on the stove-fire. The recruiter sat me at one side. Seeing these
> women, I thought, these men are going off to work, but where are these women
> going? At that time, the recruiter completely forbade making conversation

with these women. No one could go outside from there and no one from out-side could come in. The recruiter said to me, "You should cook some rice here, I'll give you some rice right away." I said, "I don't know how to cook rice. I'll eat with these Brahmins who are cooking." . . .

After three days the recruiter began to prepare us all to be brought before the magistrate. Altogether there were 165 men and women. We were closed into cars, and arrived at the court-house in a half-hour. The recruiter had said to us before, that when the magistrate asked us any question we should say "yes." If we didn't do this then we would be charged and thrown into jail. Everyone was brought one by one before the magistrate. He asked each one, "Tell me. Have you agreed to go to Fiji?" The magistrate did not tell each person where Fiji was, what work they would do there, or what punishment they would be given on not doing the work. This magistrate registered 165 people in some twenty minutes. From this the reader can estimate how the magistrate wanted to free himself from the work. Why else would he do it so quickly?

Going from here we were all loaded onto rail cars. We could not talk to the people sitting in the cars or to people outside. If someone wanted to talk to himself it was allowed. Yes, I forgot to say that this was a special train and we went straight to Havra, stopping nowhere in between. From Havra station we were all put into closed cars and taken to the depot. Here the immigration officer stood us all in a line and said, "You are going to Fiji. You will get 12 annas a day there, and you will have to do field work for five years." . . .

When the officer was explaining things to us, a doubt was born in my heart. . . . I said, "I don't want to go to Fiji. I have never done field labor. Look at my hands. They can never do field work. I won't go to Fiji." Hearing this the officer gave me over to two Bengali babus, and said to them, "Explain things to this one and fix it up." To them also I made the denial, and said, "My brother is here in Calcutta in some building. Let me meet with him. Then we'll see what happens." But who listens? The door keeper stayed with me all the time. When I would not agree to their explanations, I was locked into a room. For one day and one night I was in that room, hungry and thirsty. Helpless in the end, I was forced to say that I agreed to go to Fiji. There were none of my own people there who I could tell about this incident of suffering.

When I was brought from the cell I saw that Chamar, Koli, Brahmin and so forth [castes mixed low to high] were all seated in one place and forced to have their meals together. Just about everyone was forced to have their meal on re-used plates [deliberately polluting], and was forced to drink water. When anyone said anything, then what but he was beaten specially. Seeing this situation I said, "I will not eat with these people even if I die of hunger." The officer said, "Die. No one fears that. We'll throw you in the river." In the end I was ordered to eat with the cook. (Sanadhya 1991 [1914]:33–35)

A major role in the campaigns in India that led to the abolition of indenture was played by polemical accounts such as this one. Sanadhya's story in particular was translated into many South Asian languages and circulated widely, making Fiji infamous among the indenture destinations. Where the Gandhian campaign against indenture emphasized trickery, deliberate pollution, and exploitation of women, some historians have since argued that the image of passive, deluded, and coerced recruits was overdrawn.[3] No doubt Sanadhya and Chaturvedi were tugging hard at their audiences' heartstrings (and no doubt the white settlers and company overseers had it harder than the *Cyclopedia* would imply). But note that Sanadhya's story was not simply of deception and delusion, but of the mechanisms of a system designed to homogenize a dependent social standing and to limit his options once he entered the first depot. In its control of communication ("there were none of my own people there") and food pollution (Sanadhya, a Brahman, no doubt felt the issue extremely), the system changed the social field of its workers from the minute they crossed the first threshold. Clothes were taken away and replaced with standard issue. The managers of the system in India were clearly sensitive to caste and other differences of background, with an eye to preventing its disruption of their system. In some sense, they must have been aware of the degree to which coolies were made, rather than born, and made by pollution and isolation. Ships surgeons, paid according to the number of coolies they delivered alive, were specifically warned to watch out for suicide attempts (Gillion 1962:62). But by the time the indentured laborers met the young Australians recruited by the company to be overseers, they were largely beyond managers with sophistication about caste and status differences in India, and what was clearest about the education of a coolie was the need to teach them about industrial production of sugar. Once the coolies reached Fiji, their standardization was by law complete. They worked by task, with task sizes and wages variant only according to gender, women's three-quarters of men's. While by law the task was required to be what was reasonable for the average able worker, in practice it was whatever the overseer said it was. The overseer was paid, at rates set by CSR, according to the yield of his fields. Or, as the *Cyclopedia* put it, "So as to indemnify the overseers as far as possible against loss [not to mention limiting their gains] the company guarantees them a fixed price for their cane for periods of five years, the price being regulated by the sweetness of the cane" (172). The overseers, thus, could seek to maximize the volume and sweetness of the cane they produced. The coolies were not expected to maximize anything, but only to work.

The indenture contracts were known among the immigrants to Fiji as the *girmit*, a redaction in Fiji Hindi of the English word "agreement." These workers called "coolies" called themselves *girmitiyas*, the people of the agreement. It was very clear to them that their degradation was determined by a contract. But how clear was that to Fiji's "Europeans"? We return to the *Cyclopedia:*

> The sugar industry is at the present time so allied with the question of coloured labour that a few remarks on that subject will be made in passing. It would be impossible to impose similar restrictions on the islands of Fiji [banning "coloured labour"] as have been made in the case of the growers in Queensland. Coloured labour is here quite necessary, and the workers are permitted to rise to whatever positions they are intellectually capable of filling. In Fiji alone the company has nearly 7,000 indentured East Indians, while there are only desirable places for from 200 to 300 Europeans, who are engaged in the various responsible positions. (169–70)

Crucial to this configuration was not merely the brute economics of the racial segmentation of wage levels in this colonial world: eight shillings a day for white field workers in Queensland versus one shilling a day in Fiji.[4] It was also the surmise of essential content to the racial differences, including but not limited to intellectual capacities:

> The coolie has proved most satisfactory as a field hand. They are quiet, steady, reasonably quick to learn, and always willing. They are somewhat quick at a fight among themselves, but as these occur usually at night the routine of work is little interfered with. (170)

The work pattern displayed a racial essence. And part of that essence projected by the colonial design was that while "Europeans" could respond well to income incentives like the overseers' pay contingent on productivity, the coolies required control and the threat of physical and penal discipline. Therefore the wage rates for the Indians were flat, incentives for extra work absent, and the top position generally available to them was that of *sardar,* work boss, assistant to the roving overseer, supervising the work site. It was a promotion from disciplined to discipliner, still with a fixed wage.[5]

In the tropics, the *Cyclopedia* assured, "coloured labour" was necessary. But the progressive company did not simply accept givens. No, indeed, its early adventures led to its successes precisely because of its scientific spirit:

> In experimenting with coloured races the company had some peculiar experiences. The natives were found to be impossible, kanakas developed an alarming death rate, and a shipment of 300 Japanese, which promised well enough, was settled by an outbreak of *beri beri*, an Eastern scourge. (170)

Thus the recognition of the Indians as the best obtainable workers was the result of experience, even experiment. And thus it was Indians who were "imported in batches from time to time by the sugar planters unable to procure local labourers" (25). By the 1910s inquiries into alternative labor sources, especially Chinese, were still made on occasion, especially as protest against the indenture system grew in India, but after the failed episode with Japanese, no other experiments were actually conducted.[6]

The narrative of this *Cyclopedia* correlates interestingly with that in one of its predecessors, the 1879 *Fiji Planting and Commercial Directory*. There, in the section called "labour," it was written that

> There are about 120,000 natives in the group, and of these at least 20,000 would be available for agricultural work; but an experiment that the Government is trying, prevents more than a very few of these being employed. It is believed that, this experiment having proved a failure, the labour of the Fijians will shortly be available for agricultural purposes. (18)

If that was the fondest, doomed hope of the planters in 1879, they also had their second strategy ready: "There is an inexhaustible supply to fall back upon from India" (19). There is more to note about the indenture contract and its consequences than the economic pragmatics and the racial essentialism that were its first two premises. We need to examine actual dealing that gave it its form, deals that set the contours for future pragmatic calculations: the deal that made Fiji a colony, and deals negotiated between the colonial government of Fiji, CSR, and the colonial government of India. First we will examine this other so-called "experiment," the one protecting Fijian labor, and the negotiated arrangements at its core.

THE DEED OF CESSION

In its hopes to generate white settlers, the *Cyclopedia* was as skeptical as was the 1879 planting directory about the government protections of Fijian land and labor. And it was as wrong in its predictions of their abolition. Everard im Thurn, the Governor who sponsored the 1907 *Cyclopedia*, became enmeshed in 1907 in a public debate with his predecessors about the advisability of maintaining the long series of ordinances, with titles such as "Better Regulation of Contracts and Dealings with the Natives of the Colony," that protected Fijians from economic exploitation. The government forbade not only indigenous alienation of land, but also almost every form of contract with individual indigenous Fijians. Labor contracts not only had to provide generous and specified benefits, but had to be registered and approved by a growing bureaucracy of European and chiefly Fijian authorities. No contract of any kind with an indigenous Fijian was enforceable if it involved goods or money over £5 in value, unless it was specifically approved and registered by a magistrate, who was responsible to judge its clearness, propriety, conformity with the growing code of Native Regulations, and even whether it was "contrary to equity or sound public policy" (Fiji Ordinance No. IV, 1881).

In the 1900s Governor im Thurn began reforms intended to undo most of this. But some of his new ordinances ran into serious trouble in London.[7] Ex-governor Des Voeux wrote to the Colonial Office:

> All the Fijians, the chiefs included, are in some respects much like children, and several generations will have to pass before they will be fit to do without protection in their important transactions.

Im Thurn replied:

> I am most anxious for the welfare of these interesting natives, and that if I ever do anything which may seem like relaxing the former protection, it is only in order to leave greater freedom to them now that they are adolescent—or would be but for the over-protection of recent years—and entitled to claim their position, in the near future, as full British subjects.

Im Thurn lost this debate. The august first governor of Fiji, Lord Stanmore (Sir Arthur Gordon) turned the House of Lords against the reforms in the interests, as he saw them, of the Fijians. Many revisionist historians critical of Fijian chiefly power have correctly located the defeat of im Thurn's reform plans as a key moment in the cementing of chiefly privilege (see especially France 1969; B. Lal 1992). We can go far in casting im Thurn as a failed champion for what have come to be known as common or commoner Fijians. But not too far. We would be wise, also, to remember the goal openly promoted in the *Cyclopedia* he sponsored:

> That the fertile lands of Fiji . . . should present so low an increase in the European population leads one to suspect the existence of obstacles arising from artificial conditions in her path to prosperity. . . . Eschewing the policy of their no doubt well-meaning, but ill-advised, predecessors the present Administration has removed some of the obstacles in the way of intending settlers; the native lands have been opened up; facilities are offered for leasing and purchasing them; and with judicious advertising of these and other inducements to the outside world there is little fear that in a very short time the white population will increase by leaps and bounds, and a new era of prosperity be ushered in on a substantial basis. (25)

The point here is not only the attitude, as we quoted from the *Cyclopedia* earlier, that Fiji was "this promising colony, practically yet to be exploited."

It is also the reliance on a motif of evolution. From the debate over whether Fijians were more like children or adolescents, to this version of a nature precut by the "path to prosperity," the social imaginary in Fiji at the turn of the century was increasingly naturalized in its evolutionisms.

In 1874 Sir Hercules Robinson exceeded his instructions from London. He not only inquired into the advisability of accepting the latest of a long series of Fijian chiefly offers of cession of Fiji to the British Empire, but he signed a Deed of Cession along with the group of Fijian chiefs assembled for the purpose. He and Fiji's first governor, aristocrat Sir Arthur Gordon (once private secretary to a prime minister of England, his father; student of evolutionary theories, especially of Henry Maine; admirer of the colonial theory of J. W. B. Money; deliberately chosen by London for his longing to be a Roman-style lawgiver), also used social evolutionary categories to typify Fijians and the Crown's negotiations with them. Gordon frequently wrote of the Great Council of Chiefs, an institution he was the first to assemble, in comparative terms, aligning them with various ancient, medieval, and Scottish political assemblies. And Gordon, twice before governor of plantation colonies in Trinidad and Mauritius and a strong backer of reliance on Indian indentured laborers to secure the colony's industry, had a clear sense of the relative evolutionary rank of Fijians and Indians; Indians ranked higher. But nevertheless, or one could argue, precisely because this was so, his sympathies overwhelmingly ran with the Fijians, as in his intervention in 1907 in the House of Lords. Designing a colony that paid for itself while also protecting their truest interests was precisely what he had set out to do in the network of deals that established Fiji's original social organization and opened the path, in fact, to current predicaments.

Of all of the deals of Fiji's 1870s, it is the Deed of Cession that is talked about most, still, in Fiji politics. In fact, reification of a duty of Europeans to protect Fijians, allegedly established by the Deed of Cession, has been a primary theme of Fiji's twentieth-century history. After World War II, anger at Indo-Fijian nonparticipation in defense of the British Empire was channeled, in a contentious 1946 Legislative Council debate, into a motion that affirmed and officialized the standing of the Deed of Cession as a charter. And at independence, the issue such Deed-centric politics raised was whether it mandated ethnic Fijian paramountcy. But there were more deals than the Deed of Cession made in the 1870s, and a review of them and their connections will put us in a better position to contextualize the deals made and broken in the 1990s and in 2000, as lawgivers in Fiji struggle again to formulate a workable political order. "What makes the task of the lawgiver so difficult is less what has to be established than what has to be destroyed" (Rousseau 1968:95).

GORDON'S SOCIAL CONTRACTS

There is no doubt whatsoever that the basic difference between the Deed of Cession and the *girmit* contracts goes far to explain the differences in social relations and standing in law between "Fijians" and "Indians" in early Fiji (see Kaplan 1988a). With many elaborations, reformulations, and reestablishments, the ethnic Fijians had their social and legal standing in the colonial order mediated by their relations to "their" chiefs. Land ownership rights were established as inalienable and vested not in individuals but in kin groups, *mataqali,* groups defined by their ownership of titles and rituals as well as lands, and by traditions of service to specific chiefs. Taxation also followed lines of chiefship-centric social organization, and with variation in colonial history, Fijian villagers needed chiefly permission not only to take up employment for money, but even to leave their village and travel to the city or town. The Native Administration, later the Fijian Administration, in many ways governed a polity within the polity. The Indo-Fijians, on the other hand, were legally atomized. Nothing and no one mediated between them and colonial officials, except their employers, and that relationship only lasted until the end of the five years service, whereupon, as the *Cyclopedia* put it, "he can obtain a certificate from his employer, entitling him to retire on his own responsibility" (25). The *girmit* constituted the Indians as absolute legal individuals and cast them off without any given connections or prefigured place (except possibly the spot-market for wage labor). Indians' political struggles were then largely failing efforts to establish, on the one hand, legal standing for their own real and invented customary laws (in marriage, concerning *panchayats,* etc., see Kelly 1991) and, on the other hand, to realize the equality of citizenship that their legal individuality and freedom might seem to imply.

They had, and on frequent political occasions invoked, a preferred constitutional document of their own, what came to be known as the Salisbury Despatch. When in 1875 West Indian planters proposed new terms for indentured emigration, a proposal to support and even foster such migration was written by Lord Salisbury, then Secretary of State for India. Salisbury argued that emigration was in the interests of India's poor but made it "an indispensable condition of the proposed arrangements" that after indenture, the Indian migrants to any colony "will be in all respects free men, with privileges no whit inferior to those of any other class of Her Majesty's subjects resident in the Colonies." Vishnu Deo cited it in his 1929 election speech, for example, and again in the 1946 Deed of Cession Debate. But while it was the fate of the Deed of Cession to be explicitly labeled a charter in Fiji, the Salisbury Despatch had a different fate. Never part of any actual legal arrangement, it also never congealed into a reality deemed irreversible. Fiji's best historians note that Indo-Fijians explicitly cited it as their "charter" in contest with the Deed of Cession (B. Lal 1992:16; Gillion 1977:69–70). But efforts to use the Salisbury Despatch to counter the Deed of Cession have not met general acceptance. The claim to Fijian paramountcy taken as intrinsic to the Deed of Cession was also connected heavily to Fiji's legal history, while the legal irrelevance of the dispatch was palpable, pointing to asymmetries intrinsic to the colonial experiences of Fiji's two "races." While Fijian authorities from the earliest days of the Great Council of Chiefs elaborated on the legal structures emanating from their original deal, Indo-Fijian politicians preferred to cite a legally distant official proclamation rather than review their actual contractual history.[8] To understand this, we have to understand the rest of Gordon's dealings, and then the naturalization of the racial categories intrinsic to them.

Gordon's experiments in Fijian affairs are famous. He creatively interpreted clauses of the Deed of Cession to reserve 83 percent of Fiji's land for permanent ownership by Fijian *mataqalis*. The struggles to establish those land rights and to make workable a system of tax payment in kind rather than in cash were major preoccupations of his administration. But he was also, from the outset, under pressure to make his administration pay for itself at a level of costs that taxation on Fijians in any form could never sustain. That, and his experience in Trinidad and Mauritius, led him to some very deliberate goals. The white settler riffraff that had flowed to Fiji in the 1860s cotton boom was not going to be his answer. Their cotton boom was destroyed by the end of Civil War in the United States, just as it had been created by the outset of that war. Gordon's governorship in Mauritius had been devoted to largely failed efforts to get an economically struggling settler-run plantation colony under imperial control, as much as his tenure in Trinidad was famous for largely successful efforts to settle ex-slaves and time-expired plantation labor on surveyed, titled smallholdings, in order to make them taxpayers. Gordon had no fear of settling "coloured labor" on small farms, but much distaste for low-class whites who, in his mind, might conceivably challenge imperial control of law and order. What was necessary were corporate capital and management and a truly proper and well-regulated labor supply.

Toward this end, Gordon sought deals with Australian capitalists. A deal with Spence Brothers of Melbourne fell through, a deal that would have sold 400 to 500 acres of land, conditional on a £20,000 investment in a sugar mill. But in the same year, 1880, the sale was made of 1,000 acres to the Colonial Sugar Refining Company, conditional on a large-scale investment in sugar refining (Moynagh 1981:24). The Colonial Office asked Gordon how this sale was possible, if *mataqali* land was not alienable. Gordon replied that the sale took place before passage of the law, with full consent of the local indigenes and at a fair price, and that it was not only to their benefit, but was "a great object to the Colony at large" (quoted in Chapman 1964:210). Gordon was willing to compromise the principle of Fijian ownership only to secure his deal with serious capitalists. By 1902 CSR had invested £1,373,000 in Fiji, and sugar exports, mainly to the CSR refinery in New Zealand, were worth £403,318 in 1903, more than 73 percent of Fiji's total exports. Gordon set in motion the kind of economy he had wanted. But what was in it for CSR?

By 1880 CSR had been a dividend-paying joint-stock company for twenty-five years, with sugar refineries in Sydney and Melbourne, and shortly thereafter in Auckland. Starting in 1869, CSR began to expand aggressively, not into new colonies but into vertical integration of its Australian sugar business, building mills in New South Wales. As Moynagh (1981) details, by being in both the milling and refining businesses, CSR was much better able to insure a healthy overall profit, despite the fact that the supply and price of raw cane fluctuated much more than the demand for refined sugar (29). And what CSR really preferred was monopsony, control as single buyer over the price and terms of sale of the raw cane: precisely what it was able, after a shakeout, to achieve in Fiji. CSR was a production company focused on its input numbers, and sought, in its negotiations with Fiji, freedom from serious competition and from all other interference in corporate operations, and government guarantees of factor costs and levels. As Thurston informed Gordon after abortive 1878 negotiations:

> They stand out for conditions—viz. Government to guarantee so many tons of cane per annum; contract to last for five or ten years; Government to "assist" in finding "labour" for the mill; Government to find fuel! or to assist in finding fuel; the "miller and his men" to be placed beyond the limits of native jurisdiction; no Roko or Buli to interfere with any man wanting to work at the mill, etc., etc.; and above all, Government to *give* a block of land as an "inducement"!! (quoted in Moynagh 1981:22)

Gordon had made Fiji a suitable field for this particular—monopsonic—sort of large-scale investment.[9] Seeing his reforms, CSR did get interested, fast, precisely because of its fear of competition. Moynagh quotes E. W. Knox in 1879, the year before he became general manager of CSR: "Personally I should wish our operations could be restricted to New South Wales, but as sugar will be produced in Fiji sooner or later which will come into competition with ours, it is a question whether it will not be better for us to take a share in the development of the industry and in the profits" (1981:29). As Moynagh summarizes the negotiations between CSR and official Fiji, both in 1880 and thereafter, "neither side was able to dictate terms." CSR got few of the things on the list brought to Gordon by Thurston, but it did receive its land at only £2 an acre, other land options, and later on lucrative import duty concessions in exchange for further investments. Compromises were founded on identity of interest and mutual dependence (Moynagh 1981:25).

"Needless to say, the labour question soon arose," as the *Cyclopedia* noted. As the *Cyclopedia* told the story, the company solved the problem. But in fact, long before concluding either his land registries or his deal to bring CSR to Fiji, Gordon had set out to replace the existing sources of labor for Fiji's plantations—mainly Fijians assigned by chiefs, and "blackbirded" islanders recruited, often by force, from elsewhere in the Pacific—with indentured Indians. By 1878 the *Fiji Royal Gazette* was publishing "for general information" the ongoing correspondence between Gordon's Agent-General of Immigration (Charles Mitchell, who had worked with Gordon in Mauritius) and the Indian government.

India was pleased to note that official Fiji had so many officers, including Gordon, "well acquainted with the experience of coolie immigration in the West Indies" and was concerned mainly that Fiji be able to live up to existing standards for indentured emigration. And among more specific and technical queries about the terms and financing of the indenture, official India asked official Fiji:[10]

> What is the constitution of the colony? What is its form of Government, and the law administered? Describe the organization, powers, numbers, and distribution of the judicial and executive staff. The Governor General in Council wishes particularly to be informed of the *quality* of the agency on which devolves the decision of disputes between master and servant. From what class are the magistrates and police drawn? By whom are they appointed?

The tone here is remarkable, as the arrogant, large government of the jewel in the Crown looks down its nose at the tiny beginning government of Fiji. But in this opening query lies a crucial detail about the British indenture system as it emerged. What *quality* of agency would decide disputes between master and servant? Both imperial interlocutors, here, presumed the same thing from the outset: the relations between "master" and "servant" would not be left to any market to determine. India specifically requested that "as in the West India colonies, the labourers should be engaged directly by Government, and allotted under Government supervision to the estates." To this Fiji readily agreed: "The labourers would be engaged directly by Government, and allotted under Government supervision, as in the West Indies" (*FRG* 1878:33). No slave auctions. No private suppliers. No contracts, swaps, or independent rearrangements of the terms. And certainly, no ongoing negotiation with the laborers. This labor was a government monopoly, to be allotted at a fixed price, and paid fixed wages, both to be set by government.

Fiji answered this query fulsomely, agreeing that these questions

> are no doubt questions of the first importance when considering whether emigration . . . may be permitted with due regard to the welfare of the immigrant.
>
> When the position of the Governor is such that the influence of the landed proprietor of immigrants cannot be brought to bear on him, either directly or indirectly, to any great extent, and where he is responsible to the Imperial Government alone for his actions, the Indian Government has the best guarantee for the protection and welfare of the immigrant. That the Governor of Fiji occupies such a position, the following paragraphs . . . will place beyond question. . . . (33)

The Fiji official went on to describe Fiji's top-down, governor-centered constitution and promised specifically that all magistrates would be "British subjects, paid by Government, and appointed by the Governor." In all this India was satisfied and in later correspondence (*FRG* 1878:66–74) requested more specific changes in Fiji's rules, regarding things such as rations (addition of ghee, masala, and more sugar, as in British Guiana), and the penal sanctions for various work crimes (for desertion, instead of a twenty-dollar fine or else imprisonment with hard labor for three months, a ten-dollar fine and/or imprisonment with hard labor for one month, as in British Guiana). Once Fiji adopted the specific changes India dictated, the system was approved and the flow of *girmitiyas* commenced.

The government of India clearly shared Gordon's fear of settlers and planters. Knowing what they did about such places as Mauritius, both had good reason to. Much more could be said than we have space for concerning the efficacy of their solution of top-down government control and protection.[11] The issue for us is, instead, the political memory of these deals. For much of the first half of the twentieth century, Fiji Indians often did look to India, not only to Gandhi's Indian National Congress but also to the colonial government of India, for protective intervention into social and legal affairs in Fiji. For example, after bitter strikes over working conditions just after the end of indenture, Fiji Indians were thrilled by the arrival of an official committee of inquiry from India in 1922, and crowds gathered to receive it and make complaints. The committee, brought by official Fiji with naive hopes of finding a formula for new "assisted immigration" of some kind of contracted labor, wrote in its report, "Wherever we have gone we have been welcomed with cries of '*Mahatma Gandhi ki jai*' ["Hail Mahatma Gandhi"], a piquant experience for a deputation from the Government of India" (quoted in Gillion 1977:56). But if official India was stumbling its way toward ceding actual authority and power to that Congress (a history of those deals requiring its own treatment), official Fiji was appalled and contemptuous of everything the Indian National Congress represented and foretold (and, not incidentally, that "native" Indians had been included on the official committee). They had the commission's report, critical of Fiji, suppressed from publication, and Fiji's governor singled out the Gandhi reference as evidence that the committee was biased: "The enthusiastic cries of 'Mahatma Gandhi ki jai' presents to my mind a contemptible rather than a 'piquant' picture" (quoted in Gillion 1977:97).

Intrinsic to the vision of government protection of Indians, as well as Fijians, from rapacious unfettered capital was the propriety of resting the coolies' interests in government hands. By this measure *girmit* was less different than cession than they obviously were by the measure of legal recognition of individual competence to make contracts. But while government protections of Fijians established first by Gordon and Thurston in the name of cession continued to ramify and routinize in colonial bureaucracy and law, the commitment to use government, any government, to defend Indian welfare atrophied. By the late 1920s and 1930s, even the Indian National Congress was strongly advising "overseas Indians" against reliance on any agency in India and toward self-help. And in Fiji the Indian settlers not only found their own ways and means in capitalist markets, eventually becoming the predominant local capitalists, but faced the long struggle to establish their political place and rights. It was neither their at least formally similar commitments to paternalist protectionism, nor the differences in their premises of individualism versus Fijian collectivism, that most directly connected the formal properties of *girmit* versus cession to their historic fates. The third, crucial feature was another difference: that cession was, after all, a deal with local political agencies of representation, agents that flourished by the deal and had a stake in maintaining it, while Fiji's real partner in *girmit* was not local, but was the government of India, which developed a positive antipathy to it, and indeed canceled it, but had no stake in its aftermath in Fiji.

In this context then, it is not surprising that apart from the Salisbury Despatch, Indo-Fijian politicians in the twentieth century saw no foundations for their rights in the deals constituting their local place. Even in 1943 when Swami Rudrananda and A. D. Patel offered the boycotting cane growers' cane as a gift to the government, in their failed effort to force the government to regulate the equities of cane price, they did not recall this charter for government commitment to regulate the terms of Indo-Fijian work. The social contracts that had established the Indo-Fijians' place had long since broken down, leaving CSR to dictate terms to Indo-Fijian small farmers until the unions rose. And Indo-Fijians weren't really sorry to see the atrophy of the "coolie inspector" form of government regulation of their rights and place. They had little worth remembering or salvaging from either the agreement to protect coolies from settlers between the colonial governments of Fiji and India, or the promise by Fiji to CSR to provide contracted, penally disciplined labor. They instead had to find ways and means to take their own initiatives, and to do so in a political space already filled and indeed chartered by the efflorescing relationship between colonials and the nouveau Fijian aristocrats. On the one hand, by way of strikes as well as arguments, Indo-Fijians in the new cane growers' unions gradually gained the power to renegotiate their actual labor relationships with CSR and others. And some Indo-Fijians found great success as small and even big-time capitalists on their own. But political rights and representation were the arena most fraught with contradictions. As Indo-Fijians sought the expression of their freedom, Europeans discovered the fundamentality of race.

RACE OR WHAT? OR, WHO SAW THE NATION-STATE COMING?

In fact it was originally the government of Fiji, not the Indo-Fijians, who proposed the idea of writing the wording of the Salisbury Despatch into law in the late 1910s and drafted an ordinance "to guarantee the equal status of Indians" as part of their doomed efforts to revive labor immigration. But nothing came of it, and in any case the government assured CSR that the ordinance merely guaranteed existing rights, that "shall be equal" merely meant "are equal" (Gillion 1977:70). Official Fiji relied on the fact that it recognized the legal freedom intrinsic in the implications of the end of indenture. What separated the Indian community from the European community, in the imaginations, in the social routines, and in the legal arguments of those taking themselves to be the latter, was not law but nature. And this itself—that Indians were different by race, by nature—had, ironically, itself found its way into law as early as the 1910s.

The wording of the Salisbury Despatch actually reflected the imprecision of the terminology for social grouping that was characteristic of its time, 1875, or perhaps a different precision. Colonial documents of the period are innocent of the Marxist centering of the category "class" on economic strata or places constituted within the relations of production. Thus Salisbury wrote of "privileges no whit inferior to any other class of Her Majesty's subjects resident in the Colonies." But regardless of the fact that the Indians were, after all, there to be "a working population and nothing more," the original racial conceptions intrinsic to the very idea of coolie labor or colored labor hardened, even as the Indians' roles diversified in Fiji's economy and society, to a vocabulary centered on differences of race in nature and of "community" in social relations inevitably consequent on those differences of racial nature.

The plantations in Fiji had recognized and maintained differences between classes of labor even before the Indians arrived. Different kinds of workers were housed separately and worked under different contracts. And from the outset of Indian immigration, efforts were made to keep the plantations and the Fijian villages sharply separate. In particular, village officials were instructed that no runaway coolies should ever receive shelter in Fijian villages. A most unambiguous test of the difference in law came when Jiale Taragi, a time-expired *girmitiya* who had married a Fijian woman and had lived in a Fijian village for twenty years, applied through his local *buli*, or Fijian district official, to be "treated as a native."[12] He was willing to assume all tax and communal work duties, and in fact was performing them already. Jiale Taragi's very name suggested the social difference he had traveled, "Taragi" clearly a Fijian word and "Jiale" the Fijianization of "Charlie." His request was supported by the Roko Tui Ra, a Fijian chief and the highest government officer of his province, who minuted that the man was "energetic concerning the work of the land." The Secretary for Native Affairs William Sutherland also minuted support.

> I have only known of one case similar to this one and that was many years ago at Nadroga. I see no objection to the Indian being recognized as a native and a taxpayer. They will doubtless allot him some land or rather the use of some land as there is no provision for the N.L.C. [Native Lands Commission] registering him as a member of a mataqali.
>
> A number of Polynesians have joined native communities and been recognized as natives.

But the Colonial Secretary Eyre Hutson was dubious, concerned about "creating or recognizing an undesirable precedent and opening the door to E. Indians securing by marriage with Fijians the use of native land without paying rent. Would his children have the right to be registered as member of mataqali?" At stake, then, was the contradiction of social units, as free but land-right-less Jiale Taragi created offspring potentially within the social boundaries of an inalienably land-owning, highly duty-bound collective. At stake was opening the door to a right to be registered. This may sound legal. But Fiji's government determined that, in fact, ostensible nature would rule. Fiji's Executive Council had it announced that "it was considered and advised that it was not competent for the Governor in Council to sanction the formal recognition of an Indian as a Fijian." There would be no doorways across boundaries of race, especially for Fiji's Indians.

From the 1910s to the present, in multiple ways, race has been more fundamental and apparently inescapable than any other form of social distinction in Fiji. But since 1945, and the onset of the post-imperial, UN era, Fiji has been the site of continuing failures to articulate this racialist bedrock with the other, newer, inescapable social form forced on Fiji by the world: the nation-state. The first site wherein this collision, and an unambiguous effort to cement the priority of race, can be observed is the Deed of Cession Debate, (as it was titled even in the official 1947 parliamentary report on it) in 1946. The debate began with a motion by elected "European" A. A. Ragg, "that in the opinion of this Council the time has arrived—in view of the great increase in the non-Fijian inhabitants and its consequential political development—to emphasize the terms of the Deed of Cession to assure that the interests of the Fijian race are safeguarded and a guarantee given that Fiji is to be preserved and kept as a Fijian country for all time." [13]

To Ragg, launching the debate, all of Fiji's social and political issues were matters of fact and policy about race. "It will be necessary for me," he argued, to discuss "many facts which will be unpalatable to other races but I wish it to be understood that I have no racial prejudice" (1). By his reading of the Deed, "the duty of trusteeship devolves upon Europeans and in this duty the Indians have no part" (8). And the core issue was "whether the Fiji Government, with the consent of the Imperial Government, has the right to allow the Indians to usurp the heritage of the Fijians" (8). To address this, the core of his remarks was an "enquiry" into the "contributions" of each race to Fiji and therefore to "the prescriptive rights to which they are entitled"(8). What he found was that while the Fijians were Fiji's original owners and were committed loyally to the British Crown, and while the Europeans had turned Fiji "from a barbarous country into a civilised one," the Indians were like Europeans, "aliens," but without duty of trusteeship. Among them "the spirit to dominate" was growing. "This spirit takes its origin from the Indian leaders in India" (9). The solution he saw was his motion, which he intended to "awaken the Imperial Government to the necessity" of a clear statement of policy "implementing the Deed of Cession so that the integrity of the Fijian people and their heritage may be preserved for all time" (10).

Ragg insisted on aligning all political and historical questions to bedrock narratives of racial pasts, presents, and futures. His insistence was suffused with anxieties that make his arguments, but for the stakes, quaint in hindsight. His premise that the imperial government would rule Fiji for all time was, understandably in 1946, matched with fear and loathing for India's leadership and its influence. He and other European and Fijian speakers for Ragg's motion raised the specter that an independent India might try to interfere more in Fiji's affairs, even try to make Fiji an Indian colony. Furthermore, as discussed in chapters 3 and 4, Ragg's motion came on the heels of the departure of another invading army, the Americans. Fiji's sovereignty had been virtually segmented by years of American military suzerainty, by the American presence and the British Empire's cession to the United States of command over the defense of the islands. Everyone in Fiji in 1946 remembered the very different mana of the American youths, their wealth and technology, their insouciance toward authority, and, despite their own racial segregation, their widespread willingness to drink, eat, and otherwise "fraternize" across all colonial race lines. The Deed of Cession Debate was also, then, about reasserting and resetting colonial relationships in the era of rising American power. And Fiji's establishment had to reckon, in particular, with the rise of the Indo-Fijian population to majority and the reality of Indo-Fijian disaffection from empire. They had many reasons for their sense of crisis.

The anger of the imperial loyalists, including officials, "European" settlers, and Fijian chiefs, and also the skill and will of the Indo-Fijian politicians in deflecting, containing, and mitigating the political consequences of that anger, can be felt by tracking the motions offered in this debate, ending with the one adopted unanimously, including the elected Indo-Fijians. To recall, Ragg's first motion was "that in the opinion of this Council the time has arrived—in view of the great increase in the non-Fijian inhabitants and its consequential political development—to emphasize the terms of the Deed of Cession to assure that the interests of the Fijian race are safeguarded and a guarantee given that Fiji is to be preserved and kept as a Fijian country for all time." Halfway through the debate, at the Colonial Secretary's request, everything after the word "safeguarded" was dropped, in the interest of promoting "harmony and co-operation amongst the various races in the Colony" (25). The next version, another twenty-seven pages of recorded debate later, was "that in the opinion of this Council the time has arrived to emphasize the terms of the Deed of Cession to ensure that the interests of the Fijian race are safeguarded." Shortly thereafter, the final version was drafted that secured Indo-Fijian support and passed unanimously: "That in the opinion of this Council the Government and the non-Fijian inhabitants of this Colony stand by the terms of the Deed of Cession and shall consider that document as a Charter of the Fijian people." In deflecting the harsher versions of the motion, the Indo-Fijian politicians were successful. But Ragg wanted a specific affirmation of the foundation of social order in Fiji, and he got what he wanted. At a certain point toward the end of the debate, the Governor had asked Ragg if he wished to withdraw his motion in view of the fact that government had reiterated its adherence to the Deed of Cession. Ragg replied not, "as I think it will in the future be a sort of milestone in the history of this Colony, something for the people to go on."

What could the Indo-Fijian representatives argue? Opposing Ragg's racialism, what arguments and alliances could the Indo-Fijians mobilize? A. D.

Patel reviewed the Deed of Cession clause by clause, showing that no clauses had ever been violated by anything Indians in Fiji had ever or could ever do, and brilliantly argued that it was Indians whose labor had saved Fijians from exploitation and whose initiatives had led to the greatest improvements in Fijians' political and economic lives. Explicitly confronting the claims of "my honourable colleagues who have taken upon themselves the white man's burden of being their trustee," A. D. Patel argued that it was Europeans, not Indians, who had taken land from Fijians. When the Indians came and worked for Europeans who had "gobbled up a half a million acres of freehold land from the Fijian owners," it saved the Fijians from indentured exploitation. Thus,

> the coming of my people to this country gave the Fijians their honour, their prestige, nay indeed their very soul. Otherwise I have no hesitation in saying that the Fijians of this Colony would have met with the same fate that some other indigenous races in parts of Africa met. I would ask my honourable colleagues to consider that aspect of it before they condemn my people . . .
>
> Let me go a step further, politically. We had penal labour laws in this Colony, we did not have any provision for trade union laws in this Colony, we did not have any laws regarding compensation to workmen; as far as the brown men of the Colony were concerned life and limbs of the Indians and Fijians had no value at all. Who fought for them? Those of my honourable colleagues who claim to be the trustees of the Fijian race or we who have been made out, or an attempt has been made to make us out to be the menace of the Fijian race? We have fought that common battle. (48–49)

Patel, K. B. Singh, B. M. Gyaneshwar, and Vishnu Deo all argued that, in fact, the Deed devolved trusteeship on the Crown, not local Europeans, and was without reference to any races among British subjects. But their very standing in the debate, and in the Legislative Council, was to represent a race. To argue for alternatives for Fiji's future, Vishnu Deo turned from local benchmarks and bedrock to global events and trends. In chapter 4, the Deed of Cession Debate was analyzed particularly in light of the decline of the British Empire. The rise of racialism in Fiji was explained in part as a response to the decline of the Raj. Here, we reconsider the debate and the Indo-Fijian arguments in light of what was rising in the world. Vishnu Deo extensively quoted the new Colonial Policy announced days before in London by the Secretary of State for the Colonies, "and that Policy, Sir, is to be the guiding principle for all colonies, not only Fiji." All the colonies were, explicitly, "a great trust," but toward one goal, "responsible self-government." It was to come "as soon as may be practicable," "a goal toward which His Majesty's Government will assist them with all the means in its power. They shall go as fast as they show themselves capable of going." And, "every endeavor is being made to accelerate progress toward self-government" (28).

Vishnu Deo invoked as well the emerging United Nations. Fiji's officials and Europeans were thunderously silent, throughout the debate, about all aspects of the world's new order except the threats they feared from the impending end of the Raj in India. Ratu T. W. T. Vuiyasawa, one of the Fijian representatives supporting the motion, mentioned the United Nations. He compared his people's interests to those of minority parties in India, in effect positioning Fiji as something like Pakistan. "What we want, Sir, is our right place under the sun as echoed in the Conference of the United Nations held in San Francisco in 1945" (10). But it was Patel, Deo, and the other Indian representatives who were truly eager to envision Fiji's new future, and Deo explicitly aligned his hopes with the vision of the new Colonial Policy, an idea whose time had come. No longer merely an empire. He again quoted the Secretary of State for the Colonies: the colonies required "more liberty" and "larger opportunities."

> Then we shall have carried out our trust and the expanding prosperity and happiness of the 60,000,000 of our Colonial peoples will be assured. We are with them on the threshold of a great opportunity. A strong united Colonial Empire in a strong united British Commonwealth can make the greatest possible contribution to the world problems that face us. . . . [W]e can look into the future with every confidence. (Deo quoting Secretary of State, 28)

Vishnu Deo argued for the need to prepare Fiji, not to sustain a racially divided past but to join 60 million others in the present and future. Commonwealth was to supersede empire. Other new regional and global political associations were coming into being. With the Secretary of State, Deo found Fiji on the threshold of something new. Excluded, rendered alien, in the routinized and racialized local alignment, Deo, Patel, and the others looked to wider political fields for more liberal allies and for exigencies to pose against local fetters. The Indo-Fijians had found a new door.

CONSTITUTING INDEPENDENT FIJI

For a long period the rules for elected representation in Fiji sought to contain the tensions of race in geometries of elegant proportions and balances. Vishnu Deo himself, in his Deed of Cession Debate speech, described the patterns. (Note, among other things, that in the colonial period the official members always outnumbered, by two and then by one, the representatives, however chosen, of any "community." And we include his palpable sarcasm concerning the Deed of Cession.)

> Before 1904, Sir, there were six Official and four Nominated European members in this Council and no Fijian Members. The absence of Fijian members up to that time could have been regarded as inconsistent with the terms of the Deed of Cession but that was not done, Sir. Since March, 1904, there were ten Officials, six Elected Europeans and two Nominated Fijians. That development did not constitute a departure from the obligations created in the Deed of Cession. Then in 1914 and 1916 further amendments were made in the constitution providing thereby eleven Official Members, seven Elected Europeans, two Natives Nominated and one Indian Nominated. Even that amendment did not constitute a departure from the obligation of trust created under the Deed of Cession. In 1929 a new constitution was granted of 13 Official Members, six European Elected, three Indian Elected, three Fijian Nominated Members. No Fijian Member raised his voice against that, nobody said that was against the terms of the Deed of Cession and, Sir, you will see that under the 1929 constitution there were six Unofficial Europeans in this Council, and only three Fijians were nominated and three Indians to keep the balance three Indians and three Fijians, and on the other hand six Europeans against them to counter-balance. Well, Sir, it should have been clear to the Fijian people that they were to be with the Indians in this Council so that six Europeans could not do just what they would like. That constitution, Sir, was later amended to provide for the sixteen Official Members who sit here opposite us and five Europeans and five Indians Elected, and again five Fijians Nominated. (34)

Neglecting the differences of representation by nomination versus election,[14] then, we can spot a geometry of European retreat across the colonial history, trumped in reality by the unyielding official majority. From all European, to three-to-one European over Fijian in 1904, then by 1916 one Indian added and another European also added, a balancing move leaving an inelegant seven-to-three "white"-"black" ratio. Then came 1929, the very locally controversial reduction of the Europeans from seven to six while the "coloureds" rose to three and three, a deliberate symmetry of race, white versus others.[15] In the 1930s, after the Indian boycott over common roll, Fiji's governor sought an all-nominated Legislative Council, and in fact did roll back electoral representation. The new Letters Patent gave Fiji a mixed scheme (see note 14) whereby "moderates" could be nominated to balance against "radicals" sure to be elected (e.g., Vishnu Deo). But together with that came the new symmetry, five seats for each of the three races, what Vishnu Deo himself, in the Deed of Cession Debate, termed the system of "equal racial representation" the reckoning of equality captured in Sukuna's evocation of a "three-legged stool." Where it was electoral at all, voting was entirely by communal roll.

So constituted, Fiji approached independence, with the Indo-Fijians most enthusiastic all along. (For excellent and detailed narratives of the writing of the 1970 constitution, including the discussions of the Deed of Cession, demographics, and conflicting premises of democracy versus chiefly and ethnic Fijian paramountcy, see B. Lal 1992, 1997.) Here let us simply recall the geometry that eventuated in the actual 1970 constitution: parity in representation of "Indians" and "Fijians," twenty-two seats reserved for each, and the "European" share vastly reduced, eight seats for "General Electors" including Chinese, other Islanders, and mixed-race voters as well as Euro-Fijians, a group still vastly overrepresented, gaining over 15 percent of the seats while only 4 percent of the population. Recalling that ethnic Fijian paramountcy and more specifically chiefly paramountcy was also assured by special rules constituting the all-nominated Senate, it does not take an expert to see that if politics in fact continued to be conducted on racial premises, and the General Electors allied with the ethnic Fijian leadership, this alliance was assured control of government, continuing the pattern of the late colonial era (in which the chiefs sit on the stool). And this alliance in fact kept Ratu Mara's Alliance Party in power from 1970 to 1987. However, the 1970 constitution had another feature that made its "communal" racial premises and operating procedures less bleak. Of the twenty-two seats allotted "Fijians" and "Indians," only twelve were constituted by racially exclusive electorates. The other ten, called "national" as against "communal" seats, required the candidates to be of a specific race but mandated electorates of all voters in a given district. Such "national" seats proved crucial in the near overturning of Alliance rule in the 1977 election and then in the victory of the Labour Party coalition, a month before the first coup d'état, in 1987.

We hope it surprises less, now, that it was the essentially all-ethnic Fijian army undertaking the 1987 coup d'état after democratic processes first worked to replace an unpopular government, that it was the locals thought greatest allies to empire who led Fiji out of the Commonwealth. The point is not that the Indo-Fijians were a more intrinsically cosmopolitan race or people, the ethnic Fijians less educated, more insular or traditional by nature or culture. The point is that the ethnic Fijian leadership was over the very long run, and is still, invested in maintaining a Fiji exceptionalism, requiring chiefly mediation and protection of Fijian commoners against all things outside. The Fiji Indians were far less literate than the Fijians in days when the state provided essentially no education for "Indians." But even then, as now when racially separate admission standards for tertiary education are strongly tilted against them, they have always sought and found their strongest social, political, and economic allies outside Fiji in the wider world. From decolonization to globalization, the Indo-Fijians have always had the greatest interests, strictly speaking, in throwing the doors open widest, while ethnic Fijian leaders proclaiming threats to indigenous culture, tradition, and way of life have always and not incidentally been defending also some bedrock political privileges that were colonially constituted for chiefs misrecognized as aristocrats. Ethnic Fijians tend to seek their social contracts in some kind of extension of their colonial and precolonial deals, starting with gifts between chiefs and people, while Indo-Fijians hope to make theirs in relation to wider world practices and institutions.

A NEW DEAL FOR FIJI?

After both coups in 1987, there were spaces of confusion. After the second, September coup destroyed plans for a government of national unity, the British Commonwealth expelled Fiji, and the Republic of Fiji was declared. Few points of legal continuity remained. In many respects it was only the Great Council of Chiefs that endured, meeting with great fanfare at several points in 1987 and beyond, an ironic playing out of the Deed of Cession rhetoric. Everything happened as if, in effect, the chiefs had simply taken back their gift of sovereignty. When the "Interim Government" was installed, constitutions were debated both in the Great Council and within the Interim Government, until in 1990 a new constitution was approved and promulgated by both. This constitution mandated a 70-seat House of Representatives (37 Fijians, 27 Indians, 5 General Electors and 1 Rotuman) and a 34-seat Senate (24 Fijians, 9 others, and 1 Rotuman), and it reserved major offices for ethnic Fijians. It would seem that the ethnic Fijian elite held all the cards, and the constitutions they debated and the one they promulgated reflected that sensibility. The various geometries of parity and equality of races were replaced by a more nakedly imbalanced and restrictively racial voting system. Not only were the races out of both balance and demographic proportion and major offices reserved for ethnic Fijians, but also the "national" seats were gone.

Still, the most total control does not easily translate into a livable social and cultural hegemony. The ethnic Fijian political leadership could not avoid political infighting, and a long shakeout ensued among competing new political parties founded on Christian, regional, and even simply personal bases, before control was established by the Soqosoqo ni Vakavulewa ni Taukei (SVT), the party of the chiefs that dislikes having its name translated into English ("Fijian Political Party" is one rendering, but the local media has settled on using the Fijian language name). And while such fragmentation created opportunities for non-Fijian parties to control the formation of gov-

ernments, much to the consternation of the architects of the new racial hierarchy, it was not the only, and probably not even the main, force producing
the Fiji Constitution Review Commission of 1996 that led to the new constitution of 1997. In the face of all the real political turmoil, amidst rumors,
reports, and fears of insider dealing and corruption, and no doubt with apprehensions over potential future political crisis, new capital investment in
the islands dried up in the 1990s. Despite a tourist industry running near to
capacity and advantageous "free trade zone" tax schemes, new money was
not pouring in. And global capital had, in its effects, become an ally of all
seeking more egalitarian and democratic forms of government in Fiji.

The Fiji Constitution Review Commission was chaired by Sir Paul
Reeves of New Zealand and also included onetime parliamentary Speaker
Tomasi Vakatora and Brij Lal, a professor at Australian National University.
(The commission was thus chaired by a Maori knight and included a long-
time Alliance Party ethnic Fijian politician and the most distinguished historian of Indo-Fijians, himself grandson of *girmitiyas.*) The commission's 1996
report was titled with unambiguous emphasis on Fiji's common future over
its divided past, "The Fiji Islands: Towards a United Future," and led rapidly to adoption of a new constitution in 1997. While the 1997 constitution
continued the 1990 constitution's variety of concessions to Fijian custom and
chiefly power (the Great Council of Chiefs appointed the president, the purportedly ceremonial head of state), it altered the "racial" composition of representation in important ways. The House of Representatives consisted of
71 members, elected from 5 electoral rolls (23 by Fijians, 19 by Indians, 1 by
Rotumans, 3 by others, and 25 by all voters on an "Open Roll"). And the
prime minister was required to invite into his cabinet members from other
parties that occupied 10 percent of the seats or more in the House of Representatives, in numbers corresponding to total percentage of members in the
House.

Did global forces or agencies require Fiji to take a specific shape as a
nation-state? The Fiji of the second coup in 1987 was punished for its instability and racialism, excluded from the British Commonwealth, feared by
investors. In 1997 Fiji gained readmission to the Commonwealth for its pains
to meet global civil standards, a cherished membership in a place that never
took the British royalty off its coins and bills despite a decade as an independent republic—and a membership again in jeopardy in 2000. But how, exactly, did Fiji find and address itself to global civil standards?

Among the most interesting aspects of Fiji's recent history, we think, was
the effort of the Reeves Commission to grapple with the advice delivered to
it from political authorities of the wider world. In its report the commission
reviewed provisions in many national constitutions concerning rights to ex-

ceptional treatment of various kinds of groups, especially indigenous, and also reviewed a remarkable collection of international conventions and declarations: the Universal Declaration of Human Rights, the International Covenant on Civil and Political Rights, the Convention on the Elimination of All Forms of Racial Discrimination, the Convention on the Elimination of All Forms of Discrimination Against Women, the ILO Convention No. 169 concerning Indigenous and Tribal Peoples, and the draft Declaration on the Rights of Indigenous Peoples.

And what Fiji's commission found, in short, was that the world had no unambiguous advice for them. The first two documents listed above made no mention of justifications for affirmative action programs. "As well as requiring equality in according human rights and fundamental freedoms to all members of society, those instruments specifically recognize the right of everyone to equal access to public service in their country" (232). But the Convention on the Elimination of All Forms of Racial Discrimination "not only permits, but also requires 'special measures' to secure the adequate advancement, development and protection of 'certain racial groups and individuals belonging to them,' but only for the purpose of securing them the equal enjoyment of 'human rights and fundamental freedoms'" (233). The Convention on the Elimination of All Forms of Discrimination Against Women bases its provision justifying special measures aimed at protecting maternity on the standard used in the Convention on the Elimination of All Forms of Racial Discrimination, the aim of "accelerating *de facto* equality," especially equality of opportunity and treatment, but fails to address whether such special treatment, when permanent, is discrimination *against men*, a crucial parallel for Fiji's half-and-half social situation. Finally, the convention and draft Declaration on the Rights of Indigenous Peoples "require[s] states to take 'special measures' for the benefit of such peoples in certain specified contexts," but fails to address "whether these special measures are to be temporary or permanent, and how they are to be justified in relation to the equality rights of the population as a whole" (233).

Casting its net to the world for examples of legal solutions, Fiji's commission found not only the tensions prevalent in the world's varied versions of affirmative action programs and 1990s multiculturalist initiatives, but also a conspicuous failure of the world's meta-legislators to envision the predicaments Fiji's new lawgivers faced: a state in which the allegedly vulnerable indigenous people were half the population, a state in which the claimants to special treatment were precisely the politically dominant group. Unambiguously, Fiji had to be a nation-state. But how the nation-state form, especially in its entitlements, was expected to fit Fiji's situation was utterly ambiguous.

RABUKA'S CHOICE

In chapter 4 we labeled as "Sukuna's choice" what we think was a crucial decision in 1943. In 1943 A. D. Patel, Swami Rudrananda, and other leaders of the cane-cutting boycott had offered a gift to Ratu Sukuna and Fiji's colonial government. They offered the cane that striking workers did not want to cut for the price offered by CSR. Sukuna, high chief and Secretary of Fijian Affairs, accepted the offer. Then, after consulting with the Governor, he reversed himself and refused the gift, writing that he wished for things to return to "normal." Though this reversal was no doubt at the behest of Governor Mitchell, we call it Sukuna's choice both because of his startling turnabout and because he was in a position of leverage, in both the Fijian and colonial bureaucratic hierarchies, to have pushed for a different outcome. By refusing the gift of the cane, the chiefly-colonial rulers of Fiji entrenched a status quo of increasing racialism at a time of great possibilities, turning down the chance to create a new unified political field, and yet one still constituted by graciousness in gift exchange hierarchies. The Indo-Fijians would not have established their equality with the colonial elite had the gift of the cane been accepted; they simply would have been owed, by government, some kind of intervention or arbitration that London, also, pressed Fiji's government to establish, some kind of process whereby government owed the Indo-Fijians help in securing a fair price for the product of their labor. The gift could have founded a core nonadversarial relationship between the cane growers and the colonial elite. Instead, the colonial government closed ranks with the Australian company, and the "normality" that was reinstituted was one of racial difference and the measurement of every "Indian" gain as someone else's loss. In following years, a cascade of new institutions routinized this racialist normality, most notably, of course, the Deed of Cession Debate in 1946, and in many ways also the constitution at independence in 1970.

In 1997 Sitiveni Rabuka made a different choice, in favor of a Fijian nation of citizens, rather than a polity insistently cloven by communal racial groupings. Prime Minister ex–Brigadier General Rabuka was a surprising advocate for such a Fiji. In 1987, then simply as Colonel Rabuka, he had led the two military coups that seized power from a Fijian-headed Labour–National Federation Party coalition government. Leader of the almost completely ethnic Fijian army, his early pronouncements championed ethnic Fijians, bashed Indians, and advocated a Fijian-headed Christian polity (see Rutz 1995). He had abrogated the 1970 constitution, ruled by decree, reinstated the losers of the 1987 election, then promulgated his own new constitution in 1990.

Yet remarkably, it was Rabuka who lent his mana, here his control—even embodiment—of sovereignty, to the 1997 constitution, joining particularly with Jai Ram Reddy, the leader of the National Federation Party, to embody the Reeves Commission's phrase "Towards a United Future." Reddy became the first Indo-Fijian to address a meeting of the Great Council of Chiefs and to inform them that they were his chiefs also, the chiefs of all Fiji citizens, and Rabuka shepherded the new constitution through a rapid enactment. Rabuka oversaw at least two significant changes to the constitution proposed by the Reeves Commission. First, while the commission had suggested that the president of Fiji be elected by an "electoral college" composed of House and Senate members, from among several nominees by the Great Council of Chiefs, the actual 1997 constitution, to Rabuka's great satisfaction, made the president simply an appointee of the Great Council. Rabuka explained, in a 1997 interview, that in this, "the objectives of the coups [of 1987] have been achieved because the position of Fijian leadership has been secured. . . . [T]he pinnacle of leadership would be the president who is to be appointed by the Great Council" (quoted in Hussein 1997:20). Second, the number of parliamentary seats to be elected by "communal roll" was increased. The proportion recommended by the commission, two-thirds elected by "common roll," that is, by all voters of all race in a district, was reversed, and in the 1999 constitution, almost two-thirds of the seats were "communal." In a third, more minor revision, the number of Indo-Fijian "communal" seats was dropped one below the number demographically justified, twenty to nineteen, and the number of General Electors increased by one.

All of the tinkering was in favor of the chiefly interests, but the outcome was still praised by Fiji's pro-democracy modernists. In an interview run by *Pacific Islands Monthly* in 1997, next to the interview with Rabuka, Brij Lal said, "I think it's a major breakthrough. I can't imagine the consequences, if they had failed" (quoted in Seneviratne 1997:21). Rabuka reported his own motives as pragmatic, for a Fiji still founded on racial differences. When asked, "Is the constitution really going to promote national unity as everyone hopes?" he answered:

> The new constitution will not. The new constitution will be the document to guide the people on how they coexist, on how they interrelate, how they interact and how they govern. The constitution will force us to work together whether we like it or not because we are here together. (Quoted in Hussein 1997:19)

Rabuka envisioned his new document guiding the people to "coexist" and "interrelate." He envisioned especially the provisions allowing all significant parties into cabinet as a vehicle to "force us to work together," and in all probability, a vehicle especially to force the Labour Party to work with *him*.

Asked, in the same interview, about Labour criticism of both the communal electoral rolls and SVT policies, Rabuka was sanguine: "I agree that the Fiji Labour Party will not come in unless we have written down rules, regulations and policies which they agree with. But the NFP has agreed to work with us and I am sure that in time the FLP will also come in" (quoted in Hussein 1997:20). But on election night, the shoe was on the other foot.

To the great surprise of Prime Minister Rabuka and his allies, the 1999 elections led to an absolute majority of seats for the Labour Party, the party most resisted by the chiefly establishment. In the wake of Labour's absolute majority victory, the mechanisms for power sharing worked extremely well, but in reverse of what the designers had intended. While Fiji gained its first Indo-Fijian (and first labor-union leader) prime minister in the Labour Prime Minister Mahendra Chaudhry, his government gained the support of 58 out of 71 parliamentarians. Chaudhry's cabinet included 12 ethnic Fijians among its 18 members and included members of all significant ethnic Fijian parties except the bitter holdout SVT. It was the SVT, not Labour, that resisted "coming in" to government as the constitution allowed. One other party was also absent from the cabinet of the "People's Coalition," as the new government came to be called: the NFP, the largely Indo-Fijian-supported party that had been Labour's coalition partner in 1987 and then Rabuka's ally in constitutional reforms in 1997. Cabinet positions would have been offered to the NFP, but for the fact that the NFP failed to elect a single parliamentarian in the 1999 elections, a stinging rebuke for its alliance with Rabuka.

Fijian nationalists initiated protests and marches against the People's Coalition government as the government began efforts to address the major problems facing Fiji, notably the fact that almost all of the leases by which Indo-Fijians controlled sugarcane farms had run out and were up for renewal or termination. Rabuka seemed at first bitter, then resigned to his defeat, accepting an invitation to become a peace adviser in the Solomon Islands. Then, on May 19, came another coup d'état.

MAY–JULY 2000: REPRESENTATION AND COERCION

On May 19, 2000, the anniversary of the Labour Party victory, seven armed men stormed the Parliament building and took Prime Minister Mahendra Chaudhry and thirty members of parliament hostage. The coup leader and spokesman was George Speight, who issued several decrees to the press, claiming his own authority and revoking Fiji's constitution.[16] In response, on May 20 Fiji's president, Ratu Sir Kamisese Mara, asserted that the 1997 constitution was still in place, declared a state of emergency, and claimed executive authority. He attempted negotiations with the Speight group. The Great Council of Chiefs was convened by its president, the 1987 coups leader Sitiveni Rabuka, and it declared its support for Mara. On May 28 Mara consolidated the coup; he declared that, under the 1997 constitution, in the event that the prime minister was "absent from duty . . . or unable to perform the functions of his office," the president was obligated to appoint an acting prime minister. Mara appointed a temporary prime minister, who dismissed the cabinet ministers, prorogued Parliament, and then resigned, leaving Mara with executive authority (Fiji Government Press Releases, www.fiji.gov.fj, 5/28/00). For two days, then, Mara sought to settle the crisis as Fiji's chief executive himself. Then he too resigned, removed to a naval vessel, and handed over power to the head of Fiji's military, Commodore Frank Bainimarama. Bainimarama "assumed Executive Authority," created an Interim Military Government and declared martial law ("Announcement to the Nation by Commodore Bainimarama," fiji.gov.fj, 5/29/00). On May 30 Bainimarama revoked, by decree, the 1997 constitution. After weeks of talks with the Speight group that failed to release the hostages, Bainimarama announced a civilian government, headed by former Fiji Development Bank director Laisenia Qarase and including no Indo-Fijians as ministers. As they sensed their power to shape government slipping, the Speight group grew more restive, and friction led to violence on July 4, when threatened soldiers shot one of Speight's supporters. The event seems to have rebounded against the military and its civilian government. Thereafter and perhaps in part in consequence, groups of ethnic Fijians throughout the islands seized public and private property as "landowners," usually also announcing their support for the Speight group and its agenda. The military and Speight reopened their negotiations, and on July 9 signed the Muanikau Accord. Following the terms of the accord, the Speight group released all the hostages on the day the Great Council of Chiefs met to replace the military government with a new president, and on that day the Great Council consolidated ethnic Fijian interests as they saw them by appointing Speight's candidates president and vice president of Fiji. The next day it became clear that Laisenia Qarase, the "civilian" prime minister appointed by the military, would continue as prime minister, and that the cabinet would include none of the Speight group (strictly defined).

This outline of events would seem to begin with an opposition of terrorist hostage takers versus those upholding law, order, and "normalcy." But this seeming opposition is immediately belied by the participation of all involved in the revocation of the 1997 constitution and the willingness of all in power to sacrifice Chaudhry's position as democratically elected prime minister by assuming the right to replace and even bar him from further governing. If the events had any overall structure, perhaps the best depiction is that at least two coups were under way simultaneously and had continuing difficulty settling up with each other.

These events are still in the making, our information is incomplete, and we do not propose an in-depth analysis. But we do want to explore five themes related to representation and sovereignty: Rabuka's constitutional "transprovisions," the struggles among ethnic Fijians, control of the means of representation, Indo-Fijian dilemmas, and world reactions.

Rabuka's Transprovisions

An institutional structure came to the fore as this coup has unfolded, in a way that Rabuka had no doubt anticipated when he oversaw the constitutional drafting. Asked in 1997 whether his 1987 coups were a waste of effort, since the new constitution allowed Indo-Fijians to become prime minister, he answered:

> It's very difficult to identify how you secure Fijian dominance. With the 1997 constitution, we will now have transprovisions. We have the highest assembly in the land to appoint the head of state and that is a Fijian institution, the Bose Levu Vakaturaga, or the Great Council of Chiefs. That is what is political dominance—Fijians deciding who will be the leader of the land. (Quoted in Hussein 1997:20)

After the hostages were seized, much hung on a meeting of the Great Council. Before the meeting Fiji President Ratu Mara had deployed the army to contain the coup makers on the Parliament grounds, and Rabuka (head of the Great Council, who had mysteriously emerged as a mediator between the coup makers and the rest of the government) had more than hinted that the Great Council might ask the President, Ratu Mara, to resign. Instead, on May 23 the Great Council dramatically resolved to "give its full support" to Mara in his effort to restore "normalcy," while also calling for major pro-Fijian constitutional reforms and full pardons for the coup makers. Between Rabuka as alleged mediator and Mara, there continued to be complex maneuvering. On May 25 Rabuka announced to the media that the Great Council was determined to remove Prime Minister Chaudhry, "outside the Constitution," if he refused to resign, and to change the constitution itself, to "change a document that brought about this situation." He represented himself as a defender of the constitution he had led into being ("Chaudhry removal 'Necessary,'" www.Fijilive.com, 5/25/00). On May 27, then, Mara found highly tenuous grounds to claim that he was removing the prime minister "right on the edge but still within" the constitution ("New PM by Monday?" Fijilive, 5/27/00). Essentially, Mara sent a secretary to find the prime minister, discovered that he was unavailable (being a hostage), determined that he was unable to perform the functions of his office, appointed a very temporary acting prime minister, under the condition that he advise the president to dismiss the government and prorogue the Parliament and then resign, which he did ("President Assumes Executive Authority," fiji. gov.fj, 5/27/00). In this Mara was supported by Fiji's Chief Justice, though other judges were resigning.

For two days, then, Mara sought to settle the crisis as Fiji's chief executive himself. Then he too resigned, at which point Bainimarama "assumed Executive Authority" and declared martial law ("Announcement to the Nation by Commodore Bainimarama," fiji.gov.fj, 5/29/00). Rabuka's transprovisions had indeed secured "Fijian dominance." Sovereign power was exercised solely by ethnic Fijians as the coup began to unfold. But his transprovisions did not keep power in the Great Council's hands, let alone his own. The structure did not stop the process from becoming a multisided struggle.

Struggles among and for Ethnic Fijians

Instead, as in the wake of the 1987 coups, struggle reopened. Outsiders tried to intervene. Kofi Annan sent an official UN delegation headed by Sergio Viera de Melo to inquire and advise, but they left the country without any apparent influence on the sprawling process. On June 3 the World Bank threatened sanctions ("World Bank warns Fiji," Fijilive, 6/4/00). Labor organizations in Australia, New Zealand, and elsewhere began organizing boycotts of Fiji goods and transport that quickly throttled Fiji's economy; now, at the outset of crushing season, the European Union contemplates terminating all purchases of Fiji sugar. The British Commonwealth partially suspended Fiji's membership, clearly contemplating a new expulsion. The prime ministers of Australia and New Zealand condemned the coup but then backed away from insisting on Chaudhry's reinstatement.

However, the truly efflorescing, revived, loudest, and most-sustained complex of contending argumentation about sovereignty clearly came from the many spokespeople, established and would-be, among and for ethnic Fijians. As Rutz comments about 1987, "Henceforth, the contest over 'the nation' would be de-centered, resurfacing within the Fijian community itself" (1995:75). What ethnic Fijians do and should own, whether Fiji should be a Christian nation (while Fiji's Council of Churches condemned the coup), what respect and power is owed to chiefs, and to the Great Council in particular, whether Fijians only should be allowed to head government, and which confederacies of chiefs among the ethnic Fijians should have how much authority, all came anew into public controversy. Efforts to measure the influence of the three major confederacies of Fijian chiefs in the unfolding negotiations of sovereignty led also to discussion of the "fourth" confederacy in western Fiji, and even to proposals for secession of the west from the rest of Fiji.

Speight's disrespect for Ratu Mara raised anew the question of chiefly rights generally. There are echoes in rhetoric against Speight of 1987's disquiet in many Fijian circles over Rabuka's replacement of chiefly leadership with his own. Also, in opposition to this, Speight supporters renew the Taukei narrative Henry Rutz has called "betrayal of the land," the championing of all Fijians as equivalent to the clans that "own the land" and install chiefs, betrayed by twentieth-century chiefly leadership (1995). Speight went much further in his disrespect than Rabuka, who always claimed to support the chiefs as the arbiters of Fijian sovereignty even as he, not a chief, became the chairman of the Great Council. Speight began his first decree, the Fiji Constitution Revocation Decree 2000, by claiming his own authority: "In exercise of the powers vested in me as Taukei Civilian Takeover leader, I hereby make the following decree" (Fijilive, 5/22/00). He portrayed his possession of the parliamentarians and buildings as a total act of assuming sovereignty: "Through these actions I am asserting ownership, I am asserting control and I am asserting executive power over Fiji. We have revoked the constitution and have set that aside" (quoted in Stackhouse 2000).[17] In contrast, when the military took executive authority, "a group of senior army officers approached Mara in the traditional way and presented a *tabua* (whale's tooth) asking [him] to step aside to allow them to impose martial law in order to solve the current political impasse" ("Mara accepted Army request," Fijilive, 5/30/00).

The mutually contradictory Fijian views being expressed were never really absent from the scene in Fiji. The constitutional review process had led to many of them being expressed in formal documents submitted to the committee (see Lal and Vakatora 1997). But the bluntness of Speight's views and the violence of his acts returned an atmosphere of free-for-all, enabling not only debate but also episodes of lawlessness and retribution. While looters in Suva lived out a vision of ethnic Fijian paramountcy as simply taking what you want (some later to repent in public Christian forums), other confrontations followed from the reopening of long-standing local conflicts and controversies, as kin groups all through the islands blocked access to public, private, and government facilities on their traditional lands (roads, power plants, police stations, even resorts, industrial plants, and military bases) to extort payoffs or force renegotiations. Such conflicts intertwined with the standoff in Suva, especially when Fijian kin groups with a grievance sided with Speight. The physical cordon around the parliamentary complex was porous, with supporters gaining access and Speight and others coming and going. The ambiguity that surrounded who did and did not get to pass through checkpoints was matched by the ambiguities in who was allied with whom in what project, particularly as factions in both the military and the Great Council of Chiefs sought to intervene.

Controlling the Means of Representation

Third, there was a struggle, amidst this free-for-all of argument and violence, over controlling the means of representation, representation both in the sense of news reporting and in the sense of king making. Speight began issuing "Decrees" soon after the takeover, in part by having them posted on the Fijilive website. Fijilive preceded his decrees with an interesting disclaimer: "Note: The following decrees have been printed by the self-proclaimed Taukei civilian takeover leader, George Speight." Swiftly Ratu Mara deployed police and military force to limit Speight's powers of self-representation. Speight sought and failed to have his decrees printed at the government printing office. On May 21 Mara directed Fiji TV, a national monopoly, not to broadcast statements from Speight or his supporters, and "to remove all cameras and broadcasting equipment to a one kilometre radius from Parliament" ("TV ban on Speight," Fijilive, 5/21/00). On the night of May 28, after Fiji TV broadcast a live interview with a Speight critic, about a hundred Speight supporters with rocks and guns attacked the Fiji TV studios and destroyed broadcasting equipment, keeping Fiji TV off the air for a day. Private radio station FM 96 was also subject to several bomb threats from Speight supporters. Speight never gained access to the official Fiji government website, fiji.gov.fj, which implacably reflected the "trans-provisions" chain of sovereignty, from President Mara to martial law under Bainimarama. Fiji's journalists, especially via their Pacific Islands News Association, "appealed to all sides" on May 29, the day after the TV station attack, to let them play their role, decrying "attacks on the right of the people to be fully informed," and had their press release printed on the government website ("Let News Media Inform People Fully, PINA Appeals," fiji.gov.fj, 5/29/00). But on June 13 the government site posted Bainimarama's "Briefing to the Media," cautioning Fiji's media to "exercise restraint," and to be "accountable" rather than "neutral." Stating baldly that his Interim Military Government would be setting in place a new constitution, one that would "take into account the aspirations of the indigenous community as well as the concerns of the community at large . . . one that may not satisfy the international community," he called upon the media to "help" and "assist" in thus returning the country "to normality." While "a number of influential people and entities are clamouring for their own political agendas," and "various chiefs, provincial councils, political organizations, trade unions and other parties and individuals wish to impose their own agendas on the current situation," Bainimarama called on the media not to "take sides which may lead to further fragmentation of relationships between the various ethnic communities," and in effect to take great caution in taking any side other than his own.

Meanwhile, the military sought to ensure that no other groups would meet to claim a sovereign power rival to its own. By June 10 the Military Council had announced a clear political agenda for its nation-state: first, release of the hostages with full amnesty for all involved in the coup attempt, then three months of "Interim Government," which would put in place a new constitution, then elections, and then, and only then, a convening of the Great Council of Chiefs. Thereafter, the Speight group struggled to schedule a meeting of the Great Council sooner, hoping to gain support against the military. And in fact, in the end, the Great Council (meeting at Speight's insistence but in the military barracks) folded both groups back under its own aegis.

Indo-Fijian Dilemmas

From the outset of his assumption of executive authority, Bainimarama made clear that Chaudhry would not return to office and that a new constitution would be written. Yet all signs of civil war emerged among the factions of the army and the Great Council of Chiefs, or came couched in calls for regional secession. All threats of violence came from ethnic Fijian interest groups, and, indeed, martial law was focused on such threats. Once again, the people truly wronged, those with civil and political rights truly violated, threatened no violence.

We have written about Sukuna's choice and Rabuka's choice, decisions each took in situations great with possibility. Will there ever be an opportunity to analyze Chaudhry's choice? In an eerie repetition of the period after the coups in 1987, the news was full of debates among Fijians about nation and constitution, and the voices of Indo-Fijians were scarcely heard, rarely responded to. Both the Labour Party and the NFP have unstintingly protested the coup and called for return to the 1997 constitution. Yet in the fifty-five days Chaudhry was a hostage, there were no signs of any serious negotiations involving Mara, Rabuka, or Bainimarama, let alone Speight, with either party. The hostage-takers weren't negotiating with the supporters of the government held hostage. Leading religious organizations, the Sanatan Dharm Pratinidhi Sabha and the Fiji Muslim League, issued clear, strongly argued press statements, but in response and dissent, against calls that Fiji become an officially Christian nation. Protesters planned to march from Lautoka to Suva and were stopped by police: they did not seek a new constitution or a change in the government, but simply protested the violence, sought return to the 1997 constitution and release of the hostages. Lawsuits have been filed. Meanwhile emigration remained a major vehicle for exercising political will. The passport office ran out of forms.[18]

In these and other ways, the events of 2000 thus resemble those of 1987. But in some ways they also remind us of 1943 to 1946. "Cut the cane or else, says army" was the headline on the Fijilive website, reprinted from Fiji's *Daily Post*, June 8, 2000.

The Fiji Military Forces warned yesterday that the sugarcane farmers should harvest their cane or face prosecution under martial law. Army spokesman Captain Howard Politini said the head of the military government, Commodore Frank Bainimarama, has appealed to farmers to start the harvest.

"We are waiting for the farmers to go ahead," said Captain Politini. "We have the option to order them to harvest." Captain Politini said the army can prosecute farmers for refusing to abide by the order under martial law. . . .

The two main sugar unions, the Fiji Cane Grower's Association and the National Farmer's Union, have boycotted the harvest, demanding the immediate release of the hostages. Cane Grower's Association general secretary Jagannath Sami said yesterday that it is the farmers' own decision to stop harvesting. "I must emphasize that the farmers are doing this of their own free will and, believe me, no one is forcing them," he said. "They have the courage to do it, and they are doing it to make a point, and they have the right to do it."

"The farmers are demanding the immediate release of the hostages because their main concern right now is the release of the democratically-elected Prime Minister Mahendra Chaudhry and his Cabinet." He said that out of the 23,000 cane-farmers, the unions have 50 per cent support. He hopes that more farmers will join the protest.

"Many would be questioning the time limit of the protest, and how long the farmers can afford to go on," he said. "But the point is some thing's got to be done to uphold rule of law and order in the country. In this case, the farmers are prepared to sacrifice and fight for the right.

"This political crisis will leave many families to suffer the huge financial burden." He said that the delayed harvest may bring substantial damage to the economy. Some effects include devaluation later in the year, fall in price of cane, and limited market for Fiji sugar. "I don't blame the European Union for threatening to stop buying sugar, for they have all the right to protest," Mr. Sami said.

"I mean democracy and the value of human rights do mean something to them, and if they are prepared to do it, I don't see why farmers can't express their rights by boycotting." Mr. Sami said another reason why some farmers are hesitant to harvest their cane is the fear for their safety. "There is no law and order in this country and anything can happen, so who will take the responsibility of their safety when they move around from their farms to their homes?" He said that there are 4.5 million tonnes of standing cane, which means 400,000 tonnes of sugar is in question during the political unrest.

Meanwhile, the Fiji Trade Union Congress general secretary Felix Anthony, said that the farmers' commitment to protest is widely admired nationally and internationally. "I salute the farmers who have decided to protest and voice their rights and for the rule of law and order. If they can do it . . . I think every worker should consider protesting," he said.

"FTUC never asked the farmers for this boycott and people should understand that they are doing it of their own decision and, of course, they have the support of their union leaders." Mr. Anthony said that the congress is monitoring developments and will seek a national protest if there is no genuine improvement.

"I must say that we, as workers and people of Fiji, have to make some sacrifices for the betterment of this country and we, the trade union leaders, are also prepared to go through the financial sacrifices together with all the workers, if the situation doesn't improve," Mr. Anthony said. (6/8/00; we reproduce the story as written.)

As in 1943, cane farmers, overwhelmingly Indo-Fijian, faced excruciating dilemmas of representation and agency. In the end, in 2000 there was neither a full boycott nor a proper crushing season. The mills stayed open and barely met quotas for shipment. There were important differences between the dilemmas of 2000 and those of the crises amidst world war. In 2000 the cosmopolitan world was more likely to be sympathetic if the farmers refused to cut their crop. But a full-scale boycott faced far more economic jeopardy in the long run. In 1943 London offered to pay more for the crop, to Fiji's governor's refusal (see chapter 4) while in 2000, the European Union contemplates canceling its subsidy at the very moment the growers contemplate refusing to harvest. More importantly, in 2000 the farmers' leases have run out or are running out. Their land tenure was in extreme jeopardy as they contemplated extreme boycott. Chaudhry was elected as their leader.

And of course, the cane farmers of 2000 acted under the shadow of the memory of the wartime boycott and had every reason to fear that a boycott in 2000 would retrospectively (and unfairly) be blamed for the significant economic damages Fiji sustained.[19] To this day, the events of 1943 are told as a story of Indo-Fijian disloyalty to an anachronistically figured nation. In 2000 their choice to act politically on behalf of their elected leader was taken as a gauge of their loyalty to a nation once again constituted by Fijian-colonial military rule. They could not win as "Indians," and very significantly, as in 1943, they did not try to do so. Note in the quotations above, not only the emphases on *human* rights and democracy, but also the self-identifications as laborers and farmers, especially in connection with the future of the nation, as in Felix Anthony's "we, as workers and people of Fiji, have to make some sacrifices for the betterment of this country."

Political stances have been taken by groups organized to represent "Indians" (e.g., the International Congress of Fiji Indians), but anticoup rhetoric far more commonly seeks to avoid reinscribing race or "community" as the location for establishing grievance or allocating rights. In contrast, "community" has been foundational to the rhetoric of the Speight group and of the Interim Military Government and its civilian appointees. In his July 9 "Address to the Nation," the military's interim prime minister Qarase revived the analytic style of A. A. Ragg, assessing future constitutional rights according to group histories:

> We are absolutely mindful of the special needs of the different communities of the country. The vast contributions of our brothers and sisters in the Indian and other communities has been crucial in our development as a nation.
> But the most important contribution has been from the indigenous Fijian and Rotuman community. They are the majority landowners in this country and it is through their good will and generosity that today we are a multiethnic and multicultural society. ("New PM addresses nation," Fijilive, 7/9/00)

In Qarase's history of Fiji, the British don't figure, and everyone is always in debt to the chiefs for their generosity, especially for land that the ethnic Fijians never did, after all, actually have to cede to anyone. But Qarase's vision of Fiji, dominated by debts to the ethnic Fijians, was still too multicultural for the extremists in the Speight faction, such as Ratu Tevita Vakalalabure Jr., son of a Cakaudrove chief, who spoke to journalists the same day, after he took possession of the Savusavu police station. He said that his people wanted a government "which can entrench Fijian grievances as rights," that he had no confidence in Qarase, that "we want a government that is deaf to everybody but Fijian aspirations." Possibly borrowing metaphors from evangelical preaching ("blind to all but Christ"), he argued, "We want a government that is blind to the world at large and puts in place Fijian rights. . . . We are armed only with our hearts" ("Chief wants new govt," Fijilive, 7/9/00).

In contrast, consider remarks by Satendra Nandan, a professor in Canberra and, before the 1987 coups, a government minister in Fiji. Invited as the second guest onto the Australian television news program *Lateline*, Nandan found himself the counterweight to George Speight on July 12, the eve of the climactic meeting of the Great Council of Chiefs. After Speight argued that Fiji needed new constitutional provisions restricting key offices to ethnic Fijians and to Christians, Nandan replied in terms that remarkably echo those of A. D. Patel responding to Ragg. Then he moved firmly away from the role of spokesperson of an ethnic group, seeking a more global perspective—and alliance:

Fijian interests—let me say this very clearly in the beginning—that the Fijians are the most privileged indigenous community in the world in any migrant post-colonial society and the only reason for being like that is, of course, the presence of Indians. If you go back into the history, you will find that the Fijian culture and way of life has been preserved with a great sense of integrity, because of the presence of endangered Indians over the last 120 years. If Indians had not been there, then God knows what would have happened to their way of life because of the colonial capitalism that was rampant in Fiji at that time, including the CSR company.

So George's concern that Fijian interests should be paramount. If you look at the 1970 constitution, which was formulated when the Indian population in Fiji was 52 per cent. Now it is about 44 per cent. And no country in the world has given the indigenous people the rights and privileges that you will find the majority community, migrant community, gave to the Fijian people. We are very proud of it. We felt very deeply happy that almost 89 per cent of all land belongs to Fijians and that dispossession, or lack of that dispossession, has prevented Fijian society from disintegrating. And that is a great strength of Fiji even to this day.

So if you look at the kinds of things George wants, I think first, it will be very difficult for him to achieve that, because one of the forces he's fighting against is not Fijian nationalism. He's fighting against the democratic process, the most powerful force at the end of the 20th century and the beginning of the 21st century. (www.ABC.net.au, 7/13/00)

In countering Speight, Nandan is willing to narrate a history made by ethnic collectivities; his account of generous Indo-Fijians granting indigenes their rights is a counterpoint to Qarase's account of generous ethnic Fijian landowners making Fiji multicultural, both willfully neglecting the large role of the colonizers. But Nandan's generosity is strikingly more real. He seeks nothing more than democracy for the minority he is called to speak for. In fact, he makes no effort to portray them as an ethnicity in struggle against ethnic Fijians, but rather claims pride in ethnic Fijian successes. His point is absolutely not the assertion of an Indian identity. It is rather to define Speight's nemesis as democratization, and thereby to ally, against Speight, with "the most powerful force" in the world.

Fiji and the World, 2000

Sukuna chose not to make a relationship with Indo-Fijians in 1943. Rabuka chose to support a multiculturalist democratic constitution in 1997. From many sides Fijian nationalists attacked and overturned that constitution in 2000. The apparent structure of public order in Fiji is that it is determined by ethnic Fijian leadership (something Rabuka sought to ensure, after all, with his "transprovisions"). But twice, under democratic conditions, Labour has been put in power. These democratic victories, reliant on more than a core of Indo-Fijian voters, represent a real rejection of both the chiefly-colonial synthesis and its corrupt embrace of transnational capital. This rejection mirrors the real rejection of the British Empire in the Gandhian 1940s, but now in fact includes a wider public of workers and cosmopolitans in Fiji, including some ethnic Fijians. In light of these two electoral victories, Rabuka's choice was a realistic effort to find a place for chiefly power and privilege in a new deal for Fiji that also grants real political rights to all. Fiji will find civil peace, not when it becomes a Christian commonwealth or under any constitution promulgated by military councils, but, rather, when and if the paramount leaders among the ethnic Fijians can stick to such a deal that grants democratic rights. At present a descent into a multisided civil conflict seems as likely, not a war between Indo-Fijians and ethnic Fijians so much as ongoing conflict among ethnic Fijians fighting for power and privilege.

The Pacific Romance clearly predominates political sentiment among ethnic Fijians at present. However, compared to 1987, in 2000 the outside world is clearly less ready to applaud, less easy to enthrall in a Pacific romance. This is both because they have heard it before, and because the world has changed in other ways. U.S. President Clinton recently told the Russian people, "The world faces a very different Russia than it did in 1991. Like all countries, Russia also faces a very different world" (speech quoted in *New York Times*, 6/6/00, A10). Clinton emphasizes globalization especially of markets and the need for all nation-states to respond to the interests of outside investors. As pertinent for cosmopolitan responses to Fiji is the rising concern for democracy anywhere and fears about ethnic violence everywhere. Global responses to calls for ethnic Fijian paramountcy are more guarded and criticisms harsher than in 1987. The transnational coordination of trade union congresses is impressive and might bear fruit, and, in other ways, many kinds of nongovernmental organizations could have increasing influence in favor of civil and political rights for all in Fiji, as had seemed to be the case in the creation of the constitution in 1997.

But sovereignty, as Weber long ago emphasized, is connected always to monopoly on means of coercion. The Pacific Romance is fundamental to the loyalties of military forces in Fiji. Colonel Ilisoni Ligairi, who led the soldiers in Speight's takeover, spoke plainly to the *Fiji Times* about it: "I believe in protecting the institution of the Taukei first before protecting the institution of the government" (*Fiji Times* posted on www.FijiVillage.com, 6/26/00). The Fiji military zealously maintains an ethnic Fijian monopoly on means of destruction,[20] a tool for guaranteeing paramountcy far blunter than Rabuka's constitutional transprovisions, and as much involved in ongoing events. The question therefore arises, what will the world do about this deployed monopoly of coercive force? And the answer is, probably very little. Consider comments by the prime minister of Australia, as reported by the Australian Broadcasting Company website on July 5, 2000:

PM SAYS COMMONWEALTH SHOULD PLAY PART IN RESOLVING FIJI CRISIS

The Prime Minister John Howard says the Commonwealth should play a role in resolving the Fiji crisis.

Mr Howard made the comment after meeting his British counterpart Tony Blair in London.

He says it is essential to consider the impact any international action would have on the Fijian people.

"I think the Commonwealth does have a role, but in all of things, it's the role of advocacy and persuasion and argument and debate and so forth from outside," he said.

"I mean, you are talking about the affairs of another country." (ABC.net.au, 7/5/00)

Even in the world of interconnection, globalization, and democratization touted by Clinton et al., Fiji can be "another country" when it is time to limit responsibility. The UN era is characterized by traumatic "affairs of another country," everywhere the actual institutions of representation and coercion take aggressive turns. The nation-state utopia invites denial of the connection of sovereignty to military control, recasting standing armies as merely matters of "defense." If the world has a general plan for military interventions, especially post–Cold War, it is to enter only when it is too late and always to call it "peacekeeping," as if sovereign powers always already lie somewhere else. Postcolonial nation-states in particular are left on their own to confront colonial legacies of uneven ethnic affiliation and other antidemocratic interests in their military forces. Fiji will be left to find out for itself whether it can keep its own peace.

The latest developments in Fiji as we write are these: By July 14, the day after Chaudhry's release, two more *soros* had been solemnly conducted, one from supporters of the Taukei Civilian Government (i.e., the Speight group) "to anyone they may have offended" and especially to the military ("Rebels hand over weapons," Fijilive, 7/15/00), and one from the military to the Great Council of Chiefs, apologizing for taking "executive authority" and ruling by martial law.[21] But on July 15 something happened outside this circuit of ritual closure. Mahendra Chaudhry read a statement to the press on behalf of the People's Coalition government, which concluded:

I am only just beginning to come to terms with the extent and depth of the trauma unleashed upon our society—the violence, the burnings, the wanton destruction and looting, in Suva, Tailevu, Naitasiri, Labasa, Rakiraki and elsewhere around the country. The scale of violence and suffering has shaken the very fabric of our peace-loving multiracial country. Indeed it is far greater and more damaging in its impact than the personal experience I have just gone through, unpleasant though that was. . . .

The institutions of the state have also suffered great damage. Police stations and military bases across the country been taken over by armed civilian groups. A spate of hostage taking incidents has erupted in Korovou, Labasa, Savusavu, Naboro Prison and other places. Internally, these institutions, particularly the security forces, are being fractured by political, provincial and racial divisions. The integrity and professionalism of our judiciary and others state services have been seriously compromised.

The lawlessness has extended to the sabotage of public utilities like electricity, water supply, public roads and airports. It includes the unlawful and violent takeover of tourist resorts and other private businesses like the Natural Waters of Fiji Ltd.

All these actions have hurt investors—both foreign and local—who have demonstrated their confidence in our economy. They have done irreparable damage to our economy and they demonstrate the loss of respect for the rule of law, constitutional government, and the dignity and rights of human beings.

Despite the havoc, destruction and anarchy sweeping through our country at this time, I believe that the vast majority of our people are peace-loving and law-abiding. A vocal and violent minority holds the whole country ransom. In this moment of national crisis, the challenge before us is to vigilantly defend our nation, its noble heritage of multiracialism, religious tolerance, human rights and constitutional government.

It is a time for courage, fortitude and unwavering commitment to the universal principles of democracy, constitutional authority, and the rule of law which are enshrined in Fiji's Constitution. Our commitment to these principles requires the reinstatement of the legitimate, democratically-elected People's Coalition Government.

As the elected leader of this country, I call upon each and every one of our citizens to join us in the struggle to defend and uphold the sanctity of our Constitution.

Prime Minister Chaudhry reclaimed his country and his constitution and claimed a wide range of allies, explicitly including a vast democratic majority built from all segments of his "peace-loving multiracial country" and implicitly also a virtual alliance with the Clintonian exigencies (N.B., the Labour Party leader's concern for global investors), as he began a quest for return.[22]

Time will tell whether this quest will constitute "Chaudhry's choice," as consequential for Fiji as others we have discussed. In any case, we want to underline the existence of such choices. There are moments when constituted spokespeople, representing large and real interests, respond to events that create real dilemmas, as when Sukuna responded to Patel and Rudrananda's offer, Rabuka to the Reeves Commission report, and now Chaudhry to Speight's and Bainimarama's strange coups. Sometimes they can constitute new social contracts, which is what Fiji would have if Chaudhry can succeed in this quest.

We cannot predict Fiji's future. More possible is to reconsider ethnographic realities in light of social theory, and the crucial reverse, to reconsider social theories in light of ethnographic reality.

THE NATION-STATE

Let us return, then, to the past, present, and future of the nation-state. In light of our analysis of Fiji's recent past, its decolonization and its failure "to come to its own" as a nation-state, let us reconsider the utility of contemporary theories of identity in modernity and the politics of recognition, the cogency of recent estimations of a crisis or decline of nation-states, and the wisdom of recent scholarly efforts to undertake heroic, Hegelian critiques of "liberal" and "neoliberal" states, societies, and nations. ("Neoliberal," it seems to us, is the term that has come to replace "late" for the Hegelian scholars now reluctant to use the word "late," as in "neoliberal" rather than "late" capitalism.) This sets a much wider field of issues than merely those provided by Anderson's *Imagined Communities* argument. But we will still keep the critique of that argument at the center of our own.

We have argued that scholars find *Imagined Communities* useful not only for its very real analytic accomplishments, but also for the quietistic form of intellectual radicalism that it enables, the Hegelian Marxist discovery that because the nation-state is modernity's culture, the failure of socialism and all anticapitalist revolutions and the successes of modern nationalism are all inevitable pending some kind of intellectual overcoming of the premises of liberal society. To many who attempt this great overcoming, Fiji can only be irrelevant. The nation-state arrived there, an alien import only in the wake of the Second World War. Its arrival was clearly impelled as much or more by global UN and U.S. pushes as by any local, especially Indo–Fijian, pulls. Could this all merely be part of what Anderson calls "the last wave"? It might worry a proponent of such a position that the massive global push of the nation-state toward the colonies such as Fiji coincides so eerily with the emergence into all the English-language dictionaries of the lexeme "nation-state" and the definitions welding the nation-state to "modern" politics generally. But an effort at absolute critique of liberal modernity might simply see in the dictionaries the scratches of the claws of an owl of Minerva finally in flight, the rise of the "nation-state" and the sign of its impending decline. What is lost in such an approach? The chance, we think, to understand what is really going on in troubled places decolonized in the twentieth century, their "historic failure" (Guha's phrase) to come into their own as nation-states. The chance is lost to refigure the global dimension of the causes of crises—not as tradition faced by modernity, nor modernity faced by tradition, but the end of the beginning of the UN era. The chance is lost, we think, when one treats the so-called "new nations" as if still, as ever, catching up to the West, derivative of discourse and practice, rather than as trapped in unprecedented predicaments derived of far more specific, even when global, dynamics of decolonization.

When George Speight became the civilian leader of the May 19 coup, he declared himself the voice of an angry Fijian nation, out to restore its own sovereignty. But he launched his coup just a month and two days after the Fiji press began to investigate the payoffs alleged in his failed efforts to direct major pine and mahogany contracts to an American business ally. Was George Speight's coup a call for the kind of "recognition" theorized by Charles Taylor and/or evidence of a crisis of "the liberal state"? In order to take Speight's coup seriously, we have to reckon with the elements of fraud and farce, as well as terrorism, that clearly characterized it. When Speight told journalists that he gained a right to rule Fiji because he used guns to take over the Parliament complex, he was reminiscent of another predecessor, not Rabuka but an unremembered ethnic Fijian man who broke into a Fiji Museum case to appropriate Cakobau's throwing club, thinking it would give him the power to restore Cakobau's style of mana to Fiji's public life. (It later transpired that the Speight group stole the parliamentary speaker's mace, a club of similar provenance, when they abandoned their occupation of Parliament.) To claim analytically that his actions reflect a politics of recognition or any kind of critique of the liberal nation-state paradigm would be to neglect the obvious—that Speight patently, scrupulously, ham-fistedly deployed such critique. Speight's coup attempt was not even a clever manipulation of global disquiets. It was a crude exploitation of them. And to see this is to take him more seriously. Theories of identity in modernity or of nationalism as modern culture are not going to help us understand his kind or degree of effectiveness. There is no real reason to believe that this American-oriented businessman believed himself when he decried the ways of the outside world. We should not be too ready to locate his voice anywhere on the maps of an Anderson or Taylor depicting a vast liberal universalism emanating out of the West, a culture of modernity, provoking souls everywhere to quest for community and civility. Lost, then, is the possibility that the community invoked in Speight's claims to sovereignty has a colonial history, that the recognition Speight sought had less to do with efforts to renovate some non-Western folkways amidst the exigencies of a "modern" civil society than to rebuild on the foundation that A. A. Ragg molded and poured in 1946. But, of course, the golden ring of recognition that even the crudely lunging Speight was out to grab is not merely one of many homogeneous, deeply horizontal equivalents in a transversely symmetric rack. What Speight (and, after all, in their own ways, Rabuka, Mara, Bainimarama, Qarase, and a host of others) want recognized is hierarchy, a hierarchy remembered as ramifying both within Fijian society from village households to Great Council, and also between Fijian society and the rest of a multicommunitied empire, a hierarchy in which ethnic Fijians spread widely in status, but always with some close to the top.

In sum, the continuing significance of colonial deals, of the cornerstones laid by Sukunas and Raggs perhaps even because they felt the building pressures of UN-style symmetries, cannot but be underestimated in the literature on identity in modernity, a literature that proceeds as if the deepest issues always really concern some kind of consciousness, subjective lack, or anxiety, never also, let alone mainly, a landscape of instituted rights and extremely practical interests. And the study of what was and wasn't undone, how and why, by actual processes of decolonization, is barely capable of beginning. If this is our negative critique, what are we saying more positively about how to conduct a political anthropology?

SOCIAL CONTRACTS

The constituting moments in colonial history, the deals we have figured here as actually existing social contracts, were designed not just to keep races in their places, but in fact to make the places for races. The political universalisms of self-determination, civil society, and democracy would seem to constitute a separate universe. When Benedict Anderson renders the distinction as a crucial world-historical transformation (see Anderson 1983:40; 1991:36; and our chapter 2), he renews the multistranded tradition that Bruno Latour (1988) has called "Great Divide" theorizing, a tradition in Western social theory that includes even such antithetical characters as Rousseau and Maine. Maine's trenchant criticism of Enlightenment philosophers and political economists, and their failures to understand governments, economies, and societies past, has this in common with Rousseau's pessimistic, idealist search for a just social contract: insistence that the contract is modern. In Maine's terms, the society constituted by contracts is the antithesis as well as outgrowth of societies based on status; in Rousseau's, it is still a utopia. But in both cases, there is a great divide, and only on the modern (or modern utopian) side of the divide exists the self-constitutive, self-regulating, self-determining subject. Even when Foucaultians made this creature of contract look more sinister in her self-disciplines, the great divide still stands. Here in a specific way, Mauss was more insightful. Unfortunately, by regarding the gift and the commodity exchange as the two great species of contract, he, after all, reproduced the great divide. But Mauss depicted both as total social facts, as constitutive, performative scripts for relations between subjects and between subjects and objects that simultaneously set rigid rules of place on all the participants, but could only be felicitous when the subjects and the objects returned when, where, and how they were supposed to. For all societies, some kind of contract was in force, remembered, performed, and renewed, with only the state of war, the negation of society, as the alternative.

The forms of self-determination claimed to reside in a modern liberal nation-state are resolutely criticized from many perspectives at present, but rarely, we think, by way of recognition (after all) of the far broader reality of actual social contracts. We argue not from the premise that the self-determination claimed by the liberal nation-state is a fantasy, but that a fantasy begins whenever a monopoly on social contracting and self-determining power over life, and so on, is claimed by any form of modernist. But is there a distinction—after all, a great divide—still to be drawn here? If not a distinction between status and contract or tradition and modernity, then can perhaps a distinction be drawn between top-down, all-determining social contracts and bottom-up, Rousseauian-dream, possibly even redemptive self-determining ones?

After all, as we have seen, when colonial social contracts not only put races in their places but made the places for races—as in the deals constituting the places for Indians in Fiji and constituting the difference between classes of chiefly and "commoner" Fijians—they were not generally negotiated with them or by them. Instead, these places were constituted for specific groups by representatives themselves nominated by colonial powers: chiefs assembled for the purpose in Fiji, and for the Indians, the colonial government of India itself. Counterarguments could be made that some Fijian "owners of the land" for some part of Fiji had installed every one of the chiefs signing the Deed of Cession, or that Cakobau's conquests and short-lived, settler-dominated government justified his claim to be king of Fiji, with sovereignty to transfer in cession. Counterarguments could be made even about the realities of acceptance of domination in colonial India licensing the Raj to deal. Nevertheless, not only race but also "community" is a conception grounded in large part, at least in the British Empire, in specifically colonial practices of social contract, deals *for* peoples rather than *with* them. Does this mean, after all, that in finding a top-down quality to these deals, we need to distinguish them radically from the bottom-up constituting of nation-states? Only if we can spot a truly bottom-up constituting of the nation-state in contrast—an idea that merely flies in the face of every bit of ethnography of decolonization reported in these chapters. Vishnu Deo, in the Deed of Cession Debates, relied on his alliance not with Indo-Fijian folk aspirations or with Gandhi or an impendingly independent India, but with the San Francisco conference and the new policies of the Secretary of State for the Colonies. When an actual constitution for an independent Fiji was first written, it was written in London, the deal done behind closed doors, by eager colonial administrators holding egalitarian Indo-Fijians at bay and trading concessions for support with recalcitrant chiefs. The rituals of independence, then, relied on royalty to express and explain the new arrangement (see chapter 5), and despite the shower of honors to mark the new horizontal comradeship, none managed to recognize the contributions of the foremost advocate of a Fijian nation-state, A. D. Patel (B. Lal 1997). And as Bill Clinton reminds us, while we are all free to choose our future, we all, always, have to play by the investors' rules if we want to prosper.

We don't think this means that Fiji was never actually a nation-state, though it has definitely always been a strange one. We think that all of these actually existing social contracts—colonial, decolonizing, and otherwise—have both top-down and bottom-up moments. There are always top-down negotiations by what Latour calls spokespeople (in Fiji, consider Britain's Robinson's successful quest for a Deed of Cession and the UN's Viera de Melo's unsuccessful quest for a freeing of hostages) that sometimes produce radically new deals. And there are always bottom-up dilemmas in role inhabitance, recognition, and resistance. Even an initiative that starts bottom-up cannot negotiate without spokespeople, such as those of the Kisan Sangh after its strike actions forced CSR to the bargaining table; and then it is involved in new, complex formal and informal circuits to sustain its standing and ensure its own continuing ratification, as the Kisan Sangh learned the hard way with the rise of the Maha Sangh. As Kaplan has argued elsewhere (1995a:208), the routinization process is not the attenuation but the constitution of the charisma of the prophets, the authenticity of the representatives. In his analysis of the failure of a project intended to build Paris a flexible, high-tech mass transit system, Latour was fascinated by the fragility of spokespeople at the moment they make their deals: representatives of government and corporations signing onto a research, development, and construction plan, all doomed to be voted out of office, fired by their boards, dumped by their shareholders, their very quality as representatives of real organizations and interest groups done in as their deal unraveled. The point is not only that spokespeople's reputations wax and wane and that technological objects come into and out of existence, as deals consolidate or unravel, but also that whole instituted social groups come into and out of reality along with their institutions of representation. Historical ethnography can track the constitutive deals and specific routinizations that made them lived realities that seem irreversible, foundational givens, and thus recognize that they are, historically, made concrete by processes that can be better specified and compared than they have been heretofore, not fictitious when discovered to be invented traditions but real precisely in the crystallizations of collective memory and the institutions they charter.[23]

With this in mind, let us conclude by returning to connect two points we have made about Benedict Anderson's model of nations as "imagined communities." First, in his account, colonial histories are generally elided: a chapter on colonial processes inadvertently inspiring nationalist imaginaries is an afterthought tacked onto the second edition, while the first simply presented colonies as doomed contradictions between two modes, in effect traditional versus modern, of political imagination. Second, despite clear overall evolutionism, Anderson reverses a classic sociological motif. Instead of the nostalgic story of *Gesellschaft* and *Gemeinschaft*, community giving way to society (omnipresent in comparative methods from Maine to Marx and reproduced in Fiji's bureaucratic routines by elite Fijians with anthropological training), Anderson puts the communities at the end of the story. These two points connect precisely where the *Imagined Communities* analysis, with its emphasis on quiescent role inhabitance (reading newspapers, thinking in bounded or unbounded seriality), fails to seek the history of community representation, especially in the sense of the history of institutions and spokespeople as well as a history of concepts and images.

We seek to recover the third life of the concept of community, as neither the "before" nor the "after" picture of any great human transformation, not the icon of organic communism, wholeness, and harmony, nor a universally adopted modern imaginary. We see "communities" as creatures with an extraordinary and actually, to liberals like ourselves, quite sinister political life in the vast ground of real history. It never comes up in the Andersonian inquiry. But with increasing deliberation capped by the resolution of "communal" electoral rules for Kenya, Fiji, and elsewhere, "community" was a foundational political category in the European and especially British Empires. In places such as Fiji, "community" clearly emerged as a new name for race. And everywhere in the British Empire, regardless whether it covered for race, community was an alibi against contradictions of citizen and subject of British nation and Empire (see also Mamdani 1996; Pandey 1990). Varieties of "communalism" were a predictable response to distinction-enshrining political arrangements, a predictable response far more welcome to divide-and-rule imperials than freedom movements. "Nation," "nature," and "native" stem from the same Latin original (nat-, nasci, to be born). Community, communalism, communism. Both trios gyrate in connotation from inevitable givenness, even primordiality in reference, to utopian dissatisfaction, to the politics of the ideal. Politics oriented by them is hamstrung between utopian telos and fatalisms of givenness. Stuart Hall's argument that there are no identities without representation is correct but marred by the time line projected when he argues that *now* it is the imagined identities and the narrated ones that are the only real ones. What we need is a political anthropology that rejects both primordialist, indigenist "before" pictures and harmonic utopian telos claims that, as in Marxism, primordialist fantasies actually license. That there is also no community without representation is also palpable but is not the only point. What nations, communities, and natives all have in common is relationships of place and connection that are not given by nature but by culture, and in fact by agreement on procedures of representation and relationship in connected semiotic and sociological senses. Nations and communities have to be seen as, indeed, properties of humanity, but like land tenures, properties made by contracts, properties constituted not by nature but in histories of culture, and renewed in the rituals and routines of actual institutions of representation.

Notes

CHAPTER ONE

1. Consider some examples. *Webster's Third New International Dictionary of the English Language*, unabridged, of 1961 (G. & C. Merriam), and the 1950 *Encyclopedia of World Politics*, each explain the term with a brief historical narrative setting the nation-state's emergence in early modern Europe: "a form of international political organization developing in the 16th century from earlier feudal units . . ."; "Absolutism paved the way for the modern nation-state marked by sovereignty and the repudiation of any superior authority." And most extremely, *Webster's New World Dictionary*, 2nd college edition, 1974 (William Collins and World Publishing), defines "nation-state" as archetypally modern, as ". . . the representative unit of political organization in modern times." (And yet *Webster's New Twentieth Century Dictionary of the English Language*, unabridged, 2nd edition, 1968 [World Publishing], had no entry for "nation-state"!)

2. Another caveat: we have looked at English-language dictionaries only here. The English language, like the British Empire, was obviously more than one among equals by the outset of the twentieth century. Still we not only admit but underline that other languages need looking at on this very interesting question.

3. The examples of "nation-state" and "industrial revolution" are more comparable if, as we propose, the "nation-state" was not constituted in fact before the twentieth century. If the nation-state as the paradigmatic unit of the world's political culture begins to replace empire in fact at Versailles, then the standardization of its name follows its reality, after all, by mere decades. Clearly the idea of an intrinsic, necessary connection between nations and states is present in all but name in Wilson's fourteenth point, proclaiming need for a League of Nations: "A general association of nations must be formed under specific covenants for the purpose of affording mutual guarantees of political independence and territorial integrity to great and small States alike" (quoted in Marriott 1939:174). Of course the phenomenon of imperial amnesia, the insistence on projecting this nation-state idea back even to the sixteenth cen-

tury under the sign of the "modern," still remains. The principle of self-determination, so basic to the Wilsonian program, was clearly not merely a product of American bourgeois ideology; it was proclaimed by Lenin before Wilson hitched his wagon to its star, though we don't know whether Wilson ever knew that.

4. Lenin led the Communist International to strongly support strategic "United Front" alliances of communist parties in colonies with emergent bourgeois nationalists, against capitalist imperialist great powers. But the communists should never submerge into the bourgeois parties. "There is some similarity between the way mankind should arrive at the abolition of classes and the way it should subsequently arrive at the fusion of nations. Thus, only a transition stage of dictatorship by the oppressed class leads to the abolition of classes, only the liberation of the oppressed nations and real eradication of national oppression leads to the fusion of nations, and the political criterion of the feasibility of this lies precisely in the freedom to secede. Freedom to secede is the best and only *political* means against the idiotic system of petty states and national isolation which, to mankind's good fortune, is being inexorably destroyed by the whole course of capitalist development" (Lenin, "Note to the Theses 'Socialist Revolution and the Right of Nations to Self-Determination,'" 1916, quoted in Aarons 1970:61).

5. General Smuts was a member of the commission that drafted the Covenant of the League of Nations and took particular interest in how to articulate the principle of "no annexations, and the self-determination of nations" with the cases in which "barbarian" populations were wholly unable to rule themselves. Joint administration by League of Nations officials, he argued, would lead to administrative staffs that did not work "smoothly or loyally together," and thus to "paralysis tempered by intrigue." Either the league would risk "discrediting itself," or it should adopt the only workable solution and nominate particular states with proven records of success to act on its behalf in government of particular territories requiring "assistance, advice or control." Ever the sponsor of political development, he added that "wherever possible the agent or mandatory so appointed shall be nominated or approved by the autonomous people or territory" (J. C. Smuts, "General Smuts's Plan for the League of Nations," *The Nation* 108:226–28, Feb. 8, 1919, quoted in Hicks 1920:181–83).

6. Our world tends to take for granted this delegitimization of war between nation-states, but it is an extraordinary accomplishment. By one estimate, there were approximately 20 million war dead from 1850 to 1900 (world population below 2 billion) and 58 million from 1900 to 1950 (world population still below 3 billion) but since 1950, with all the civil conflicts and even genocides of the 1990s included, perhaps 17 million war dead for a world of over 5 billion. (See Castells 1996:458; he cites statistics to the 1980s, and we have added 5 million for the 1990s, the figure named by Bill Clinton before the UN on September 6, 2000.) Endemic civil wars, and perhaps most tellingly, so-called ethnic cleansing are also part of the world of the nation-state. But criticism of the nation-state and the UN era should start with recognition of its general success in banning state-sponsored conquest, a major delimitation of all national political will.

7. Of course we are not the first to emphasize World War II in the punctuation of world history. We are aware that different fields of scholarship periodize differently and that World War II is recognized as a major watershed in world history, for example, among scholars of international relations. Our point here is especially for discussions in historical anthropology and adjacent fields: attention to World War II as

a global watershed profoundly disrupts the periodizations of things "late" and "post," periodizations that emphasize a modernity beginning long before World War II and then a watershed of lateness, post-ness, or neo-ness long after it.

8. Anderson is not consistent in modeling the nation as a cultural universal, a type of culture, or a stage in global history. He claims to approach nationalism "in an anthropological spirit," and he aligns it with categories such as kinship and religion (1983:5) that are usually taken to be universal analytic domains. But then, rather than expecting a vast complexity of alternative developments within his domain (in kinship, for example, variations in descent, residence, marriage, naming, etc.), Anderson gives the nation one universal definition—the nation is a community imagined limited and sovereign, with deep horizontal comradeship, and so on. Then he emphasizes "the modern culture" of it (1983:9). Looking at Anderson's argument as a whole, especially his emphasis on historic emergence of nations among New World Creoles, then the development of a European modular form, and then its global pirating, what predominates is the theme of a stage of history congruent with "modernity."

9. Weber develops the concept of routinization especially in his discussion of how the charismatic authority of religious virtuosos is transformed over time into, in his terms, a traditional or a rational-legal order. He correctly identifies "routinization" processes, processes whereby institutions are consolidated out of beliefs, plans, and arguments, as a significant sociological reality. For us, reconsidering routinization in a dialogical framework, the charismatic break of an ossified structure, routinized into a new ossification, would be an extreme case and not an inevitable one for any period of history. As Martha Kaplan has argued (1995a:208), where Weber saw routinization as the attenuation of charisma, we think it is more often the (retrospective) constitution of it, routinization the more truly creative process wherein projects constituted dialogically and responsively, such as the American plan for a globe full of quiescent, open-doored republics, get made into obligatory institutional realities.

10. On this see Bernard Semmel's *The Rise of Free Trade Imperialism* (1970), which describes both the rise of political economic rhetoric, especially quotations of Adam Smith, to join biblical and classical quotation as Holy Writ in British legislative debate in the early 1800s, and the arguments within the British Empire that advanced laissez-faire against so-called "mercantilism" on grounds of national interest.

11. For analyses of the political dynamics in the constituting of this aggressive republic, see Pocock 1975, Gustafson 1992, and Onuf and Onuf 1993. For its late-nineteenth-century rise as a world power interested in strategic bases and market access, see LaFeber, who styles the United States as a "new empire" but "an empire which differed fundamentally from the colonial holdings of the European powers" (1998 [1963]:408).

12. In the Pacific war, also, Churchill worked silently against the American efforts to plan changes to the prewar imperial order. "Roosevelt later complained to Eden that he had discussed Indochina twenty-five times with Churchill, adding, 'Perhaps discussed is the wrong word. I have spoken about it twenty-five times. But the Prime Minister has never said anything.' In March 1944 Churchill explicitly instructed his officials to 'adopt a negative and dilatory attitude' on these questions" (Aldrich 2000:4). Aldrich details how after 1942 the secret services of these allies focused their espionage in the Pacific increasingly on each other's plans and ambitions.

13. See Freeland 1972:48–49. The British agreed to major reforms of financial policy, especially a new obligation to make profits earned in pounds sterling anywhere

in the British Empire freely convertible into other currencies at the request of the holder. They also agreed "to eschew discrimination against Americans in the use of quantitative controls on imports." American negotiations with the French in 1945, a month after those with the British, successfully linked reconstruction loans with acceptance of multilateralism.

14. Discussing such phenomena as the emphasis of new Asian states on great pasts, while African states described their futures, and the choice of India to emphasize its Buddhist past on the flag and other national emblems in a nation with very few living Buddhists, Marriott acutely describes the planning of national memory, oriented in these new nations, he argues, to garner global respect and to maximize breadth of affiliations, both internationally and within polyglot populations of the new state. See Marriott 1963.

15. Anderson's 1992 essay "The New World Disorder," for example, bears superficial similarity to our own account above in stressing the importance of the collapse of empires in the twentieth century: but to Anderson, it is one unified two-century, "deep tectonic movement," in which vast political projects securely within the capitalist era, even those of the Soviets, Japanese, and Nazis, get assimilated with the "monarchical empires built up so painfully in mediaeval and early modern times" (3). "Bourgeois colonial empires" are briefly acknowledged, but only in their collapse (4–5), and not at the deep tectonic level. As in both the original *Imagined Communities* and in the second-edition chapter on empires, one gains the distinct sense that regardless of longevity or even growth during the period of so-called "modernity," these empires were at their best merely contradictory and self-destructive amalgams of traditional and modern elements and (as in the predominant Western fantasy about the Byzantine Empire) always, for centuries, in decline and fall. Finally, the inceptive fantasies of modernization theory appear most clearly in Anderson's 1998 article "Nationalism, Identity, and the World-in-Motion: On the Logics of Seriality," regarding which, see the afterword to chapter 2.

16. We would also like to add, parenthetically, a slightly more complex interruption of the metropole and diffusion story. Bernard Cohn makes the important point that many of the key techniques and practices of "modern governmentality," notably censuses and other modalities of information collection and assessment, were developed first *in the European colonies* to address colonial problems. The same is true, of course, about the most important of all European innovations in the world of markets, the joint-stock company.

CHAPTER TWO

1. To be clearer about this premise, the concept of globalization clearly refers to an ongoing process and so also implies both that there was a time when the globe was less global and that it is getting increasingly unitary as time passes. The units problem, recently renewed in anthropology by Wolf's 1982 critique of ethnographic method and theory, perhaps first emerged in late-nineteenth-century efforts to defend ambitious, evolutionary comparative methods in anthropology and other social sciences against increasing numbers of skeptics. As Stocking shows, the issue was raised by Galton against Tylor in 1888 and became known as "Galton's problem" (1987:318): when Tylor cited multiple cases of similar social phenomena, which were truly independent and which connected, or at least derived, from a common source?

Where Galton's skepticism of the separateness of social fields interrupted Tylor's effort to document a general theory of social evolution and fed directly into Boas's increasingly radical skepticism of general ethnological theories, Wolf's skepticism of separateness served his effort to resituate ethnology in a "new, historical political economy," an ultimate science of what really is, perceiving not just breaching, connecting and unifying flows, but an underlying "manifold" of social relations, a different global metaphor that I will not examine here.

2. I will also discuss other theoretical works and make references especially to Fiji and India, my two more particular area interests as a scholar. This chapter is oriented further by the premise that theory can be approached by way of critical engagement with the images, metaphors, and other touchstones that can be so useful, but also so fettering. If theory in social science is not sheer abstraction—and I think it rarely or never is—the point is rather that its tropes are not grounded in the first instance, none are safe, and all merit their moment of conscious, critical examination.

3. The quote is from the 1978 edition of *Economy and Society*, in which Guenther Roth and Claus Wittich revised all previous translations, in this case that of Ferdinand Kolegar. I am told, authoritatively, that "pathos" and "pathetic" here are lexically literalist bad translations, creating in English an overtone of dismissive pity, where "emotion" and "emotional" would better convey Weber's point. To provide the fuller form, Weber's comment, in his short chapter "Ethnic Groups" in *Economy and Society*, continues as follows:

> The more power is emphasized, the closer appears to be the link between nation and state. This pathetic pride in the power of one's own community, or this longing for it, may be much more widespread in relatively small language groups such as the Hungarians, Czechs or Greeks than in a similar but much larger community such as the Germans 150 years ago, when they were essentially a language group without pretensions to national power.

For clarifying this translation issue, I thank participants at the Conference on Globalization in Amsterdam (March 3, 1996) and Patrick Eisenlohr.

4. Anderson claims a close relationship. The first line of the acknowledgments in *Imagined Communities* is "As will be apparent to the reader, my thinking about nationalism has been deeply affected by the writings of Erich Auerbach, Walter Benjamin, and Victor Turner." Much connects these authors to Anderson: their interest in the transporting powers of literature (cf. novels, print capitalism), their studies of worldviews and what supports and overturns them (cf. the national language, the bureaucratic pilgrimage), and possibly also their searches for aesthetic solutions to political questions.

5. For a good introduction to the issues involved in sorting out Benjamin's Judaism and Marxism, see Rabinbach 1989 or the biography by Witte 1991. The crucial texts for the assertion of a Judaism deeper than and alien to his Marxism are those of his friend Gershom Scholem 1976, 1981. The literature privileging his Marxism is vast; important works include Buck-Morss 1989 and Tiedemann 1988, 1989. My own view—offered to help you understand me, not as an authority—is with those who see Benjamin as irreducibly both Marxist and Jewish, like other Marxists committed to class struggle as the real story in history, but much unlike most other Marxists, believing in revelation and redemption as actual events: revelation, to those who

can seize it, from actually existing things themselves, and redemption when victories add meaning to all prior sacrifices in struggle. Thus Scholem is insightful when he describes Benjamin as a "theologian marooned in the realm of the profane," and when he emphasizes that Benjamin's search for revelation and redemption, and his "Holy Writ" writing style, set him utterly apart from the analytical and critical style of most other twentieth-century writers (Scholem 1976:187, 193, 198). Benjamin's own answer to Scholem's vision of historical materialism as an alien, entrapping limit to his thought is clear in his perception of the theology in Marx's own Holy Writ, as the "Theses on the Philosophy of History" famously argues.

6. In fairness to Anderson and his affiliation of the angel and the historian, I should note that Benjamin certainly, in complex and changing ways over the course of his life, saw himself connected to the *Angelus Novus*, "the New Angel," a Paul Klee painting that was one of Benjamin's favorite possessions and was the direct inspiration for his description of this angel of history. Scholem 1976 traces Benjamin's changing interpretations of the angel in relationship to himself as a success and failure. Finally, in this connection, note that while Benjamin affiliates good historians with the Messiah, this does not mean he saw any such success in his own works. Benjamin's biographer Witte connects Benjamin's self-affiliation with the angel of history with Benjamin's commentary on Kafka's sense of hope: "Thus as Kafka puts it, there is an infinite amount of hope, but not for us. This statement really contains Kafka's hope; it is the source of his radiant serenity" (Scholem 1989:225; cf. Witte 1991:203).

7. For a sympathetic but devastating critique of Benjamin's "political Messianism" and dialectical tiger's leaps, see Tiedemann 1989, esp. 200–1. Regarding "Probably almost everywhere," apologies to James Boon (cf. Boon 1984:157). On the question whether the ubiquity of "gates," sites of flow, after all, is itself the homogenizing, emptying force, see the conclusion of this chapter.

8. Two other examples: "Americans, in order to understand ordinary self-disciplinary practices in Japan, therefore, have to do a kind of surgical operation on our idea of 'self-discipline'" (Benedict 1946:233). "Special Japanese meanings of this word 'sincerity' have already been referred to in passing. Makoto does not mean what sincerity does in English usage. It means both far less and far more. . . . Once one has accepted the fact that 'sincerity' does not have the American meaning it is a most useful word to note in all Japanese texts. For it almost unfailingly identifies those positive virtues the Japanese actually stress" (215, 218). Davidsonians can whine as they like about the perils of willful bad translation in ethnography. Benedict's clear, amply documented claim is that there is no simply good translation across cultural boundaries, that even closely comparable conceptions, those that cross-language dictionaries consociate, undergo a "sea-change" as they change contexts.

9. "Transcourse," "transcursion," "transcoursing agency" are terminology we have adopted to discuss precisely the cultural phenomena of complex interaction of well-articulated and instituted social-cultural systems. See Kaplan and Kelly 1994.

10. Guha's observation of the sea change suffered by political economy in empire resembles, in some ways, many other depictions of colonial social relations. It is not novel in observing that colonial practices made real the premise of "comparative method" scholarship that differences in space could be mapped as difference in time, an argument available in versions ranging from "underdevelopment" theory to the critique of Orientalism (see also discussion of Fabian's version below). An important

aspect of Guha's account is that he does not argue that the British had to do it this way. Unlike arguments, notably Said's, that seek to precipitate imposed inferiority as a logical necessity, as if the West intrinsically depended upon the maintenance of inferior difference of "the Other," Guha finds not that Europe needed India to be different, but simply that the permanent settlement and its sea-change political economy created easy channels for the exercise of colonial power.

11. Or as Macaulay puts it: "And such is this philosophy, for which the experience of three thousand years is to be discarded; this philosophy, the professors of which speak as if it had guided the world to the knowledge of navigation and alphabetical writing; as if, before its dawn, the inhabitants of Europe had lived in caverns and eaten each other! We are sick, it seems, like the children of Israel, of the objects of our old and legitimate worship. We pine for a new idolatry. All that is costly and all that is ornamental in our intellectual treasures must be delivered up, and cast into the furnace—and there comes out this calf!" (1860b:681).

12. The phrase, intentionally derisive, is from Ernst Bloch's critique of Spengler, quoted by Fabian and justifiably connected to his own critique of Benedict (Fabian 1983:44–48). Though Fabian does not note it, Benedict is explicit in connecting her own thought to Spengler's, in *Patterns of Culture* and elsewhere. I doubt the conclusion that relativism is always allochronic and wonder whether it would be fairer as a claim against Marxists and other Hegelians. In any case, I hope one need not be Hegelian in order not to be conservative.

13. I would even go so far as to argue that the *Arthaśāstra* slips the distinction between bound and unbound series, since the text (in the section quoted) provides a structure whereby a limited set of distinctions and positions—enemies and allies, weak and strong, positioned in front or in rear, adjacent or not adjacent to the focal king—can in potentially recursive combination generate an unbound set, for example, *arimitramitra*, "enemy's ally's ally," constructed as necessary to lay out strategic principles and exceptions. Of course the text presumes, precisely as Anderson has ruled impossible, that these rules applied to "a common activity—'politics'—that was self-evidently going on *everywhere*" (120).

CHAPTER THREE

1. Other studies of Hawaiian history I have relied upon include overviews by Fuchs 1961 and Daws 1968; Ogawa 1978 and Takaki 1989 as well as Okihiro 1991 on Japanese Hawaiians and other Asian immigrants; and Cameron 1994 and Bailey and Farber 1992 for history of Hawai'i during World War II.

2. The events of 2000 will be discussed in chapter 6. Even the constitution overturned in 1987 already included an open commitment to specific protections and privileges for indigenous Fijians: for example, in an all-appointed Senate, elections left the balance of power virtually unchanged. While the prime minister appointed people to seven seats and the leader of the opposition, six, the indigenous Fijian Great Council of Chiefs appointed people to eight seats, and, further, six of these eight had to assent to changes in land-ownership law or other matters impinging on legally defined indigenous customary rights. The theme of priority for state paternalist protection of indigenous Fijians, a commitment allegedly springing from the 1874 Deed of Cession that granted sovereignty to the British, runs very deeply in Fiji's colonial history. It was often used to maintain colonial state power against the political aspirations of white settlers and, increasingly in the twentieth century, those of

Indo-Fijians. For observations on this longer history see Kelly 1991, Kaplan and Kelly 1994, B. Lal 1992. Concerning the 1987 coups, see especially B. Lal 1988, V. Lal 1990, and Howard 1991.

3. While radical calls for secession from the United States have a longer history, Hawaiian nationalist projects have been vigorous in planning and protest especially in the 1990s, 1993 being the centenary of the coup that removed the last indigenous royal from even the pretense of sovereign power. In the early 1990s several organizations actively pursued and debated their plans to constitute new forms of sovereignty for indigenous Hawaiians (for an overview, see Young 1995), and in 2000 debate continues (see, e.g., the *Honolulu Star-Bulletin* roundtable on Hawaiian sovereignty, March 20, 2000). The discussion of ends as well as means is renewed in 2000 especially in the wake of a major legal defeat. The Office of Hawaiian Affairs (OHA), created by Hawai'i's state legislature in 1978, gained a firmer structure in 1980 when it was assigned a share of the revenue of Hawai'i's Public Land Trust and the power to choose its leadership by elections restricted to indigenous Hawaiians as voters. In 1996 a lawsuit was filed against this voting system (*Rice vs. Cayetano*). On February 23, 2000, the U.S. Supreme Court ruled it unconstitutional. In the late 1990s the fate of OHA became central to debates over indigenous Hawaiian self-determination, in part because of this suit, and in part because such activist leaders as Mililani Trask (from 1990 to 1998 the *kia'aina*, or "governor," of Ka Lahui Hawai'i) had become elected OHA trustees (elected with a record number of votes). For good reasons both historical and contemporary, control over large land trusts is a continuing target for indigenous Hawaiian political movements. An imperfect institution of self-determination has again been lost, with no clear alternative yet in sight.

4. For a concrete extreme example, consider the following by Hawaiian Studies scholar Lilikala Kame'eleihiwa:

> Foreigners must learn to behave as guests in our "*Aina*" [land] and give respect to the Native people. If foreigners cannot find it in their hearts to do this, they should leave Hawai'i. . . .
>
> If foreigners truly love Hawaiians they must support Hawaiian sovereignty. They must be humble and learn to serve Hawaiians. . . . They will never be Hawaiian; they are forever foreign. A foreigner who has lived here for seven generations can never be a Hawaiian who has lived here for 150 generations. Foreigners should remember who they are and should be unashamed of their race.
>
> If foreigners admire Hawaiian culture and truly want to join our society, they can start at the bottom and learn as we have how it feels to be the outcast of society. . . . [T]hey must *never* take leadership roles. Leadership must be left to Hawaiians, for we can never learn to lead our *lahui* (people) again until we do it ourselves. Foreigners can serve Hawaiians by educating other foreigners and teaching them to be humble. Foreigners who love us can donate their land and money into a trust fund for Hawaiian economic self-sufficiency, to promote agriculture, aquaculture, fishing and the Native initiative for sovereignty. (1992:325–26)

Like many in the Hawaiian nationalist movement, Kame'eleihiwa rarely registers, in this rhetoric, that there are nonwhite, nonindigenes in Hawai'i, or that anyone other than Hawaiians were ever "at the bottom" there. (Filipino Hawaiians, the last large-scale labor diaspora to Hawai'i, need also to be particularly noted in this respect, having only very recently gained any significant political representation there.) Kame'eleihiwa's history of white accumulation of Hawaiian lands almost literally ends where Okihiro's history of Japanese in Hawai'i begins. Both are seeking to reshape memory of past exploitation in the service of present political trends and movements, but their Hawai'is do not intersect. Kame'eleihiwa's Hawai'i is a paradise lost, a fantasy nation now to be made real on the foundation of its different, superior (loving, *aloha*) dispositions and values. Okihiro seeks to align the history of indigenous Hawaiians and Japanese Hawaiians with those of American Indians and African Americans, in a general narrative of "struggle that resulted in a more democratic America. . . . Such a history will go a long way toward demystifying the exoticism of Hawai'i's race relations and the Asian American experience, and it will help reshape our thinking about the nature of American society" (1991:xv). Scholars seek in the past the shapes congruent with the needs of the future, needs that they, of course, imagine; it is no accident that in the past I depict, Hawai'i and Fiji come into focus as nodes in a network of colonial capitalist labor diasporas, home to the vast discourse on race and civilization that vanishes from sight when we approach these racially ordered places with questions about nation and identity.

5. It was no accident that Gandhi found in South Africa both the need and the means to move National Congress action into a social realm wider than that of the middle class, as he confronted not only the problems faced by the exploited so-called coolies, but also the problems that the very existence of the so-called coolies posed for aspiring Indian nationalism, that is, the civil implications of a labor segmentation insistent upon deep differences of race. For two accounts of Gandhi's work in South Africa, see Swan 1985 and Gandhi's own 1928.

6. This awareness of the power of sacrifice and suffering explains Gandhi's record of participation in imperial wars, which is not what one would otherwise expect from someone committed to nonviolence. He never fought in any war, but for decades he went out of his way to provide other publicized services to the cause. In fact, it is said that seeds to Gandhi's transformation from reforming citizen of the British Empire to enemy of empire lay in his experiences as an ambulance driver and stretcher bearer during the Boer War and the Zulu "Rebellion" of 1906. In both cases, he professed after the events, his sympathies lay with the other side, but he felt that his demands for rights as a citizen brought also a duty to serve, "a genuine sense of loyalty" to the empire (Gandhi 1983 [1948]:278). The Boer War service taught him mainly that "Indians' prestige was enhanced" in the empire by war service, when newspapers that were normally anti-Indian proclaimed them "sons of Empire after all" (189). But the Zulu "Rebellion" service shocked him more profoundly; on those battlefields race took absolute precedence over civility and even decency. Whites refused to treat wounded Zulus, including Zulus fighting for the British and mistakenly shot. Gandhi trailed after an army gunning down people in hamlets, and he treated men receiving wounds long after capture, men flogged as "suspects" (279). Thereafter, Gandhi grew increasingly ambivalent about empire, and yet he still organized and publicized a volunteer ambulance service for empire in Europe in World War I. And even though he (very publicly) returned his Zulu War and Boer War medals to the Viceroy in 1920 with his decision to refuse to cooperate in empire, he was not keen to use world war to hasten the end of the Raj. In World War II Gandhi at first advised sympathy for the British insofar as their struggle was against evil and later justified the Quit India

campaign only after he convinced himself that England was no longer defending India. The most aggressive position was that of Subhas Chandra Bose, who was against neither war nor violence and was determined to end the Raj, building his Indian National Army in alliance with Japan. Both Gandhi and Bose were avidly observed in Fiji, condemned in the leading colonial newspaper, and celebrated in the leading Indo-Fijian "vernacular" newspaper, which was shut down under sedition ordinances during the war.

7. To obtain permission to see confidential minute papers in the Fiji national archives, I signed an undertaking not to name my sources when quoting from confidential documents. These debates will be discussed again in the coming chapter. See also Kaplan and Kelly 1994.

8. Observing this British favoritism is not to suggest that ancestors of contemporary ethnic Fijians didn't suffer as well as benefit from structures of paternalism (see France 1969 and B. Lal 1992). Some, notably the chiefs and peoples of the eastern kingdoms, fared far better than others, particularly hinterland and hill peoples. For a detailed study of an anticolonial hinterland movement and its aftermath, which also includes discussion of the interest in Hitler in the hills, see Kaplan 1995a.

9. In Fiji "Ratu" is an honorific used exclusively for male Fijian chiefs. "Adi" is used for chiefs who are women. Sukuna was also knighted by the British, thus the "Sir."

10. Fiji born Brij Lal, resolutely modernist and committed to seeking a democratic future for Fiji, is clearly a leader among Fiji scholars; indigenous Fijian nationalists are led by Asesela Ravuvu, an enthusiast for the rhetoric of blood sacrifice: "Today Indians talk about Fiji as their country, but to the Fijians, this is not so, because they refused to sacrifice their lives for its defence when the threat of Japanese invasion was real and close. Money and the accumulation of wealth are more important to them than defending the country which they now proudly claim as theirs too" (1991:63).

11. The CIO, established in 1935 with the support of New Deal legislation, was far more hospitable to black workers from the outset than the previously existing structure of American labor unions and was a major force in the American 1930s and 1940s, tipping the union movement away from quests to protect white workers against wage-cutting competition and toward insistence on equal wages for equal work. (The world has yet to see an organization arise equal to the same task on a global scale in response to the globalization of investment and inequalities of wages internationally.) Its efforts in Hawai'i followed its general pattern of efforts to unionize workers and to mobilize them to vote, with a major push beginning in the late years of World War II. See Sullivan 1996.

12. In fact, it has flaws and problems similar to the Congress Party and other entrenched parties. In Hawai'i, these Democrats built a liberal welfare state particularly impressive for its health-care mandates and gender rights, but alliances with developers sidetracked and redirected land reforms. See Cooper and Daws 1985.

CHAPTER FOUR

1. As we have argued in detail elsewhere (Kaplan and Kelly 1994), we think far too much has been made of Gramsci's concept of resistance, especially since it was initiatives, not mere resistance, that actually interested him both theoretically and politically. And we are actually oriented more by Bakhtin than Gramsci. We do not

doubt that social and cultural hegemonies often exist, social fields dominated by stable and ramified cultural logics that naturalize and invisibly reproduce and augment the power, status, and control of elite social classes. But we doubt that truly stable and singular hegemonies are the human norm and find much to recommend, even for such special cases, a dialogical approach that gives at least as much attention to varied points of initiative and contention as to mechanisms of fragmentation and misdirection of potential opposition, occlusion, and routinization of domination. We think that attention to dialogics can, simultaneously, track more clearly the processes by which actual hegemonies are achieved and maintained (especially, the histories of alignment of heterogeneous elements and interests) and provide more insight into actual histories and possibilities of contestation and change. And almost needless to say, attention to dialogical processes of many kinds is particularly vital in actual colonial histories, especially for a place like Fiji, where one is ill-advised to take for granted the relations between official cadets from London and Australian corporate executives, let alone the relations between "Europeans" and "others," and not even to speak of the routines of expectation and interaction between indigenous Fijians and South Asian immigrants.

2. Here and throughout this book, when speaking of race and racialization, we are referring to objects constituted by discourse and social practices, not biology.

3. For those interested, more population details: the Indo-Fijians numbered 85,002 in the 1936 census, the ethnic Fijians, 97,651; in 1946 the Indo-Fijians numbered 120,063, and the ethnic Fijians, 117,488. The census categories used in those years were simply "Indian" and "Fijian." The census also counted Chinese (2,105 by 1946), Europeans, Part-Europeans (6,142 in 1946), and "Others (mostly Islanders)" (9,246 in 1946). The "European" population grew by far the least of all categories from 1921 to 1946, from 3,878 in 1921, to 4,028 in 1936, to 4,594 in 1946. Across the same period, the "Indian" population virtually doubled (60,634 in 1921), the Chinese, Part-European, and "Others" categories more than doubled, and the ethnic Fijian population rose approximately 40 percent (84,475 in 1921). The birth rate among Indo-Fijians was higher at midcentury and has since dropped sharply. In addition, emigration from Fiji by Indo-Fijians, beginning even before the coups of 1987, has affected Fiji's population proportion. In 1970, at Fiji's independence, the Indo-Fijians were 51 percent of Fiji's population (and were given 40 percent of the racially demarcated seats in Fiji's legislature). In the 1990s, however, ethnic Fijians again slightly outnumbered Indo-Fijians, each close to 50 percent of the population of the islands. Some ethnic Fijian leaders voice open aspirations to reestablish ethnic Fijians as an absolute majority in Fiji, a status they lost before 1936. In fact, in the early twentieth century, many among Fiji's "Europeans" believed that the ethnic Fijians were dying out in a Darwinian competition (with the "Indians," of course, never mind all that good land snapped up for "European"-owned plantations; images of a rising tide and floodgates were common, and the word "teeming" was used a lot), especially since Fijian fertility had declined steeply in the wake of a major nineteenth-century measles epidemic. By 1936, however, it was clear that the ethnic Fijian population was again growing.

4. Another discussion of these two senses of representation that also addresses this quotation from Marx and Said's use of it can be found in Gayatri Spivak's 1988 essay "Can the Subaltern Speak?" Spivak emphasizes the naïveté of scholarly quests to seek out subaltern self-representations without attention to structures denying

them political representation. In this book, our ethnographic interest is to track the renegotiation of the powers of self-representation across a chain of crises in Fiji, from World War II through decolonization to the coups.

5. Some examples, heuristically categorized: (1) Efforts to add to the theory: Appadurai in *Modernity at Large* (1996) proposes that we now need a model of cultural self-consciousness connected to electronic media, parallel with the sacred text languages of traditional hierarchy, and the national language, novel, and newspaper "print capitalism" world of nations. Tololyan 1991 seeks to reposition imagined national selves in generalized opposition to diasporic others. (2) Efforts to correct the theory: for example, controversy over who was first, New World "creole pioneers" or nation-states in Europe. See, for example, Segal and Handler 1992, 1993 or Trouillot 1995 on neglect of revolution in Haiti. Efforts to address religiously articulated nationalisms, for example, for India, see Ludden 1996, McKean 1996, van der Veer 1994; many parallel literatures for other regions. (3) Efforts to complicate it: Kapferer 1988 argues that different cultural ontologies condition different imaginations of community. Verdery 1992 distinguishes three forms of state-subject relationships, two of which, citizenship and ethnicity, differently invoke a nation, while a third, socialist paternalism, does not. Foster 1995a doubts the similarity of cases where a nation struggles to capture control of a state for itself versus cases where the state precedes the national imaginary, for example, India versus Papua New Guinea.

6. Scholars of the Hispanic New World have doubted whether the model captures even the basics of their political experience, which has so fundamentally thematized mixing creole and mestizo gradations of distinction and difference (but see also Klor de Alva 1995). Scholars of East and Southeast Asia have posed complex questions about whether East Asia's state histories and forms of modernity have been adequately calibrated with the West's (e.g., Barlow 1997; Duara 1995; Ivy 1995; Pemberton 1994), while scholars of South Asia seek the theory that can explain endemic violence before as well as after elections (esp. Tambiah 1996). And scholarship on Africa turns increasingly from allegations of primitivity to inquiries into colonial history for explanations of the limits to African development, modernity, civil society, and so on (Comaroff and Comaroff 1991; Ferguson 1990; Mamdani 1996).

7. To recall only two: voting systems and land tenure rules. From its formal inception as a U.S. territory (N.B., not colony), electoral representation in Hawai'i was organized on the pattern that in Fiji was called common roll, but with voting rights only for those who were "native-born," born in Hawai'i. Neither principle was a response to conditions local to Hawai'i: the restriction to native-born was a legacy of pre-revolutionary Atlantic colony politics, and the common roll, a legacy of Northern victories in North-South U.S. pre–Civil War struggles over rules for slavery in territories. Meanwhile, by 1900 the Hawaiian aristocracy, unlike the chiefs of Fiji, had long since sold out their people, giving up land for money (it was especially lost during probates in the settlement of debts backed up by mortgages) and had themselves largely merged via intermarriage into the planter class, creating a genetically mixed and culturally complex elite now remembered nostalgically in Hawai'i by a DAR-style organization called Daughters of Old Hawaii.

8. The complexities of their composition need not detain you here, unless you are interested. The Kisan Sangh, the first union, was founded largely by North Indian immigrants and their descendants. The first three-quarters of the *girmitiyas* came largely from North India, especially what is now Uttar Pradesh, via the depot in

Calcutta. Only in the 1900s did political agitation in India lead to the closing of that depot and the turn for Fiji supply to a Madras depot sending South Indians, Tamil, Telagu speakers, and others. Out of indenture earlier, and more likely to have secured and developed good leaseholds, the North Indians were generally, still, more prosperous in the late 1930s. Apart from M. T. Khan (who, for the record, was an Ahmadiyya; the Ahmadiyya sect of Lahore had been particularly prepared in the 1920s and 1930s to meet the call from Fiji's Muslims to send preachers and teachers capable of standing up to the Arya Samaj), the leaders founding the Kisan Sangh were largely Arya Samajis. The second union, the Maha Sangh, was founded by two men, Swami Rudrananda, a Ramakrishna Mission teacher and missionary called to Fiji by South Indians (the Ramakrishna Mission ran some of the leading educational institutions in Madras), and A. D. Patel, a Gujarati barrister sent by Gandhi to aid the Indians in Fiji. The Kisan Sangh had alienated the Gujarati merchants of Fiji after several public attacks on them, and more particularly because it sought to help its members avoid debts to them via new union cooperative stores; many poor South Indians felt that the Kisan Sangh, representing growers, did not represent their interests as mere cane-cutting laborers. Finally, after A. D. Patel's articulate and dynamic leadership in opposition to CSR caused support for the Maha Sangh to swell during the strike, a new "left" faction emerged within and eventually took control of the Kisan Sangh, led by Padri Mehar Singh, a Punjabi (and also one of the original founders of the union). This group supported and on some occasions even extended the harder line taken by the Maha Sangh.

9. For readers desiring further gloss and more Fijianist authority on this subject, I quote from R. R. Nayacakalou, a Fijian who received a Ph.D. in anthropology under Raymond Firth at the University of London and later was a distinguished government official and adviser vastly influencing the Fijian Administration, the Fijian Regulations, and the Native Land Trust Board. What follows is from his 1964 Ph.D., published as a book in 1975. Discussing what official reports mean when they declare the "first purpose of the Fijian Regulations" to be to secure "the continuance of the Fijian communal system," he goes on to define that view of "the Fijian way of life," emphasizing "the continuance of traditional loyalties and respect associated with the Fijian chiefly system, and the meticulous observance of the obligations of chiefs to people and *vice versa*. . . . Underlying this interpretation is the notion of a Fijian society as a communal organization where everything is done by groups which stand in specified relationship to one another and which function together through the recognition of obligations between them, as well as between members within each" (4).

10. This and the other motions and resolutions quoted below are quoted in Gillion 1977:196–97. The quotations of speeches come from the official record of the Legislative Council debates for 1947.

CHAPTER FIVE

1. I thank the late Harigyan Samalia (who died in 1992) for talking with me in 1984.

2. On British colonial ritual, see Cohn 1983; for the phrase routines and rituals of rule, see Corrigan and Sayer 1985 and Cohn and Dirks 1988; on anticolonial and nationalist ritual, see Freitag 1990, Jolly 1991, Kelly 1988b, Lincoln 1987, LiPuma and Meltzoff 1990, Masselos 1990 and n.d., and sections of Foster's fine 1991 review

article on nations and nationalism. For a review article on ritual and the making of history, see Kelly and Kaplan 1990.

3. On flag raising as possession, see Dening 1986 on Tahiti, Masselos 1990 on India, and Sahlins 1985 on New Zealand.

4. Discussing political rhetorical narratives in postcolonial Fiji, Rutz 1995 notes that chiefly political power tended to construct chiefly legitimacy in terms of the historical relation made between Cakobau and the other signatories and the British queen. Other rhetorical claims replace the queen as source of legitimacy with the Christian God. Rutz's example is Sitiveni Rabuka—who, in his second military coup of 1987, broke Fiji's Commonwealth ties with the queen and proclaimed a Christian republic. It seems to me that this analysis of recent rhetoric has parallels in the competing claims of chiefly-colonial officials and prophet leaders in the nineteenth century.

5. Colonial Office, Great Britain (CO 83/139). Correspondence included in dispatches between the Governor of Fiji and the Colonial Office, London.

6. For parallels in the Raj, see Cohn 1983 on British Durbars.

7. As discussed in note 4, in contest with chiefly-colonial officials claiming colonial legitimacy, prophet-leaders sometimes invoked the Christian God as a source of legitimacy. In so doing, they also mobilized the narrative of the power of indigenes as opposed to all "foreign" chiefs, Fijian and British. Thus, in the 1870s and 1880s, Navosavakadua claimed Jehovah to be a Fijian god, an indigenous god.

8. In every village—even those with Tuka temples in the 1880s or branches of Apolosi Nawai's Viti Company in the 1920s—local daily, habitual institutions, rituals, and routines of rule upheld the colonial order. Such institutions were the Methodist church, the colonially designated village headmen, and the local colonially designated "traditional" chief. They included as well the moral calendars of Fijian life, the days of work allotted to church, government, and community, and the fund-raising ceremonies for church, province, and people.

In some places, the local church was the site of Viti Company persuasion, the colonially designated headman himself actually an agent of the company. And, in some very particular locales, Navosavakadua's Tuka or Apolosi's Company have themselves been steadfastly routinized, in text, in oral tradition—indeed, in the very landscape. The continuing power of their local rendering remained in constant contest with, but did not replace, the powerful centralized colonial order (Kaplan 1995a).

9. See Brown 1984 for an account of enactments of these tensions in 1970s and 1980s Indo-Fijian fire-walking rituals.

10. Also interesting in both the text of the newspaper ad and this interview is their self-referentiality, the way that Samalia refers to the dissemination of his words as part of his words. The text of the ad includes the name and date of the paper it appears in; later in the course of the interview, he referred to the number of flyers he had distributed in which he made these prophecies.

11. In my notes I have some versions saying that he spoke of a red cloud, and others saying he spoke of blood on the grass. This may well reflect a confusion of *o* ("cloud") and *co* ("grass"), perhaps my mistake when I wrote up my notes, or perhaps a transformation that took place as villagers passed on to one another and to me accounts of what had been said, or perhaps Samalia prophesied both.

12. This ritual clearly surprised some of the observers, especially when Samalia

came out in the white uniform that governors-general wore in colonial days and identified Lakshmi and Adi Sovanatabua (Hindu deity and Fijian ancestor deity, respectively) as one and the same. But he pulled off this ritual and made it relatively respectable because he had prevailed upon Ratu Sir George, the former governor-general, to attend. This came through his connection to the Indian Alliance political organization, a subgroup of the ethnic Fijian–dominated Alliance Party.

13. While Samalia used the gendered imagery to represent a complementary interrelationship, it is noteworthy that his gender imagery also replicates British colonial gendered constructions of Fijians and Fiji Indians as masculine and feminine, respectively.

14. Samalia's narrative contradicts the ethnic Fijian perspective on the Indo-Fijian presence in Fiji, which proposes it to be accidental and unnecessary. Scholars' histories, too, have tended to stress the coincidence of colonial Governor Gordon's pro-Fijian paternalism and his experience with indentured Indian labor elsewhere in the British Empire. Scholarly accounts that take "cultures" to be rooted naturally in territories have found the ethnic Fijian presence in the islands to be "natural" (taking the Indo-Fijians—but, curiously, less so the British—to be the odd and excludable members of Fiji's population). Here a world-system perspective makes a contribution—Wolf 1982, for example, would see the Indo-Fijian presence not as random, but as a typical outcome of world labor processes. For Samalia it is not political-economic forms, but divine imperatives, that have made the presence of Indo-Fijians in Fiji necessary and inevitable.

15. Here his language echoed two kinds of discourse about respect. The first claimed respect for the sacrifice and contribution of Indian (and all) laborers. Perhaps the most powerful generally known example is a speech by Indo-Fijian politician and leader of the National Federation Party A. D. Patel to the Fiji Legislative Council in 1946. Second, in the 1980s especially, debates about respect for chiefs were frequent in Fiji's Parliament, often used by Alliance politicians to disparage the opposition by claiming that any disagreement, even by the elected Indo-Fijian members of Parliament, and especially any disagreements raised by the opposition, traduced a duty to respect Fijian chiefs. This ethnic Fijian political insistence on "respect" for chiefs became increasingly strident, portending the oncoming crisis.

16. As Foster 1995a discusses, it is especially ironic that the globalizing First World now appears to be turning away from the national form while "allowing" or "insisting" on nationness for places like Fiji.

17. The Native Land Trust Board is the central agency that leases ethnic Fijian lands to Indo-Fijian sugarcane growers. As we edit in June 2000, land rights and institutions are again contested. Extensions of thirty-year land leases during preparations for independence institutionalized three decades of stability for Fiji's sugarcane regions. But all the leases in effect in 1967 have run out and are now up for renewal. No new agreement has been reached.

18. On the "coup from above" in the 1977 elections, see B. Lal 1986.

19. The party was a transformation of his India Fiji Girmit Council. In 1991 Samalia distributed an appeal for people to run as Girmit candidates. The appeal was a calendar, embellished with many of the symbols and slogans of his vision of Fiji, with "Vote Girmit 1992" heading the section of dates. The party had no tangible support in the 1992 election.

CHAPTER SIX

1. Recently the ethnic Fijian population has again become larger, because of differences in birth rate and decades of Indo-Fijian out-migration up to quota limits to Australia, New Zealand, the United States, Canada, and Britain. As a journalist has cogently summarized, fears "about Indians taking over" are unfounded. "They're not taking over. They're taking off" (Singh 1998:8).

2. For the fullest treatment of our views on colonials imagining themselves Roman-style "lawgivers," and on Macaulay and Maine in particular, see Kaplan and Kelly forthcoming.

3. See for example the early work on Fiji of Brij Lal 1983 and, more recently, Carter 1992 on indenture in Mauritius, each of whom seek to recapture affirmative agency of the indentured laborers themselves. For more extreme views, see the works of cliometrician Pieter Kemmer, who seeks to statistically deny the immorality of indentured labor migration, arguing for example that birth-rate statistics prove that workers must have been content. The point here for us is less an abstract debate about how we should judge the morality of historic realities, than to observe the role of rhetoric about deals past in such historic events as the abolition of indenture.

4. This fact was well known, discussed for example by E. F. Powell, president of the Fiji Planters' Association, in an interview with the *Auckland Star* on September 27, 1912, reprinted in the *Fiji Times* on October 1: "It would be utterly impossible for Fiji to compete with other countries and islands where tropical products are raised if she were compelled to pay white labourers 8s a day, even if they were available, as against the 1s a day paid for black labour in those other places." But this practicality was not Mr. Powell's only reason for declaring "all this wild talk about slavery" to be "downright rubbish." He likely had in mind the condemnations of indenture debated in India, and especially the motions to abolish the system entered by G. K. Gokhale in the Legislative Council of India. Gokhale's criticisms and the reforms he was inspiring were much discussed in the Fiji Planters' Association 1912 annual meeting (see *Fiji Times*, 11/7/12). It couldn't be slavery, Powell argued in his interview, because government inspectors visited estates and solicited complaints; complaints were rarely made. On this, compare Sanadhya's reports: "These great men are drinking brandy at the homes of the planters all the time" (1991 [1914]:43, see also 83). "The coolie inspector comes a few times a year, but even then he does not hear our complaints. . . . What kind of complaint can be made about those at whose place one certainly has to work for five years? Today we complain, tomorrow they will kick us with shoes, and give us more difficult work, write a shilling in the register and give us six pence. This is the consequence of our complaints" (77).

5. For the best comparative and general discussions of colonial constructions of "coolie" laborers and the role of race in work discipline, see Breman 1989, Stoler 1985 and Daniel, Bernstein, and Brass 1992. For histories of indenture in Fiji, including the "blackbirded" Pacific Islanders ("*kanakas*," etc.) as well as the Indians, see Gillion 1962, Legge 1958, and B. Lal 1992. Concerning the fights "among themselves" at night in Fiji, referred to by the *Cyclopedia*, and particularly their gendered dynamics and the role of colonial premises about race and sex in their provocation, see Kelly 1991 and 1997.

6. For example, the *Fiji Times* of September 28, 1912, reported on new information about Chinese employed elsewhere in the British Empire. It was bad news for

planters. The contract used for Chinese was less favorable, requiring them to be paid full "whether capable or not" and requiring paid cooks one per thirty men. It was said that they "cannot be managed," that they had a propensity to go to the capital and make complaints. "The only respect on which the Chinaman is a superior indentured labourer to the Indian would appear to be in the fact that he is content to return to China when his term of indenture expires."

7. The letters that follow were printed in the *Fiji Times* on December 4, 1907.

8. One has to be careful here not to let the standardized narratives of deals overshadow the actual past events. The pertinence of the Deed of Cession for law and order in Gordon's Fiji was great, but not absolute. Gordon and his Attorney General agreed, as they established the legal machinery of his colony, *not* to refer to and rely on the Deed of Cession when they took some basic steps in the establishment of law and order in colonial Fiji, preferring instead to operate by decree, direct from the Crown. Similarly, the irrelevance of the Salisbury Despatch can also be overstated. Gordon was one of the witnesses, based on his experiences in Mauritius and Trinidad and especially his Trinidad reforms, at Salisbury's inquiry leading to the dispatch. Yet no doubt, the Deed of Cession has had a dense actual history in Fiji's constitutional apparatuses, while the Salisbury Despatch has not. For more on Gordon as colonial lawgiver and the limits of his dependence on the Deed of Cession and the Great Council of Chiefs, see Kaplan and Kelly forthcoming.

9. Scholars who debate the degree to which Gordon's land policy was a romantic and/or heroic enterprise in applied anthropology (of the nineteenth-century, evolutionary sort), and/or a practical concession to chiefly interests and power, have tended to neglect this dimension of his deals. Gordon's alliance with corporate capital tends to get elided when, precisely in keeping with the Pacific Romance, people describe early Fiji as if what really mattered was the axis of interests relating ethnic Fijians and "the white man" (as pidgin elsewhere would have it). A master not only of law giving but of the big deal, Gordon in fact had more than one goal to meet and many things going on at once.

10. This quotation is from an official letter from G. H. M. Batten, Esq., Officiating Secretary to the Government of India, to C. Mitchell, Esq., Agent-General of Immigration in Fiji, dated November 6, 1877, as reprinted in the *Fiji Royal Gazette* (hereafter, *FRG*) of February 9, 1878:27–35. The *FRG* quotations above are from the same issue.

11. See note 7 above, and also Sanadhya 1991, Kelly 1991, 1993, and 1997.

12. This and all quotations concerning this case come from CSO 3657/12.

13. All quotations from this debate are from "Extracts from Debates of July Session 1946," Legislative Council of Fiji, Government Press.

14. Deo himself oversimplified these. In fact the new Letters Patent ("constitution," actually instructions from London on how the colony is allowed to operate) provided for three European and three Indian members to be elected, and two more of each group, together with five Fijians, to be nominated.

15. These changes were in part because of Fiji's promises a decade before to give the Indians elected representation, at the time that Fiji was still seeking new labor immigration from India. And it was, to recall, the era of sharpest common roll debate throughout the British Empire. Meanwhile in the 1929 election, three European incumbents vied for two seats, and anti-Indian rhetoric was a fierce part of their campaigns. See Kelly 1991.

16. Eerily, the May 19 coup caught leaders of antigovernment Taukei protest marches by surprise, disrupting their plans. Further, by numerous reports, other coup plans were preempted (e.g., "The plot to topple Chaudhry," Fijilive, 5/26/00). One of the released hostages, Minister of Agriculture Poseci Bune, was later quoted as saying that the SVT parliamentarians looked "aghast" when Speight took over Parliament, not because they opposed a coup but because they too "were pipped by George Speight" ("Coup Full of Agendas—Bune," Fijilive, 7/17/00). Speight was not a well-known Fijian nationalist visibly leading any groundswell of dissatisfaction, nor a figure from the military, but rather a failed businessman and allegedly highly corrupt bureaucrat with a financial grudge against the Labour government. Whatever transformations, like Rabuka, Speight may undergo in future, one of the immediate causes of his coup was very likely the Chaudhry government's reversal of a Rabuka government deal to sell mahogany and pine to American companies. Speight, appointed by Rabuka to chair the Fiji Hardwood Corporation and later also to chair Fiji Pine Ltd., had received "thousands of dollars of 'consultancy fees'" from a U.S. businessman in the course of the negotiations. When Chaudhry's government fired him from both posts, his deals fell apart (*Sydney Morning Herald*, 5/27/00 [posted by Pacific Peoples' Partnership, sppf@SPPF.org]). The military personnel necessary to the parliamentary takeover all came from the army's elite Counter Revolutionary Warfare Unit and were led by Ilisoni Ligairi. Later press reports suggested that Speight was a latecomer to a coup planned and executed by Ligairi.

17. Speight asserted that his coup paralleled Rabuka's of 1987 in both substance and destiny: "Two years later, everyone was patting him on the back. . . . I'm confident in five years from now . . . [the Australian prime minister] will come and shake my hand" ("You'll respect me: Speight to Howard," Fijilive, 6/4/00). However, as this book goes to press, Speight is in prison awaiting trial.

18. One example of the English-language press reports on Indo-Fijians highlights this lack of representation:

> Fiji Indians have expressed concerns about being ignored in the negotiations held by the military and coup leader George Speight.
>
> Neither of the negotiators has considered the future of Indians in Fiji, say Indian leaders who met a special envoy from India, ST Devare.
>
> Several representatives of the various Indian organizations in Fiji made submissions to Devare, who is on an information gathering mission to Fiji. The National Federation Party, Fiji Labour Party, and various religious organisations including the Arya Pratinidhi Sabha were represented.
>
> Reports state that Devare did not choose to react to the submissions. The talks between the military and Speight are primarily focusing on indigenous rights. ("Indians voice concern," Fijilive, 4/6/00)

It should be noted that an analysis by Dr. Brij Lal, who was a member of the Constitution Review Commission that assembled the 1996 report, was posted on Fijilive a couple of days after the coup attempt and has been kept there since, on the home page along with each day's breaking news. However, on Fijilive and elsewhere, only a tiny number of news stories were about Indo-Fijians and their rights and representation.

19. While no current statistics are reliable, there is no doubt that Fiji has suffered tremendous economic losses in the 2000 coup, in tourism and in fact almost every

sector of the economy. Many investments were reconsidered, and outside investors have become extremely wary of Fiji. But the greatest loss is no doubt in human capital, as skilled workers including an extraordinary number of professionals emigrate in response to events.

20. A recent incident illustrates the extreme to which this impulse to disarm can be taken by Fiji's police and military. In early July 2000, in the rural district of Viria, while some Indo-Fijian farmers left their farms after threats of violence, one Indo-Fijian farmer with a gun fired warning shots in the air and scared off looters who had threatened to rob his house. Investigating police confiscated the gun. ("Police take gun," Fijilive, 7/5/00).

21. The Fijilive posting describing this event is worth quoting at length:

ARMY SAYS SORRY
Saturday, July 15, 2000
The military apologised to the Great Council of Chiefs on Thursday in the traditional manner.

A group of senior officers led by Army Commander Commodore Voreqe Bainimarama, presented their mata ni gasau before the GCC meeting began on Thursday and accepted. The whale's tooth was accepted by the Tui Vuda Ratu Josefa Iloilo, on behalf of the GCC. In the presentation, the army explained in full the reason why they took over power from former president Ratu Sir Kamisese Mara when the GCC had given their full support to him.

The army took over from Ratu Sir Kamisese on May 29 after they traditionally asked him to step down. As soon as they took over government, the 1997 Constitution was abrogated and executive power was vested on Commodore Bainimarama. There was a lot of negative reaction from the international community when martial law was put in place. Bans were imposed on Fiji which resulted in loss of jobs. Fiji felt the brunt of international focus when the nation was temporarily suspended from the Commonwealth.

The very reason the military took over was because of the lawlessness in the country and many civilians had been threatening police and members of the public with guns. While in power, the safety of the hostages was their main objective and even though talks broke down, they continued their negotiation with the rebels until the objective was successfully achieved.

Their second was to bring normalcy into the country. Two people were killed during the 56-day ordeal and the use of guns was the military's last resort of action. In true Fijian protocol the military asked for the forgiveness from the GCC for what they had done. The GCC thanked the military for the role they played during the political crisis that started on May 19. (Fiji's *Daily Post*, posted on Fijilive, 7/15/00)

22. Chaudhry also had the Australians as an explicit ally, at least for the moment. The day before this statement, John Howard told the press that Australia was disposed to reinstate pressures on Fiji to restore democracy and was awaiting his advice. Chaudhry read this statement after speaking with Howard, and Australian high officials were quick to add harsh criticism of the Great Council of Chiefs for failing to defend democracy.

23. To illustrate this, a final moment of Bill Clinton's 1998 speech: "Now, this is not an American agenda. I will say it again. This is not an American agenda. These

are the imperatives of the global marketplace, and you can see them repeated over and over and over again. . . ." To understand that these global imperatives realized over and over again are part of an instituted American agenda, as we have argued, is not merely to falsify Clinton's perspective, but also to understand that these imperatives are now lived and narrated as laws of nature, not culture or history, and that the Clintons of the world want it that way.

Bibliography

Aarons, Eric. 1970. *Lenin's Theories on Revolution*. Sydney: Communist Party of Australia.

Abu-Lughod, Janet. 1989. *Before European Hegemony: The World System A.D. 1250–1350*. New York: Oxford University Press.

Aldrich, Richard J. 2000. *Intelligence and the War Against Japan: Britain, America, and the Politics of Secret Service*. Cambridge: Cambridge University Press.

Ali, Ahmed, ed. 1979. *Girmit: The Indenture Experience in Fiji*. Suva: Fiji Museum.

Anderson, Benedict. 1983. *Imagined Communities: Reflections on the Origin and Spread of Nationalism*. London: Verso.

———. 1991. *Imagined Communities*. Rev. ed. London: Verso.

———. 1992. "The New World Disorder." *New Left Review* 193:3–13.

———. 1998. "Nationalism, Identity, and the World-in-Motion: On the Logics of Seriality." In *Cosmopolitics: Thinking and Feeling Beyond the Nation*. Vol. 14, Cultural Politics, edited by Pheng Cheah and Bruce Robbins, 117–33. Minneapolis: University of Minnesota Press.

Appadurai, Arjun. 1993. "Patriotism and Its Futures." *Public Culture* 5:411–29.

———. 1996. *Modernity at Large*. Minneapolis: University of Minnesota Press.

Asad, Talal, ed. 1973. *Anthropology and the Colonial Encounter*. London: Ithaca Press.

———. 1993. *Genealogies of Religion: Discipline and Reasons of Power in Christianity and Islam*. Baltimore: Johns Hopkins University Press.

Ashmore, Malcolm, Derek Edwards, and Jonathan Potter. 1994. "The Bottom Line: The Rhetoric of Reality Demonstrations." *Configurations* 2:1–14.

Bachelard, Gaston. 1984 [1934]. *The New Scientific Spirit*. Boston: Beacon Press.

Bailey, Beth, and David Farber. 1992. *The First Strange Place: The Alchemy of Race and Sex in World War II Hawaii*. New York: Free Press.

Bakhtin, M. M. 1981. *The Dialogic Imagination*. Austin: University of Texas Press.

Balibar, Etienne. 1994. *Masses, Classes, Ideas*. London: Routledge.

Barlow, Tani E., ed. 1997. *Formations of Colonial Modernity in East Asia*. Durham, N.C.: Duke University Press.

Benedict, Ruth. 1934. *Patterns of Culture*. Boston: Houghton Mifflin.

————. 1946. *The Chrysanthemum and the Sword: Patterns of Japanese Culture*. New York: New American Library.

Benjamin, Walter. 1968. "Theses on the Philosophy of History." *Illuminations*, 253–64. New York: Schocken Books.

————. 1989. "N (Re the Theory of Knowledge, Theory of Progress)" In *Benjamin: Philosophy, History, Aesthetics*, edited by Gary Smith, 43–83. Chicago: University of Chicago Press.

Berman, Marshall. 1988. *All That's Solid Melts into the Air: The Experience of Modernity*. New York: Penguin.

Bhabha, Homi K., ed. 1990. *Nation and Narration*. London: Routledge.

Boon, James. 1984. "Folly, Bali, and Anthropology, or Satire Across Cultures." In *Text, Play, and Story*, edited by E. Bruner, 156–77. Washington, D.C.: Proceedings of the American Ethnological Society for 1983.

Breman, Jan. 1989. *Taming the Coolie Beast: Plantation Society and the Colonial Order in Southeast Asia*. Delhi: Oxford University Press.

Brown, Carolyn Henning. 1984. "Tourism and Ethnic Competition in a Ritual Form: The Firewalkers of Fiji." *Oceania* 54:223–44.

Buck-Morss, Susan. 1989. *The Dialectics of Seeing: Walter Benjamin and the Arcades Project*. Cambridge: MIT Press.

Burridge, Kenelm. 1969. *New Heaven, New Earth: A Study of Millenarian Activities*. Oxford: Basil Blackwell.

Cameron, Craig M. 1994. *American Samurai: Myth, Imagination, and the Conduct of Battle in the First Marine Division, 1941–1951*. Cambridge: Cambridge University Press.

Carter, Marina. 1992. "Strategies of Labour Mobilisation in Colonial India: The Recruitment of Indentured Workers for Mauritius." *Journal of Peasant Studies* 19.3/4:229–45.

Castells, Manuel. 1996. *The Rise of the Network Society*. Oxford: Blackwell.

Chakrabarty, Dipesh. 1989. *Rethinking Working-Class History: Bengal 1890–1940*. Delhi: Oxford University Press.

————. 2000. *Provincializing Europe: Postcolonial Thought and Historical Difference*. Princeton: Princeton University Press.

Chandra, Bipan, et al. 1989. *India's Struggle for Independence 1857–1947*. Delhi: Penguin.

Chapman, J. K. 1964. *The Career of Arthur Hamilton Gordon First Lord Stanmore 1829–1912*. Toronto: University of Toronto Press.

Chatterjee, Partha. 1986. *Nationalist Thought and the Colonial World: A Derivative Discourse?* Avon, UK: Zed Books.

————. 1993. *The Nation and Its Fragments: Colonial and Postcolonial Histories*. Princeton: Princeton University Press.

Chaudhuri, K. N. 1990. *Asia Before Europe: Economy and Civilization of the Indian Ocean from the Rise of Islam to 1750*. Cambridge: Cambridge University Press.

Cho, Hae-Joang. 1992–94. *T'alsikminji Chisikin ui Kullikki wa Samilkki* [Reading Texts, Reading Life: The Point of View of a Post-Colonial Intellectual], 3 vols. Seoul: Ttohaniuimunhwa Press.

————. 1998. "Constructing and Deconstructing 'Koreanness.'" In *Making Majorities: Constituting the Nation in Japan, Korea, China, Malaysia, Fiji, Turkey, and the*

United States, edited by Dru C. Gladney, 73–91. Stanford: Stanford University Press.

Chow, Rey. 1993. *Writing Diaspora: Tactics of Intervention in Contemporary Cultural Studies.* Bloomington: Indiana University Press.

Clinton, William J. 1998. Speech at the Moscow State University for International Relations. *New York Times,* September 2, A8.

Cohn, Bernard S. 1983. "Representing Authority in Victorian India." In *The Invention of Tradition,* edited by Eric Hobsbawm and Terence Ranger, 165–209. Cambridge: Cambridge University Press.

———. 1987. *An Anthropologist among the Historians and Other Essays.* Delhi: Oxford University Press.

———. 1996. *Colonialism and Its Forms of Knowledge.* Princeton: Princeton University Press.

Cohn, Bernard S., and Nicholas B. Dirks. 1988. "Beyond the Fringe: The Nation State, Colonialism, and the Technologies of Power." *Journal of Historical Sociology* 1:224–29.

Colonial Secretary's Office (CSO). 1875–1955. Minute papers. National Archives of Fiji, Suva.

Comaroff, Jean, and John Comaroff. 1991. *Of Revolation and Revolution: Christianity, Colonialism, and Consciousness in South Africa,* vol.1. Chicago: University of Chicago Press.

Cooper, George, and Gavan Daws. 1985. *Land and Power in Hawaii: The Democratic Years.* Honolulu: Benchmark Books.

Corrigan, Philip, and Derek Sayer. 1985. *The Great Arch: English State Formation as Cultural Revolution.* Oxford: Basil Blackwell.

Curtin, Philip. 1984. *Cross-Cultural Trade in World History.* Cambridge: Cambridge University Press.

Cyclopedia of Fiji. 1907. Sydney: The Cyclopedia Company of Fiji. Reprinted by the Fiji Museum, 1984.

Daniel, E. Valentine, Henry Bernstein, and Tom Brass, eds. 1992. *Plantations, Peasants and Proletarians in Colonial Asia.* London: Frank Cass. Also printed in a special issue of *Journal of Peasant Studies* 19 3/4

Darnton, Robert. 1984. *The Great Cat Massacre and Other Episodes in French Cultural History.* New York: Basic Books.

Daws, Gavan. 1968. *The Shoal of Time: A History of the Hawaiian Islands.* New York: Macmillan.

Dening, Greg. 1986. "Possessing Tahiti." *Archaeology in Oceania* 21:103–18.

Dower, John. 1986. *War without Mercy: Race and Power in the Pacific War.* New York: Pantheon Books.

Duara, Prasenjit. 1995. *Rescuing History from the Nation: Questioning Narratives of Modern China.* Chicago: University of Chicago Press.

———. 1996. "Historicizing National Identity, or Who Imagines What When." In *Becoming National,* edited by Geoff Eley and Ronald Grigor Suny, 151–77. New York: Oxford University Press.

Duncan, David D. 1945. "Fiji Patrol on Bougainville." *National Geographic Magazine* 87:87–104.

Eagleton, Terry, Frederick Jameson, and Edward Said. 1990. *Nationalism, Colonialism and Literature.* Minneapolis: University of Minnesota Press.

Fabian, Johannes. 1983. *Time and the Other: How Anthropology Makes Its Object.* New York: Columbia University Press.

Fanon, Frantz. 1968. *The Wretched of the Earth.* New York: Grove Press.

Fardon, Richard. 1995. "Introduction: Counterworks." In *Counterworks: Managing the Diversity of Knowledge,* edited by Richard Fardon, 1–22. London: Routledge.

Ferguson, James. 1990. *The Anti-Politics Machine: "Development," Depoliticization, and Bureaucratic Power in Lesotho.* Cambridge: Cambridge University Press.

Fiji Constitution Review Commission. 1996. "Report, The Fiji Islands: Towards a United Future." Parliamentary Paper No. 34 of 1996. Suva: Parliament of Fiji.

Firth, Stewart. 2000. "Decolonization." In *Remembrance of Pacific Pasts: An Invitation to Remake History,* edited by Robert Borofsky. Honolulu: University of Hawaii Press.

Foster, Robert J. 1991. "Making National Cultures in the Global Ecumene." *Annual Review of Anthropology* 20:235–60.

———. 1995a. "Introduction: The Work of Nation Making." In *Nation Making: Emergent Identities in Postcolonial Melanesia,* edited by Foster, 1–30.

———, ed. 1995b. *Nation Making: Emergent Identities in Postcolonial Melanesia.* Ann Arbor: University of Michigan Press.

Fox, Richard G. 1985. *Lions of the Punjab: Culture in the Making.* Berkeley: University of California Press.

France, Peter. 1969. *The Charter of the Land.* Melbourne: Oxford University Press.

Frank, Andre Gunder. 1998. *ReORIENT: Global Economy in the Asian Age.* Berkeley: University of California Press.

Freeland, Richard M. 1972. *The Truman Doctrine and the Origins of McCarthyism.* New York: Alfred A. Knopf.

Freitag, Sandria B. 1990. *Collective Action and Community: Public Arenas and the Emergence of Communalism in North India.* Delhi: Oxford University Press.

Friedman, Thomas L. 1996. "Big Mac II." *New York Times,* December 11, A27.

Fuchs, Lawrence. 1961. *Hawaii Pono: A Social History.* San Diego: Harcourt Brace Jovanovich.

Gandhi, Mohandas K. 1928. *Satyagraha in South Africa.* Ahmedabad: Navajivan Publishing House.

———. 1983 [1948]. *Autobiography: The Story of My Experiments with Truth.* New York: Dover.

———. 1986. *The Moral and Political Writings of Mahatma Gandhi.* Vol. 3: *Non-Violent Resistance and Social Transformation.* Edited by Raghavan Iyer. Oxford: Clarendon Press.

Geertz, Clifford, ed. 1963. *Old Societies and New States: The Quest for Modernity in Asia and Africa.* Glencoe, Ill.: Free Press.

———. 1973a. "Deep play: Notes on the Balinese Cock Fight." *The Interpretation of Cultures,* 412–53. New York: Basic Books.

———. 1973b. "The Integrative Revolution: Primordial Sentiments and Civil Politics in the New States." *The Interpretation of Cultures,* 255–310. New York: Basic Books. Published originally in Geertz, ed., 1963. *Old Societies and New States,* 105–57.

Gillion, Kenneth L. 1962. *Fiji's Indian Migrants.* Melbourne: Oxford University Press.

————. 1977. *The Fiji Indians: Challenge to European Dominance, 1920–1946.* Canberra: Australian National University Press.

Goldsmith, Michael. 1991. "Speech Acts, Silence and Myth: Rhetorical Dimensions of the Fiji Coup." Paper presented to the Conference of the Pacific Islands Political Studies Association, Monash University, Melbourne, Victoria, December.

Gordon, Arthur Hamilton. 1879a. *Letters and Notes Written During the Disturbances in the Highlands. . . .* Edinburgh: privately printed.

————. 1879b. "On the System of Taxation in Force in Fiji." Paper read before the Royal Colonial Institute, March 18. Privately printed by R. and R. Clarke. Newberry Library, Chicago.

Gordon, Leonard A. 1989. *Brothers Against the Raj: A Biography of Sarat and Subhas Chandra Bose.* New Delhi: Viking.

Guha, Ranajit. 1981. *A Rule of Property for Bengal.* Delhi: Orient Longman.

————. 1982. "On Some Aspects of the Historiography of Colonial India." In *Subaltern Studies I,* edited by Ranajit Guha. Delhi: Oxford University Press.

Gustafson, Thomas. 1992. *Representative Words: Politics, Literature, and the American Language, 1776–1865.* Cambridge: Cambridge University Press.

Handler, Richard, and Daniel A. Segal. 1993. "Introduction: Nations, Colonies and Metropoles." In Nations, Colonies and Metropoles, edited by Daniel A. Segal and Richard Handler. Special issue, *Social Analysis* 33:3–8.

Hannerz, Ulf. 1992. *Cultural Complexity: Studies in the Social Organization of Meaning.* New York: Columbia University Press.

Hicks, Frederick Charles. 1920. *The New World Order.* Garden City: Doubleday.

Hobsbawm, Eric. 1983. "Introduction: Inventing Traditions." In *The Invention of Tradition,* edited by Eric Hobsbawm and Terence Ranger, 1–14. Cambridge: Cambridge University Press.

————. 1987. *The Age of Empire 1875–1914.* New York: Vintage Books.

————. 1990. *Nations and Nationalism Since 1780.* Cambridge: Cambridge University Press.

Hobsbawm, Eric, and Terence Ranger, eds. 1983. *The Invention of Tradition.* Cambridge: Cambridge University Press.

Hocart, A. M. 1969 [1927]. *Kingship.* Oxford: Oxford University Press.

Hont, Istvan. 1995. "The Permanent Crisis of a Divided Mankind: 'Contemporary Crisis of the Nation-State' in Historical Perspective." In *Contemporary Crisis of the Nation-State?,* edited by John Dunn, 166–231. Oxford: Blackwell.

Howard, Michael. 1991. *Fiji: Race and Politics in an Island State.* Vancouver: University of British Columbia Press.

Hussein, Bernadette. 1997. "Speaking to the PM." *Pacific Islands Monthly* 67.9 (September):19–21.

Huxley, Julian, and A. C. Haddon. 1935. *We Europeans: A Survey of 'Racial' Problems.* London: Jonathan Cape.

Hymes, Dell, ed. 1969. *Reinventing Anthropology.* New York: Random House.

Inouye, Daniel K. 1978. "A Reckoning in Ballots." In *Kodomo no tame ni—For the Sake of the Children,* edited by Dennis Ogawa, 389–96. Honolulu: University Press of Hawaii.

Ivy, Marilyn. 1995. *Discourses of the Vanishing: Modernity, Phantasm, Japan.* Chicago: University of Chicago Press.

Jolly, Margaret. 1991. "Verbal and Visual Creoles: Symbols of Nation and Secession in Vanuatu." Paper presented at the Annual Meetings of the American Anthropological Association, Chicago, December.

Kame'eleihiwa, Lilikala. 1992. *Native Land and Foreign Desires.* Honolulu: Bishop Museum Press.

Kapferer, Bruce. 1988. *Legends of People, Myths of State: Violence, Intolerance and Political Culture in Sri Lanka and Australia.* Washington: Smithsonian Press.

Kaplan, Martha. 1988a. "The Coups in Fiji: Colonial Contradictions and the Postcolonial Crisis." *Critique of Anthropology* 8.3:93–116.

———. 1988b. "Land and Sea and the New White Men: A Reconsideration of the Fijian Tuka Movement." Ph.D. diss., Department of Anthropology, University of Chicago.

———. 1989. "The 'Dangerous and Disaffected Native' in Fiji: British Colonial Constructions of the Tuka Movement." *Social Analysis* 26:22–45.

———. 1990a. "Christianity, People of the Land, and Chiefs in Fiji." In *Christianity in Oceania,* edited by John Barker, 189–207. Lanham, Md.: University Press of America.

———. 1990b. "Meaning, Agency and Colonial History: Navosavakadua and the Tuka Movement in Fiji." *American Ethnologist* 17:3–22.

———. 1995a. *Neither Cargo nor Cult: Ritual Politics and the Colonial Imagination in Fiji.* Durham, N.C.: Duke University Press.

———. 1995b. "Panopticon in Poona: An Essay on Foucault and Colonialism." *Cultural Anthropology* 10.1: 85–98.

Kaplan, Martha, and John D. Kelly. 1994. "Rethinking Resistance: Dialogics of 'Disaffection' in Colonial Fiji." *American Ethnologist* 21.1:123–51.

———. Forthcoming. *Laws Like Bullets: Imagined Disorder in British Colonial Worlds.* Durham, N.C.: Duke University Press.

Kawahara, Kirnie, and Yuriko Hatanaka. 1943. "The Impact of War on an Immigrant Culture." *Social Process in Hawaii* 8.

Kelly, John D. 1988a. "Fiji Indians and Political Discourse in Fiji: From the Pacific Romance to the Coups." *Journal of Historical Sociology* 1:399–422.

———. 1988b. "From *Holi* to *Diwali* in Fiji: An Essay on Ritual and History." *Man,* n.s., 23:40–55.

———. 1989. "Fear of Culture: British Regulation of Indian Marriage in Post-Indenture Fiji." *Ethnohistory* 36.4:372–91.

———. 1991. *A Politics of Virtue: Hinduism, Sexuality, and Countercolonial Discourse in Fiji.* Chicago: University of Chicago Press.

———. 1992. "Fiji Indians and 'Commoditization of Labor.'" *American Ethnologist* 19:97–120.

———. 1993. "'Coolie' as a Labor Commodity: Race, Sex, and European Dignity in Colonial Fiji." *Journal of Peasant Studies* 19.3/4:246–67. Special issue, edited by Jan Breman, Val Daniel, Henry Bernstein.

———. 1995a. "*Bhakti* and Post-Colonial Politics: Hindu Missions to Fiji." In *Nation and Migration: The Politics of Space in the South Asian Diaspora,* edited by Peter van der Veer, 43–72. Philadelphia: University of Pennsylvania Press.

———. 1995b. "The Privileges of Citizenship: Nations, States, Markets and Narratives." In *Nation Making: Emergent Identities in Postcolonial Melanesia,* edited by Robert J. Foster, 253–73. Ann Arbor: University of Michigan Press.

————. 1995c. "Threats to Difference in Colonial Fiji." *Cultural Anthropology* 10.1:64–84.

————. 1997. "Gaze and Grasp: Plantations, Desires, and Colonial Law in Fiji." In *Sites of Desire / Economies of Pleasure: Sexualities in Asia and the Pacific,* edited by Margaret Jolly and Lenore Manderson, 72–98. Chicago: University of Chicago Press.

————. 1998. "Aspiring to Minority and Other Tactics Against Violence in Fiji." In *Making Majorities: Constituting the Nation in Japan, China, Korea, Fiji, Malaysia, Turkey, and the United States,* edited by Dru Gladney, 173–197. Stanford: Stanford University Press.

Kelly, John D., and Martha Kaplan. 1990. "History, Structure, and Ritual." *Annual Review of Anthropology* 19:119–50.

Klor de Alva, Jorge. 1995. "The Postcolonization of the (Latin) American Experience: A Reconsideration of 'Colonialism,' 'Postcolonialism,' and 'Mestizaje.'" In *After Colonialism: Imperial Histories and Postcolonial Displacements,* edited by Gyan Prakash, 241–75. Princeton: Princeton University Press.

LaFeber, Walter. 1998 [1963]. *The New Empire: An Interpretation of American Expansion 1860–1898.* Ithaca: Cornell University Press.

Lal, Brij V. 1983. *Girmitiyas: The Origins of the Fiji Indians.* Canberra: Journal of Pacific History.

————. 1988. *Power and Prejudice: The Making of the Fiji Crisis.* Wellington: New Zealand Institute of International Affairs.

————. 1992. *Broken Waves: A History of the Fiji Islands in the Twentieth Century.* Honolulu: University of Hawaii Press.

————. 1997. *A Vision for Change: A. D. Patel and the Politics of Fiji.* Canberra: National Centre for Development Studies, Australian National University.

————, ed. 1986. *Politics in Fiji: Studies in Contemporary History.* Sydney: Allen and Unwin.

Lal, Brij V., and Tomasi Rayalu Vakatora, eds. 1997. *Fiji Constitution Review Committee Research Papers* (vol. 1, *Fiji in Transition;* vol. 2, *Fiji and the World*). Suva: School of Social and Economic Development, University of the South Pacific.

Lal, Victor. 1990. *Fiji: Coups in Paradise.* London: Zed Books.

Latour, Bruno. 1988. *The Pasteurization of France.* Cambridge: Harvard University Press.

Le Carré, John. 1994. "The Shame of the West." *New York Times,* December 14.

Legge, J. D. 1958. *Britain in Fiji 1858–1880.* London: Macmillan.

Legislative Council of Fiji. 1946. *Extract from Debates of July Session 1946.* Suva: Government Press.

Lincoln, Bruce. 1987. "Ritual, Rebellion, Resistance: Once More the Swazi *Ncwala.*" *Man,* n.s., 22:132–56.

Linnekin, Jocelyn. 1983. "Defining Traditions: Variations on Hawaiian Identity." *American Ethnologist* 10:241–52.

LiPuma, Edward, and Sarah Keene Meltzoff. 1990. "Ceremonies of Independence and Public Culture in the Solomon Islands." *Public Culture* 3:77–92.

Louis, William Roger. 1977. *Imperialism at Bay: The United States and the Decolonisation of the British Empire, 1941–1945.* Oxford: Clarendon Press.

Ludden, David, ed. 1996. *Contesting the Nation: Religion, Community, and the Politics of Democracy in India.* Philadelphia: University of Pennsylvania Press.

Luke, Harry. 1945. *From a South Seas Diary, 1938–42.* London: Nicholson and Watson.

Macaulay, Thomas Babington. 1833. "Government of India, A Speech Delivered in the House of Commons on the 10th of July, 1833." *The Complete Works of Lord Macaulay.* Vol. 9: *Miscellaneous Works,* 146–93. Philadelphia: University Library Association, 1910.

———. 1860a. "Church and State." *Essays, Critical and Miscellaneous,* 378–400. New York: D. Appleton and Co. Reprinted from *Edinburgh Review,* April 1839.

———. 1860b. "Mill's Essay on Government." *Essays, Critical and Miscellaneous,* 670–83. New York: D. Appleton and Co. Reprinted from *Edinburgh Review,* March 1829.

———. 1910. "War with China, A Speech Delivered in the House of Commons on the 7th of April, 1840." *The Complete Works of Lord Macaulay.* Vol. 10: *Miscellaneous Works,* 247–69. Philadelphia: University Library Association.

———. 1972 [February 2, 1835]. "Minute on Indian Education." *Thomas Babington Macaulay: Selected Writings,* 237–51. Edited by John Clive and Thomas Pinney. Chicago: University of Chicago Press.

Macnaught, Timothy J. 1982. *The Fijian Colonial Experience.* Pacific Research Monograph No. 7. Canberra: Australian National University.

Mamdani, Mahmood. 1996. *Citizen and Subject: Contemporary Africa and the Legacy of Late Colonialism.* Princeton: Princeton University Press.

Marriott, John A. R. 1927. *The Mechanism of the Modern State: A Treatise on the Science and Art of Government.* Oxford: Clarendon Press.

———. 1939. *Commonwealth or Anarchy? A Survey of Projects for Peace.* New York: Columbia University Press.

Marriott, McKim. 1963. "Cultural Policy in the New States." In *Old Societies and New States,* edited by Clifford Geertz, 27–56. Glencoe, Ill.: Free Press.

Marx, Karl. 1977. *Capital,* vol. 1. New York: Vintage Books.

———. 1978 [1859]. "Preface to a Contribution to the Critique of Political Economy." *The Marx-Engels Reader,* 3–8. 2nd ed. Edited by Robert C. Tucker. New York: W. W. Norton.

Masselos, Jim. 1990. "The Magic Touch of Being Free: The Rituals of Independence on August 15." In *India: Creating a Modern Nation,* edited by Jim Masselos, 37–53. New Delhi: Sterling.

———. n.d. "India's Republic Day: The Other 26th January." Unpublished manuscript.

Mauss, Marcel. 1967. *The Gift.* New York: W. W. Norton.

Mayer, Adrian C. 1963. *Indians in Fiji.* London: Oxford University Press.

McCullough, David. 1992. *Truman.* New York: Simon and Schuster.

McKean, Lise. 1996. *Divine Enterprise: Gurus and the Hindu Nationalist Movement.* Chicago: University of Chicago Press.

Moulton, Edward C. 1991. "The Early Congress, and the Idea of Representative and Self-Governing Institutions on the Colonial Canadian Model." In *The Congress and Indian Nationalism: Historical Perspectives,* edited by John L. Hill, 222–58. London: Curzon Press.

Moynagh, Michael. 1981. *Brown or White? A History of the Fiji Sugar Industry 1873–1973.* Pacific Research Monograph No. 5. Canberra: Australian National University.

Nandy, Ashis. 1983. *The Intimate Enemy: Loss and Recovery of Self Under Colonialism.* Delhi: Oxford University Press.

Nayacakalou, R. R. 1975. *Leadership in Fiji.* Melbourne: Oxford University Press.

Nietzsche, Friedrich. 1989 [1886]. *Beyond Good and Evil.* New York: Vintage Books.

Ogawa, Dennis. 1978. *Kodomo no tame ni—For the Sake of the Children.* Honolulu: University Press of Hawaii.

O'Hanlon, Rosalind. 1989. "Cultures of Rule, Communities of Resistance: Gender, Discourse and Tradition in Recent South Asian Historiographies." *Social Analysis* 25:94–114.

Okihiro, Gary. 1991. *Cane Fires: The Anti-Japanese Movement in Hawaii, 1865–1945.* Philadelphia: Temple University Press.

Onuf, Peter, and Onuf, Nicholas. 1993. *Federal Union, Modern World: The Law of Nations in an Age of Revolutions 1776–1814.* Madison, Wis.: Madison House.

Pandey, Gyanendra. 1978. *The Ascendancy of the Congress in Uttar Pradesh 1926–34: A Study in Imperfect Mobilization.* Delhi: Oxford University Press.

———. 1990. *The Construction of Communalism in Colonial North India.* Delhi: Oxford University Press.

Pemberton, John. 1994. *On the Subject of "Java."* Ithaca: Cornell University Press.

Pletsch, Carl E. 1981. "The Three Worlds, or the Division of Social Scientific Labor, circa 1950–1975." *Comparative Studies in Society and History* 23.4:565–90.

Pocock, J. G. A. 1975. *The Machiavellian Moment: Florentine Political Thought and the Atlantic Republican Tradition.* Princeton: Princeton University Press.

Polanyi, Karl. 1944. *The Great Transformation.* Boston: Beacon Press.

Pollock, Sheldon. 1996. "The Sanskrit Cosmopolis, 300–1300 CE: Transculturalism, Vernacularization, and the Question of Ideology." In *Ideology and Status of Sanskrit: Contributions to the History of the Sanskrit Language,* edited by Jan E. M. Houben, 197–247. Leiden: EJ Brill.

Rabinbach, Anson. 1989. "Introduction." In *The Correspondence of Walter Benjamin and Gershom Scholem, 1932–1940,* edited by Gershom Scholem, vii–xxxviii. New York: Schocken Books.

Ralston, David B. 1990. *Importing the European Army: The Introduction of European Military Techniques and Institutions into the Extra-European World, 1600–1914.* Chicago: University of Chicago Press.

Ravuvu, Asesela. 1974. *Fijians at War, 1939–1945.* Suva: University of the South Pacific, Institute of Pacific Studies.

———. 1991. *The Facade of Democracy: Fijian Struggles for Political Control 1830–1987.* Suva: Reader Publishing House.

Renan, Ernest. 1990 [1882]. "What Is a Nation?" In *Nation and Narration,* edited by Homi Bhabha, 8–22. London: Routledge. (Also in Geoff Eley and Ronald Grigor Suny, eds. 1996. *Becoming National,* 42–55. New York: Oxford University Press.)

Rousseau, Jean Jacques. 1968. *The Social Contract.* London: Penguin.

Rutz, Henry. 1995. "Occupying the Headwaters of Tradition: Rhetorical Strategies of Nation Making in Fiji." In *Nation Making: Emergent Identities in Postcolonial Melanesia,* edited by Robert J. Foster, 71–93. Ann Arbor: University of Michigan Press.

Sahlins, Marshall. 1972. *Stone Age Economics.* New York: Aldine.

———. 1976. *Culture and Practical Reason.* Chicago: University of Chicago Press.

————. 1985. *Islands of History*. Chicago: University of Chicago Press.

————. 1988. "Cosmologies of Capitalism: The Transpacific Sector of 'The World System.'" *Proceedings of the British Academy* 73:1–51.

Said, Edward. 1979. *Orientalism*. New York: Vintage Books.

————. 1994. *Orientalism*. 2nd ed. New York: Vintage Books.

Sanadhya, Totaram. 1991 [1914]. *My Twenty-One Years in the Fiji Islands*. Translated and edited by John D. Kelly and Uttra Kumari Singh. Suva, Fiji: Fiji Museum.

Scarr, Deryck. 1980. *Ratu Sukuna: Soldier, Statesman, Man of Two Worlds*. London: Macmillan Education Limited, for the Ratu Sir Lala Sukuna Biography Committee.

Scholem, Gershom. 1976. *On Jews and Judaism in Crisis. Selected Essays*. New York: Schocken Books.

————. 1981. *Walter Benjamin: The Story of a Friendship*. Philadelphia: Jewish Publication Society of America.

————, ed. 1989. *The Correspondence of Walter Benjamin and Gershom Scholem, 1932–1940*. New York: Schocken Books.

Scott, David. 1999. *Refashioning Futures: Criticism After Postcoloniality*. Princeton: Princeton University Press.

Segal, Daniel, and Richard Handler. 1992. "How European Is Nationalism?" *Social Analysis* 32:1–16.

————, eds. 1993. Nations, Colonies and Metropoles. Special issue, *Social Analysis* 33. Adelaide: University of Adelaide.

Semmel, Bernard. 1970. *The Rise of Free Trade Imperialism: Classical Political Economy, the Empire of Free Trade and Imperialism, 1750–1850*. Cambridge: Cambridge University Press.

Seneviratne, Kalinga. 1997. "Moving (Slowly) in the Right Direction." *Pacific Islands Monthly* 67.9 (September):21–22.

Singer, Daniel. 1996. "The Real Eurobattle." *The Nation* (December 23):20–23.

Singh, Madhur. 1998. "The Land of Would-be Emigrants." *Fiji Islands Business*, 3.7(July):8.

Spivak, Gayatri Chakravorty. 1994. "Can the Subaltern Speak?" In *Colonial Discourse and Post-Colonial Theory*, edited by Patrick Williams and Laura Chrisman, 66–111. New York: Columbia University Press.

Stackhouse, John. 2000. "Wooden Soldiers Try to Take Over Paradise." *Toronto Globe and Mail*, May 20 (posted on asaonet@listserv.uic.edu).

Stocking, George W. 1987. *Victorian Anthropology*. New York: Free Press.

Stoler, Ann Laura. 1985. *Capitalism and Confrontation in Sumatra's Plantation Belt, 1870–1979*. New Haven: Yale University Press.

————. 1995. *Race and the Education of Desire: Foucault's History of Sexuality and the Colonial Order of Things*. Durham, N.C.: Duke University Press.

Subramani. 1995. *Altering Imagination*. Suva: Fiji Writers' Association.

Sukuna, (Ratu Sir) Lala. 1983. *The ThreeLegged Stool: Writings of Ratu Sir Lala Sukuna*. Edited by Deryck Scarr. London: Macmillan Education.

Sullivan, Patricia. 1996. *Days of Hope: Race and Democracy in the New Deal Era*. Chapel Hill: University of North Carolina Press.

Swan, Maureen. 1985. *Gandhi: The South African Experience*. Johannesburg: Ravan Press.

Takaki, Ronald. 1989. *Strangers from a Different Shore: A History of Asian Americans*. New York: Penguin.

Tambiah, Stanley J. 1985. *Culture, Thought and Social Action: An Anthropological Perspective*. Cambridge. Harvard University Press.

———. 1996. *Leveling Crowds: Ethnonationalist Conflicts and Collective Violence in South Asia*. Berkeley: University of California Press.

Taylor, Charles. 1992. "The Politics of Recognition." In *Multiculturalism and "The Politics of Recognition,"* edited by Amy Gutmann, 25–73. Princeton: Princeton University Press.

Thomas, Nicholas. 1990. "Sanitation and Seeing: The Creation of State Power in Early Colonial Fiji." *Comparative Studies in Society and History* 32:149–70.

Tiedemann, Rolf. 1988. "Dialectics at a Standstill: Approaches to the *Passagen-Werk*." In *On Walter Benjamin: Critical Essays and Reflections*, edited by Gary Smith, 260–91. Cambridge: MIT Press.

———. 1989. "Historical Materialism or Political Messianism? An Interpretation of the Theses 'On the Concept of History.'" In *Benjamin: Philosophy, History, Aesthetics*, edited by Gary Smith, 175–209. Chicago: University of Chicago Press.

Tinker, Hugh. 1976. *Separate and Unequal: India and the Indians in the British Commonwealth, 1920–1950*. Vancouver: University of British Columbia Press.

———. 1977. *Race, Conflict, and the International Order: From Empire to United Nations*. New York: St. Martin's Press.

Tipp, Dean. 1973. "Modernization Theory and the Comparative Study of Societies: A Critical Perspective." *Comparative Studies in Society and History* 15:199–226.

Tololyan, Khachig. 1991. "The Nation and Its Others." *Diaspora* 1.1: 3–7.

Toren, Christina. 1988. "Making the Present, Revealing the Past: The Mutability and Continuity of Tradition as Process." *Man*, n.s., 23:696–717.

Tribe, Keith. 1981. *Genealogies of Capitalism*. London: Macmillan.

Trouillot, Michel-Rolph. 1995. *Silencing the Past*. Boston: Beacon Press.

van der Veer, Peter. 1994. *Religious Nationalism: Hindus and Muslims in India*. Berkeley: University of California Press.

Verdery, Katherine. 1992. "Comment: Hobsbawm in the East." *Anthropology Today* 8:8–10.

Viswanathan, Gauri. 1989. *Masks of Conquest: Literary Study and British Rule in India*. London: Faber and Faber.

Weber, Max. 1949. *The Methodology of the Social Sciences*. New York: Free Press.

———. 1978. Vol. 1. *Economy and Society*. Berkeley: University of California Press.

———. 1989 [1897]. "Germany as an Industrial State." In *Reading Weber*, edited by Keith Tribe. London: Routledge.

Wells, H. G. 1940. *The New World Order: Whether It Is Attainable, How It Can Be Attained, and What Sort of World a World at Peace Will Have to Be*. New York: Alfred A. Knopf.

Williams, Brackette F. 1989. "A Class Act: Anthropology and the Race to Nation Across Ethnic Terrain." *Annual Review of Anthropology*, 401–44.

———. 1990. "Nationalism, Traditionalism, and the Problem of Cultural Inauthenticity." In *Nationalist Ideologies and the Production of National Cultures*, edited by Richard Fox, 112–29. American Ethnological Society Monograph Series, No. 2. Washington, D.C.: American Anthropological Association.

————. 1991. *Stains on My Name, War in My Veins: Guyana and the Politics of Cultural Struggle.* Durham, N.C.: Duke University Press.

Williams, Raymond. 1976. *Keywords: A Vocabulary of Culture and Society.* New York: Oxford University Press.

————. 1977. *Marxism and Literature.* London: Oxford University Press.

Witte, Bernd. 1991. *Walter Benjamin: An Intellectual Biography.* Detroit: Wayne State University Press.

Wolf, Eric. 1982. *Europe and the People without History.* Berkeley: University of California Press.

Worsley, Peter. 1968. *The Trumpet Shall Sound: A Study of "Cargo" Cults in Melanesia.* New York: Schocken Books.

Yans-McLaughlin, Virginia. 1986. "Science, Democracy and Ethics: Mobilizing Culture and Personality for World War II." In *Malinowski, Rivers, Benedict and Others: Essays on Culture and Personality,* edited by George W. Stocking Jr., 184–217. Vol. 4, History of Anthropology. Madison: University of Wisconsin Press.

Young, Kanalu G. T. 1995. "Hawaiian Issues." *The Contemporary Pacific* 7.1:148–52.

Index

plexity and, 96; of different political systems in empire, 97–99

Cohn, Bernard, xiv, 59, 204n. 16

Cold War: American power in, 18–22; decolonization and, vii–viii, 20–22; framework of commitments in, 4; three-worlds scheme of, 33–34, 58

colonialism: "community" concept in, 4, 22–23, 91–92, 197–98; ritual in, 125–28, 214n. 8; sea change under, 44–45, 57–58; techniques of governmentality of, 204n. 16, 214n. 8

Colonial Sugar Refining Company (CSR), *113;* Gordon's indenture contracts and, 162–67, 217n. 9; labor policies of, 68, 84, 88–92; romanticized history of, 153–54; strike against, 70–71, 84, 102–3; sugar prices for, 82, 90–93, 102–3, 105–7

common roll. *See* voting

Commonwealth Games, apartheid protest of, 148

communalism, in India, 25, 98, 104

communal roll. *See* voting

communal system, in Fiji: Fijian Regulations and, 213n. 9; government support and, 110–11; rhetoric of, 104–9. *See also* chiefs

Communist International (Comintern), 9–10, 18–19, 202n. 4

community: approach to, 4–5, 82–83, 199–200; colonial Europeans' use of, 4, 22–23, 91–92, 197–98; complexity of, 82–83, 95–99; in coup (2000) rhetoric, 189–90; Macaulay's notion of, 47–48; race and, 83, 109–12, 150, 168. *See also* represented communities

complexity: approach to, 82–83; Bachelard on, 83, 93–94; globalization and, 65–66; in understanding community, 95–99

Conference of New Americans (1927), 72

Congress of Industrial Organizations (CIO), 77–78, 210n. 11

consciousness, seriality concept and, 60–63

constitutions: of 1970, 132, 150, 174, 178, 207n. 2; of 1990, 175, 178; of 1997, 176–80; after coups (1987), 175; indigenous Fijians protected in, 207–8n. 2; overview of, in Fiji, 145–46; Rabuka's choice and, 178–80; Rabuka's transprovisions and, 182–83; racial patterns in, 172–74; Review Commission on, 176–79; revoked

in coup (2000), 180–82, 184. *See also* elections; Parliament; voting

contracts. *See* social contracts and contract narratives

Convention on the Elimination of All Forms of Discrimination Against Women, 177

Convention on the Elimination of All Forms of Racial Discrimination, 177

coups (1987): aftermath of, 146, 175–77; ethnic Fijians in, 174–75; justifications for, 139, 148–49; liberal support for, 147; ritual context of, 133; voting structure and, 151

coups (2000): aftermath of, 192–94; controlling representation in, 185–86; description of, 143–46, 180–82; Indo-Fijian dilemmas in, 186–90, 218n. 18; Rabuka's transprovisions and, 182–83; struggles among/for ethnic Fijians, 183–85; violence in, 181, 184–85, 186, 193, 219n. 21; world order and, 190–92

creolization, 43–44

Cripps Mission, 67–68

culture: Benedict and, 51–55, 59–60; as totalizing, 140–41

Cyclopedia Company of Fiji, 153–54, 156–59, 161, 164

Declaration of Independence (U.S.), 46

Declaration on the Rights of Indigenous People (draft), 177

decolonization: American power and, 15–17; approach to, vii–viii, 16; effacement of processes of, 21–22; in Fiji, 130, 172; nation-state and, vii, 3–6, 59, 140–41, 194–96

Deed of Cession (1874): celebration of, *119,* 126–27; debate on (1946), 84, 104, 109–10, 169–72, 197; description of, 158–60, 217n. 8; narratives of, 207–8n. 2, 214n. 4; signing of, 85, 127

Defence Force, *116;* deployed in cane fields, 69, 77, 84, 90; dismissal of Indian platoon in, 100–101. *See also* military

democracy: global pressure for, 191–92; Mill on, 47–48; violence and, 212n. 6; Wilson on, 52–53

Democratic Party (U.S.), 78–79, 210n. 12

Deo, Vishnu, *117;* Deed of Cession Debate and, 109–10, 171–74, 198; on equal citizenship, 68, 149; on history of constitu-